SCENES OF A WOOD-BURNING STOVE
AND A HAPPY CHILDHOOD
WHEN THE WORLD WAS SIMPLER . . .

We talked with people who enthusiastically shared memories of their forebears' ways with food and what it means to them today. These family recipes stir up memories for many of us of days when the family dining table was the focal point of the home— the symbol of togetherness where everyone gathered at least once a day for discussions of future plans, current happenings, dreams of the future.

For us lucky ones, the melting pot still bubbles with memories of happy family times, spilling over into our homes today, enriching our lives.

There are evidences everywhere that these heirloom recipes have become, through use and pride, truly "American"—the cooking of our nation that is matched by no other country.

—from the Preface to
**THE GREAT AMERICAN
FAMILY COOKBOOK**

Cookbooks by Maria Luisa Scott and
  Jack Denton Scott

THE COMPLETE BOOK OF PASTA
FEAST OF FRANCE WITH ANTOINE GILLY
INFORMAL DINNERS FOR EASY ENTERTAINING
MASTERING MICROWAVE COOKING
COOK LIKE A PEASANT, EAT LIKE A KING
THE BEST OF THE PACIFIC
THE GREAT POTATO COOKBOOK
THE CHICKEN AND THE EGG COOKBOOK
THE COMPLETE CONVECTION OVEN
  COOKBOOK
THE WORLD OF PASTA
THE COMPLETE BOOK OF PIES
RICE—MORE THAN 250 UNEXPECTED WAYS TO COOK THE
  PERFECT FOOD
THE GREAT AMERICAN FAMILY COOKBOOK

THE GREAT AMERICAN FAMILY COOKBOOK

■■■

Maria Luisa Scott
and
Jack Denton Scott

■■■

*America's favorite recipes are
family heirlooms*

BANTAM BOOKS

TORONTO · NEW YORK · LONDON · SYDNEY · AUCKLAND

THE GREAT AMERICAN FAMILY COOKBOOK
A Bantam Book / March 1986

ISBN 0-553-24886-3

Published simultaneously in the United States and Canada

Bantam Books are published by Bantam Books, Inc. Its trademark, consisting of the words "Bantam Books" and the portrayal of a rooster, is Registered in U.S. Patent and Trademark Office and in other countries. Marca Registrada. Bantam Books, Inc., 666 Fifth Avenue, New York, New York 10103.

CONTENTS

PROLOGUE

America is a family of nations. It is also a nation of families. And these families today cook the way they were taught by their ancestors, who came here first and led the way.

We are a unique country made up of peoples from all over the world, who have brought us their strengths, not only of character but cuisine. They have given us rich and varied table treats from the Old World, which have now become the cooking of the New World.

Those of us fortunate enough to have parents, grandparents, or great-grandparents from Europe or elsewhere know all about how certain recipes stir family memories' evoke warm feelings of togetherness.

We bring some of those memories together here, memories not only of our own families but also those of friends and acquaintances—a nostalgic springboard, we hope for a joyful leap into *The Great American Family Cookbook*.

FOREWORD

They had to use the sturdy extra leaves from the big old oak table, propping them flat on chairs on either end to form benches and make room for all of the family and in-laws. I (Jack) was one of the bench-sitting in-laws at this ritual Sunday gathering of the Limoncelli clan. Papa, my father-in-law, Pasquale, sat at the head of the table; Mama, his wife, Maria, at the other end. A human-chain embrace of family surrounded them; three sons, three daughters, three daughters-in-law, three sons-in-law.

Food was spectacular, *antipasti,* anchovies, tuna, mushrooms, beans, peppers, salami, cheese, then soup, followed by a homemade string pasta topped with a rich dark tomato sauce in which the meat course—stuffed, rolled veal, *braciole*—had cooked, sliced tender veal and baby string beans were served after the pasta, then crusty chicken roasted with potatoes arrived with a green salad. Wine, from Pasquale's grapes, flowed like the laughter around us. That regular family gathering, holding all the good things of life—love, togetherness, family loyalty, happiness—ended with a remarkable cake, *zuppa inglese,* with Amaretto substituted for rum, ice cream for custard, and dark strong coffee, espresso. And many *salutes,* good health. It was a day to make memories.

Recently, on another winter's day, my wife decided to recreate for our lunch the soup we had had at that family get-together. She brought it steaming to the table in a big, blue and white tureen and ladled it into bowls, serving it with warm, buttered Italian bread. It was *pasta e fagioli*—beans simmered in chicken broth with a touch of garlic and olive oil, chopped tomatoes, and a few *ditalini,* a short tubular pasta.

A bowl of ordinary soup?

Or a magic mixture, giving our lives a new dimension, blending canny cooking economy and superb ethnic food with memories that will warm us forever?

As we sprinkled grated Asiago cheese on the soup and dipped our spoons in we were treated to a surprising vision: we were at that family gathering again, hearing the laughter, eating the soup, twirling the pasta. Then memory did a scene switch: we saw Pasquale working in his garden, which he had learned to plant when a small boy in Italy. This soup was a specialty of his.

Now in our mind's eye he was standing in his garden. He could grow anything almost on command in that carefully regimented garden: great beefsteak tomatoes staked high, eggplants drooping on tall plants like giant purple plums, pole beans, fava beans, perfect cauliflower looking just dusted with snow, shiny emerald peppers. Pasquale's garden was a work of art.

I remembered another garden when I was growing up in upstate New York, that of our neighbor, who had come from Spain, a garden my mother dubbed "the nursery." He called his vegetables "sons of my soil" and had names for each. When he carefully watered them by hand he was giving *mios niños* (my children) a drink.

Long before most of us realized that chicken was one of our most versatile and economically valuable foods, he was teaching my mother unusual dishes. *Empanada gallega,* a chicken-filled bread pie, was a favorite—chicken, onions, garlic, sweet red pepper, chopped ham, and tomatoes, an impressive dish that puffed up and easily fed a family of six with a single chicken.

I am twelve years old again, talking over the backyard fence with that dark, gentle man, watching his brown hens do an insect-catching ballet around the perimeter of his garden, these thoughts, now with this memory-magic that has come to me, rekindled whenever I cook that Spanish chicken pie.

As we enjoyed that memory-making soup that winter's day we also spoke of Maria Limoncelli, Maria Luisa's mother, and her economic legerdemain, another asset of ethnic cooking. We remembered what she accomplished with a pot of chicken broth (from a fat fowl that she herself had raised):

First, a quick trip to Pasquale's garden for a head of romaine lettuce and a cauliflower. She peeled off the larger, outside leaves of the lettuce, leaving just the heart for salad. The large leaves were simmered briefly in the broth, then forked out and chopped, mixed with a touch of olive oil and garlic for a delicious vegetable.

Half the broth was saved for a future minestrone soup. Into the remainder of the simmering broth she stirred eggs beaten with parsley and grated Romano cheese, producing the classic *stracciatelli* soup. The results of her economic expertise: two luncheons, a different, tasty vegetable, a salad, and a dinner to come.

That evening she prepared *cavatelli,* curled, thumbnail-size pasta, tossing it with cooked flowerets of cauliflower, butter, black pepper, and grated Parmesan cheese.

It amuses us today to remember back when some of Maria's ingredients—olive oil, garlic, pasta (which nearly everyone called "spaghetti")—were regarded with curled lips. Today they are culinary status items.

My Scotch grandmother's "highlander's pie" may never be considered a status item, but it ranked high with her grandchildren and with this particular grandchild, who now prepares it often, communing with that sagacious, warm-hearted old lady every time he puts it together. Like most good dishes, it is simple. Leftover meat, any kind, but we loved beef, mixed with gravy, placed in a baking dish, lavishly smoothed over with creamy mashed potatoes, and popped into a hot oven until brown.

Our European heritage- and memory-makers had high regard for potatoes, sometimes giving them equal billing with meat, often combining them with other ingredients. We have a friend who when he smells sauerkraut always sees Holland and his family's flower farm, tulips blazing against a bleak sky, and his mother's spotless but aromatic kitchen and remembers her mixing mashed potatoes with cooked sauerkraut in a favorite family recipe.

Another friend, Barbara Valbona, revisits her mother and teen days every time she puts together *jambota*, an

Italian dish of sliced potatoes layered with onions, leftover meat, and peppers. And a friend with Austrian parents gets emotional when he talks about *hoppelpoppel*—potatoes with onions, bacon, and eggs. Thoughts of family food have the power to stir much more than just the appetite.

Take John Petrokaitis's Lithuanian mother Sofia's potato *kugeli*, a cake made with grated Idahos, seasonings, eggs, sautéed minced onion, bacon, and milk and baked until golden. "A transporter," he calls it, for as he prepares it he is growing up again on his grandparents' farm in Connecticut, seeing his father and grandfather start off early in the morning for the barn and the cows across a field silvered with frost, hearing again the big old battle-scarred rooster crowing up the dawn.

Potatoes made Jack's friend Steve Derry think of his Polish mother in Brooklyn and her potato meat loaf—raw, grated potatoes blended with ground beef, onion, tomato sauce, and cheese. They served in World War II together, and Derry never saw a potato that he didn't rattle on about his mother's clever dish, which predated today's popular hamburger helper by years. And he would talk, eyes misting, about her and his family in Greenpoint at length, about the hard years and his parents' courage. Such is the magic of the potato for some of us.

Seeing again on the table in Ireland a dinner consisting only of potatoes, Dennis Hussey's mother hopefully asked what else they were going to have. "You'll have the big ones with the little ones and the little ones with the big ones," her mother said, "and thank God you've got 'em."

But the Irish had a couple of tricks that gave those potatoes flavor variety. They mashed them and stirred in cooked onions; sometimes they also mashed them and mixed in boiled turnips. When they could scare up some bacon and sausage, they also made a potato coddle, layering potatoes, bacon, onions, and sausage, pouring in hot water, and baking it into that famous dish. Dennis Hussey's mother taught her son all of these variations, but the dish he likes best and cooks most is her mutton pie, a rare treat in Ireland because of budget.

"With its special sorcery I bring not only my mother into

the kitchen with me every time I cook it," Dennis says, "but Ireland itself. On a cold February night it's a warm and tasty reminder of all the good things."

He uses a boned leg of lamb, the bone becoming a base for the gravy that goes into the pie with the meat mixed with chopped salt pork and seasonings. Then the whole thing is covered with pie dough and baked until golden—into what Dennis calls "a memorable Irish work of art."

Winter also revives warm memories for Antoine Gilly, who became one of the world's great French chefs. It was his grandmother and her cooking in Burgundy that led Antoine into his profession. The first day of winter, especially when snow has fallen, he regularly prepares a special dish, honoring his grandmother who created it, and thereby reliving his childhood days with her. It was *mitonnée*, her first soup of the winter—chicken broth mixed with rich farm cream and stale breadcrumbs and served piping hot to the whole family as an early breakfast.

"Whenever she cooked it," Antoine recalls, "she would say, 'This is the morning to make the pot smile.' She made the whole family smile."

We've been surprised time after time by all the many families with these meaningful melting pot memories. We are indeed a land given strength for survival by the many nationalities who have brought their know-how from the Old World. At random we talked with more than a dozen people who enthusiastically shared memories of their forebears' ways with food and what those memories mean to them today. Without exception, what turned the clock back happily for them wasn't fancy, festive food—a fat goose stuffed with apples, or a prune-filled pork loin—but simple recipes. Even just those prosaic potatoes or, for Sally Kulik Noble, a cabbage.

The mere sight of that leafy head calls up scenes of a wood-burning kitchen stove and a happy childhood, when the world was simpler. It also brings her Ukrainian mother's skill to Sally's kitchen in Bedford Hills, New York. "She used what we had, what we grew, just as she did in the Ukraine," Sally remembers, adding, "but it's the pleasure, not the pennies, that we count when we cook what she taught us." The cabbage was parboiled, leaves separated, spine removed, leaves then spread with a mixture of cooked rice, onions, chopped, browned salt pork, ground pork or beef, and seasonings, rolled cigar-fashion, topped with home-canned tomatoes, then larger cabbage leaves spread flat over the rolls, and slowly baked in the oven.

Sally chuckles over the fact that her mother is sensitive about those cabbage rolls. "When a grandchild stuck up a nose at cabbage for dinner, she would snap, 'You've got to like cabbage. It's part of your heritage.' In a few minutes the child would say, 'Grandma, I like it, I like it.' "

B. J. Guidetti's heritage is a melting pot in itself, filled with dishes that fire up memories of her Korean father and German mother. Sometimes even an era is recreated when she cooks a family recipe. "We were the first Oriental family in Suffern, New York," she says, "and our dishes had to be very strange to that community. A fishmonger would come up on the train from New York City once a week and sit on the back doorsteps cleaning the fish you bought on newspaper. Lobster was very cheap, so was squid. People hadn't yet worked up the courage to eat those odd-looking creatures. Cooked Korean style they were fantastically delicious."

While the neighbors' children were eating hamburgers, hot dogs, and fried chicken, B. J. enjoyed barbecued beef short ribs, flank steak marinated in oil and spices, and smoked tongue with raisin sauce.

"Today the aroma of the kitchen drops the years away from me," B. J. says. Her late Italian husband, Ralph, a famous restauranteur, and her daughters enjoy B. J.'s melting pot of recipes; Korean short ribs with linguine, Italian-style, tossed with oil and garlic, Korean string beans with her mother's spatzle, a German pasta.

There is no generation gap with her melting pot memories: *gooksu,* a Korean cold summer soup, is now cooked by her daughters for their children—cold chicken broth blended with small pieces, of stir-fried beef or pork, lettuce in pieces, cooked vermicelli, and crushed toasted sesame seeds. "When any of us cook it," B. J. says, "it's like

••

looking at a photograph of my Korean father—a photograph come alive like a face on the TV screen."

Those who smoothed the bumpy road ahead for many
of us considered "fast food" certain meatless days when
they were fasting, and their vitamins came on a plate, not
from a bottle.

Although they knew that eggs were as valuable and
much more versatile than meat, they probably weren't
aware that that powerhouse in a shell had every vitamin
except C, plus thirteen minerals. But they were very con-
scious of the fact that the egg was the most economical
and versatile food.

The Old World ways of converting eggs into main dishes
provide countless childhood memories for many of us:
dozens of French-style rolled omelets; flat Italian cakes,
frittate; eggs scrambled with potatoes Spanish style, poached
in a spicy tomato sauce, "eggs in hell," as Bruno Valbona
called his family's dish. My father scrambled eggs with
calf's brains; my grandfather rolled hard-cooked eggs in
beaten egg, then molded them with sausage meat and
deep-fried them, and my grandmother broke them whole
atop sliced cooked potatoes and baked them with cream
and cheese in a "baker's wife" technique.

But it isn't especially the economy those of us who nostal-
gically remember and use Old World egg recipes treasure,
but their uniqueness. Brunhilde Johnson of Washington,
Connecticut, often recreates *eier nudeln,* her German parents' dish of leftover noodles fried in butter then mixed
with beaten eggs and cooked until set. Today her family
applauds the "pasta omelet" that she makes from leftover
spaghetti.

Ann Dahl, also of Washington, Connecticut, with a Swedish father and Norwegian mother, has a long list of
Scandinavian memory- and money-savers, but the one that
holds the warmest memories of what she calls her "parents' ingenious frugality" is Norwegian *aggkaka.* They often had a home-cured, smoked ham hanging in the cellar.
The egg cake was made by frying bits of ham and ham fat,
then stirring into it eggs, flour, milk, and salt beaten together, and then placing it in the oven. "It puffed up like a

popover," she recalls. "It still does, impressing the new generation just as much as it did us."

Eggs for William Bauserman bring back childhood days in Virginia (and a memory of meals that didn't include eggs), when his Swiss grandfather had him collect eggs from the henhouse every Friday and sell them at the local store to buy a big chunk of Cheddar cheese and a quarter pound of dried, chipped beef for meals the Swiss called "stomach stuffers."

The cheese (and few Swiss meals were complete without it, Bauserman remembers), generously blended with cooked elbow macaroni, butter, flour, cream, and crushed saltine crackers, became the Bauserman's classic Saturday night dinner. Midweek brought creamed chipped beef over hot cornbread.

"It was a ritual," Bauserman says, "that I continue today, not because it saves money, but because it is delicious and it is 'family.'"

These family recipes often also stir up somewhat sad memories for many of us of better days, when the family dining table was the focal point of the home, the symbol of togetherness, where everyone gathered at least once a day for discussions of current happenings, future dreams, problems. All were part of that evening meal—and everyone had better be there, or have a very good reason for not being part of the family group. Best of all was the conversation.

Regrettably, today that valuable, family-knitting relationship is lost for many of us to a too busy world, television replacing the dinner table as the modern symbol of the home, where we sit mute, staring, not sharing. But for us lucky ones, the melting pot still bubbles with memories of happy family times, spilling over into our homes today, enriching our lives.

There is evidence everywhere that these heirloom recipes now not only are America's favorite family cooking, but have become through use and pride truly "American recipes," the cooking of our nation, which is matched by no other country.

Our ethnic dishes are being used more and more not

only because of their simplicity of preparation and their cunning circumvention of inflation but because they are imaginative and delicious and lend themselves to improvisation.

Recently, the United States has been pressured by writers and media "cooks" to switch to so-called new (light) cooking, *nouvelle cuisine,* an artificial and manufactured "French" concept that the French themselves don't use. We, as a team, predicted that it wouldn't last: it was loaded with excesses; it was simple and light in concept only, not in practice. Fish were overwhelmed with so many ingredients that the delicate flavor of the fish vanished. Some of the dishes were artfully arranged, but art was never easy to eat. Sometimes two or three sauces dominated a single dish.

Famed master chef Jacques Pepin speaks for most professional and serious American cooks in his summing up of *nouvelle cuisine* in *Bon Appetit* magazine. He called it *cuisine de bébé,* or "baby food." "Nothing has texture," he said. "The dishes are overcomplex, overprecious, overworked, and with too many sauces." He added that the so-called light cuisine has become the reverse of simplicity.

Also, there is a new wave of "American cuisine," largely a fad and representing a semantic confusion. American cooking has always been a practice of improvisation, or "make do," using what one had. If a New England cook made a cranberry-nut pie, she used the old basic berry pie technique, probably originated in England, then adapted with the local cranberries and perhaps hickory nuts. Making a duck pâté French style with Long Island duckling is not new, but that is what the new wave calls "American." Throwing about everything but the boat into a Pacific Northwest stew is also "American," or regional, but an honest opinion would have to conclude that it is remarkably like a French bouillabaisse.

There are original regional dishes, good ones, and we have included some. However, because we may use Monterey Jack in some Italian recipes rather than Mozzarella doesn't make the recipe "ours." Basic recipes of most American cooking are most likely European. What gives many of these dishes their New World appeal is the use of our own fresh produce—meats, poultry and fish, unequalled in the world.

American apples, oranges, peaches, pears, raspberries, strawberries, mushrooms, onions, tomatoes, and Idaho potatoes have no counterpart anywhere. Our beef and lamb are the world's best; our poultry may not have the international respect of the famous French chickens and geese, but in world cookoffs, the United States has always emerged at the top or near the top in contests using American poultry.

So ingredients are really the key to this current cooking craze that is bent on making everything come out "American."

But the propaganda and the pretentious concept isn't working. Ethnic dishes are more popular than ever. As this is written, in Manhattan, where classic foods of the world have made the restaurants there justly famous, two simple dishes—French beef stew and an Italian offering of beans and pasta—are gathering new fans, and pasta dishes are prestige food. Look closely at the recipes that follow, forgetting the food magazines' fancy frills and way-out creations (like poaching prunes in herbal tea, or boiling red potatoes in Asti Spumante), and you will realize that our recipes are sensible, time proven, and classic. Recipes that never fade like fads.

Some are American originals, but with many, someone has been there before us: our ancestors, who made America what it is, starting in the kitchen.

Chapter 1

APPETIZERS AND SALADS

Americans are fond of little nibbles with their evening drinks before dinner, also often something more substantial that can be eaten with cocktails or as a first course at dinner. Often this special food has its genesis with our ancestors, who favored certain foods as that first offering. Our own Italian forebears liked eggplant and zucchini, and we offer a couple of examples here.

Actually, though, we in the United States are probably the most inventive at creating and assembling what has come to be called appetizers. Probably even more so than the French, with their hors d'oeuvres, even though they have been at it for a longer time. But French immigrants also gave us a head start, as did many of the other nationalities that gathered here.

Salads, too, were a hand-me-down bonus from these inventive and economical people who did so much for us. We think we invented the potato salad. We didn't. It came with the folks who checked through Ellis Island.

But again, with salads, we in the United States probably ran out ahead of everyone else, even though we use many European and Asian touches. For example, California introduced the "salad first" method of dining. We, as a team, don't care particularly for this, as it has a number of drawbacks. A lusty salad can fill you up and make the food to follow less appealing. Because many salads are made with vinegar, they destroy, or lessen, the sensitivity of the taste buds for the wine that may be drunk with the dinner, or delicate foods that follow. We've had that salad first course at friends' followed by a unique shrimp dish, and we couldn't even taste the shrimp. We solve this by asking (at restaurants) for the salad to be served with the meal, or even after it.

But such is the appeal and popularity of salads that we remain very much in the minority with our salad-first complaint. Salads are great summer fare, also make excellent luncheon entrees, and can be a dramatic and decorative addition to any meal. We offer a number that we find have turned our guests on and also honor the various nationalities that conceived some of them.

We first had a bean and tuna salad in Genoa and were somewhat shocked at the price but very taken with the combination. Since then we have served it often as a first course and have found it in various restaurants all over America.

And cole slaw! It comes in almost as many versions as there are nationalities that make up our country. But there is one fact for sure: it most certainly is an American creation. In traveling around the world a dozen times, we never saw it in any country, even the "cabbage" countries of Germany, the Baltic states, and Scandinavia.

EASY CHICKEN LIVER PÂTÉ
■■■

Makes 2½ cups, enough for 6:

1 POUND CHICKEN
   LIVERS, CLEANED
¼ TEASPOON DRIED MARJORAM
1 MEDIUM ONION, MINCED
¾ CUP PLUS 2 TABLESPOONS
   BUTTER, AT ROOM
   TEMPERATURE

1 TABLESPOON BRANDY
2 TABLESPOONS DRY SHERRY
SALT AND PEPPER TO TASTE
BUTTERED TOAST
CORNICHONS (A SMALL TARRA-
   GON-FLAVORED PICKLE)

IN A SAUCEPAN, cover the livers with water and add the marjoram. Bring to a boil and cook until done, about 8 to 10 minutes. They should be slightly pink inside. Drain and cool. Sauté the onion in 2 tablespoons of the butter until just soft (do not brown). Purée the livers and onion in a processor or push them through a sieve. In a bowl mix well with the butter, brandy, sherry, salt, and pepper and serve on buttered toast as canapés with a slice of cornichon on top. Or serve at the table on lettuce leaves with slices of buttered toast and cornichons.

CHEDDARED CLAMS

■ ■ ■

Americans have come up with more ways to cook clams than anyone, perhaps because we appear to have more than anyone. Here's a hot little number to offer with drinks.

½ POUND NEW YORK STATE
 MILD CHEDDAR CHEESE,
 SHREDDED
TWO 10½-OUNCE CANS MINCED
 CLAMS, DRAINED
3 TABLESPOONS MINCED
 PARSLEY
2 GARLIC CLOVES, MINCED

2 SMALL WHITE ONIONS,
 MINCED
⅛ TEASPOON BLACK PEPPER
⅛ TEASPOON CAYENNE, OR TO
 TASTE
20 SLICES (OR MORE) PEPPER-
 IDGE FARM PARTY RYE
 BREAD

IN A BOWL, combine and blend well all ingredients except the bread. Arrange the small bread slices on a baking sheet. Spoon a small amount of clam mixture on each slice, smoothing it so it won't topple off when passed from hand to mouth. Place under the broiler until bubbly golden. *Serves 10.*

CLAMS OREGANATO

■■■

2 MEDIUM-SIZED, RIPE, FIRM
   TOMATOES, PEELED, SEEDED,
   AND CHOPPED
½ CUP CHOPPED PARSLEY
1 LARGE GARLIC CLOVE,
   MINCED
3 TABLESPOONS OLIVE OIL
¼ TEASPOON DRIED OREGANO

3 CUPS FRESH CHOPPED
   CLAMS, OR USE MINCED
   CANNED CLAMS, DRAINED
SALT AND PEPPER TO TASTE
¾ CUP BREAD CRUMBS
½ CUP GRATED ASIAGO OR
   PARMESAN CHEESE

IN A BOWL combine and mix well all ingredients except the bread crumbs and cheese. Divide among 6 scallop shells, or 6 small ramekins. Sprinkle top with bread crumbs, then the cheese. Place under broiler until golden and cheese has melted. *Serves 6.*

Note: These can be frozen in the shells or ramekins and sprinkled with bread crumbs and cheese just before cooking.

ITALIAN COLD SLICED EGGPLANT
(with Piquant Sauce)

■ ■ ■

2 MEDIUM-SIZED EGGPLANTS,   3 TABLESPOONS OLIVE OIL
   THINLY SLICED LENGTHWISE   PIQUANT SAUCE (SEE BELOW)

IN A FRYPAN, over medium heat, heat the oil and evenly brown the eggplant on both sides. Add more oil, if needed. Drain on paper towels and cool. Serve cold with Piquant Sauce sprinkled over the top. *Serves 4 to 6.*

Piquant Sauce

6 ANCHOVY FILLETS, MASHED   ¼ CUP WINE VINEGAR
1 TABLESPOON CAPERS   PEPPER TO TASTE
1 GARLIC CLOVE, PUT THROUGH   3 TABLESPOONS MINCED
   A GARLIC PRESS   PARSLEY
¾ CUP OLIVE OIL

In a bowl combine all ingredients and blend.

MUSSELS WITH PIQUANT SAUCE
■ ■ ■

3 TABLESPOONS BUTTER
2 WHOLE SCALLIONS (GREEN
   ONIONS), MINCED
1 CUP DRY WHITE WINE
1 BAY LEAF

½ TEASPOON DRIED THYME
¼ TEASPOON PEPPER
32 MUSSELS, WELL SCRUBBED
   AND DEBEARDED
PIQUANT SAUCE (SEE BELOW)

IN A HEAVY, deep frypan, over medium heat, melt the butter and cook the scallions until soft. Add the wine, bay leaf, thyme, and pepper and simmer 5 minutes. Raise heat, add the mussels, cover tightly, and cook 5 to 6 minutes, shaking the pan several times, or until the shells open and the mussels are just firm. Do not overcook, or they'll become rubbery, but they should be separated from the shell when done. Remove from the pan with a slotted spoon and cool. Serve them on the half-shell with a spoonful of the warmed Piquant Sauce spooned over each. *Serves 4.*

Piquant Sauce

¼ POUND BUTTER, CUT INTO
   PIECES
¼ CUP STRAINED LEMON JUICE
1 TABLESPOON CHOPPED
   PARSLEY

1 TABLESPOON CAPERS, DRAINED
   (IF SMALL, LEAVE WHOLE,
   IF LARGE, CHOP)
4 ANCHOVY FILLETS, CHOPPED

Combine all ingredients in a saucepan. Heat until butter melts and blend well.

CHINCOTEAGUE OYSTERS IN PASTRY
■ ■ ■

Makes 12 pastries:

12 LARGE, DRAINED CHINCO-
  TEAGUE OYSTERS
½ CUP LEMON JUICE
2 TABLESPOONS MINCED
  SHALLOTS
SALT TO TASTE
⅛ TEASPOON CAYENNE, OR TO
  TASTE

PASTRY FOR A 2-CRUST, 9-INCH
  PIE (DOUBLE THE RECIPE
  FOR THE PASTRY IN NEW
  ENGLAND CLAM PIE, p. 82)
MELTED BUTTER
BUTTER

COMBINE THE OYSTERS, lemon juice, shallots, salt, and cayenne in a bowl, and gently mix to coat the oysters. Refrigerate
while you prepare the pastry. Roll out the pastry, and cut
it into 4-inch circles, ⅛-inch thick. Brush each circle with
melted butter. Place 1 oyster in the center of each circle,
and place a dot of butter on it. Moisten the edges of the
pastry and bring it over the oyster to form a half-moon.
Pinch the edges together to seal. Pierce the top with the
tines of a fork to allow steam to escape. Place on a baking
sheet and bake in a preheated 425° oven for 20 minutes,
or until the pastry is golden brown.

Note: If large oysters are not available, use 2 smaller
ones for each pastry.

PIZZA
■■■

Pizza, which simply means pie in Italian slang, came here with immigrants from the Naples area, where these tomato delights were perfected. They didn't originate there, however, as a kind of pizza was eaten in ancient Rome. In the United States the pizza is becoming more American than apple pie. Yearly we buy $1 billion worth of frozen and $2.5 billion worth of fresh from pizzerias.

This recipe is just a "pizza starter." Your imagination makes almost any combination possible—everything from anchovies to even a zucchini pizza, zucchini being that "everything" vegetable that appears in just about everything except ice cream.

Basic Pizza Dough

Excellent pizza dough is also available in most supermarkets, which makes making pizza even easier.
For two 12-inch pizzas:

2 PACKAGES DRY ACTIVE YEAST
¼ TEASPOON SUGAR
1 CUP WARM (NOT HOT) WATER
4 CUPS UNBLEACHED ALL-
   PURPOSE FLOUR
1½ TEASPOONS SALT
3½ TABLESPOONS OLIVE OIL

PLACE THE YEAST and sugar in a cup with the warm water. Allow to stand for 10 minutes to dissolve. Stir and place in a warm, draft-free place for several minutes, until it bubbles and expands. Place the flour and salt in a large bowl. With your fingers make a well in the center. Pour in the yeast–water mixture and the olive oil, working the flour into the liquid with your fingers and working from the center to the side of the bowl. Continue mixing until the dough can be formed into a ball. Place the ball of dough on a lightly floured board and knead for 15 minutes, or until the dough is elastic and smooth, not sticky. (If the dough is too wet and sticky, work in more flour, very small amounts at a time.) Place the ball of dough in a lightly buttered bowl, turn to lightly coat the whole ball with butter. Cover and set in a warm place to allow the dough to rise until doubled in volume, about 1 hour. A slightly warm oven (turned off) is good for this. With your fist, punch the dough down. Knead for 5 minutes and return to the warm place to rise again, until double in bulk. It is now ready to use.

Basic Tomato Sauce Pizza

Makes one 12-inch pizza:

4 TABLESPOONS OLIVE OIL
ONE 1-POUND CAN PLUM
　　TOMATOES (OR 5 FRESH,
　　RIPE PLUM TOMATOES,
　　PEELED AND SEEDED),
　　DRAINED, AND CHOPPED

1 GARLIC CLOVE, MINCED
1 SMALL ONION, MINCED
SALT AND PEPPER TO TASTE
1 TEASPOON DRIED OREGANO
BASIC PIZZA DOUGH (SEE
　　ABOVE)

Combine and blend well in a bowl 3 tablespoons of olive oil with all the other ingredients except the pizza dough. Oil a 12-inch pizza pan with the remaining olive oil. Divide the dough into halves. Save half the dough for another pizza. Roll out and place the other half in the pizza pan. With oiled fingers, stretch the dough over the rim to form a ½-inch, slightly raised rim circling the pan. Spread the tomato mixture over the dough, using the back of a spoon to distribute it evenly. Bake in a preheated 425° oven for 30 minutes, or until the rim is crusty brown. This is delicious as it is, but usually a variety of other ingredients are arranged on the tomato sauce.

Variations

Note: When additional ingredients are to be placed atop the basic pizza, cook the basic pizza with the tomato sauce 20 minutes. Remove from the oven, add the other ingredients, and cook for another 10 minutes.

CHEESE

| 1 CUP GRATED MOZZARELLA CHEESE | ½ CUP GRATED ASIAGO, PARMESAN, OR ROMANO CHEESE |

Sprinkle both cheeses evenly over the partially cooked basic pizza and cook another 10 minutes, or until the cheese has melted.

SEAFOOD

| ½ CUP GRATED MOZZARELLA CHEESE | ½ POUND SHELLED MUSSELS, CLAMS, OR DEVEINED SHRIMP, COOKED UNTIL JUST FIRM, OR ONE 2-OUNCE CAN FLAT ANCHOVIES, DRAINED |

Evenly distribute the cheese and shellfish or anchovies over the basic pizza and cook another 10 minutes, or until the cheese has melted, and shellfish are just firm.

MEAT OR VEGETABLE

| ½ CUP GRATED MOZZARELLA CHEESE | ½ POUND SLICED PEPPERONI, SLICED PRECOOKED ITALIAN SAUSAGE, OR THINLY SLICED FRESH MUSH-ROOMS, OR 1 DOZEN, PITTED, SLICED BLACK OLIVES, OR THINLY SLICED RAW VEGETA-BLES OF YOUR CHOICE (ZUCCHINI IS A FAVORITE) |

Evenly distribute the cheese and meat or vegetables over the partially cooked basic pizza and cook another 10 minutes, or until the cheese has melted.

SHANGHAI SHRIMP BALLS
■ ■ ■

This is a favorite of Chinese Americans, often served with cocktails.

1½ POUNDS SHRIMP, SHELLED, AND DEVEINED
ONE 6-OUNCE CAN WATER CHESTNUTS
3 SCALLIONS (GREEN ONIONS), INCLUDING ALL BUT THE LAST INCH OF THE GREEN PART
1 LARGE GARLIC CLOVE, PUSHED THROUGH A GARLIC PRESS

2 TEASPOONS CORNSTARCH
1 EGG, BEATEN
SALT TO TASTE
CORNSTARCH (IN WHICH TO ROLL BALLS BEFORE SAUTÉING)
PEANUT OIL
ORANGE SAUCE (SEE BELOW)

MINCE (PUT THROUGH a food chopper or processor) shrimp, water chestnuts, and scallions. In a large bowl, combine and blend well all ingredients except cornstarch and peanut oil. Form into balls slightly smaller than walnuts. Roll lightly in the cornstarch and, over medium heat, sauté in hot peanut oil until golden, turning to brown evenly. Serve hot with Orange Sauce. *Serves 8.*

Orange Sauce

1 CUP ORANGE MARMALADE
¼ CUP LEMON JUICE
1 TEASPOON FRESH GRATED HORSERADISH

¼ TEASPOON POWDERED GINGER

In a bowl combine all ingredients and blend well. Makes about 1½ cups.

STEAK TARTARE
■ ■ ■

1½ POUND TOP ROUND, FILET, OR SIRLOIN, PUT THROUGH A FOOD CHOPPER 2 OR 3 TIMES, OR USE A FOOD PROCESSOR TO PRODUCE SMOOTH, FINELY MINCED MEAT (THE PROCESSOR IS ESPECIALLY GOOD BECAUSE IT PRODUCES A PUREE-LIKE TEXTURE, BUT BE CAREFUL NOT TO OVERPROCESS)

1 JUMBO EGG YOLK OR 2 SMALLER YOLKS (INTACT)
½ CUP CHOPPED PARSLEY
⅓ CUP FINELY CHOPPED WHITE ONION
¼ CUP SMALL CAPERS, RINSED AND DRAINED (IF LARGE, CHOP)
8 ANCHOVY FILLETS
SALT AND PEPPER TO TASTE
24 SMALL PARTY ROUNDS OF RYE BREAD, BUTTERED

PLACE THE MEAT in the center of a serving dish, shaping it into a large thick patty. Make a depression in the center and slip the egg yolk into it. Arrange the parsley in a ring around the meat. Spoon the onion and capers in small mounds on the parsley. Arrange the anchovy fillets like spokes in a wheel, leading out from the egg yolk. Bring to the serving table and mix before your guests with a large spoon and fork, blending all ingredients well and adding salt and pepper. Serve on the buttered bread. *Serves 6.*

ZUCCHINI PIE

■■■

1 CUP BISQUICK OR OTHER
   BISCUIT MIX
½ CUP VEGETABLE OIL
3 CUPS THINLY SLICED
   ZUCCHINI (ABOUT 3 OR 4
   SMALL ONES)
1 CUP GRATED ASIAGO,
   PARMESAN, OR CHEESE OF
   YOUR CHOICE

4 EGGS, BEATEN
3 SCALLIONS (GREEN ONIONS),
   FINELY CHOPPED, USING
   MOST OF THE DARK GREEN
   PART
2 TABLESPOONS FINELY
   CHOPPED PARSLEY
SALT AND PEPPER TO TASTE

MIX ALL INGREDIENTS together in a large bowl. Spoon into a buttered 8-inch square baking dish. Bake in a preheated 350° oven 35 minutes, or until golden and set (a knife blade inserted just off center will come out clean). Let set a few minutes before cutting into squares. *Serves 6.*

BEANS AND TUNA

■ ■ ■

1 POUND DRY GREAT
   NORTHERN BEANS, PICKED
   OVER AND SOAKED FOR 5
   HOURS IN WATER TO COVER
ABOUT 5 CUPS CHICKEN BROTH,
   TO COVER BEANS
3 GARLIC CLOVES, PEELED
TWO 7-OUNCE CANS BUMBLE
   BEE FANCY SOLID WHITE
   TUNA, DRAINED AND BROKEN
   INTO LARGE BITE-SIZED
   PIECES

⅓ CUP OLIVE OIL
JUICE OF 1 LARGE LEMON
½ CUP CHOPPED BROADLEAF
   PARSLEY
SALT AND PEPPER TO TASTE

DRAIN THE BEANS and place them in a large pot with enough of the chicken broth to cover them well. Add the garlic, bring the liquid to a boil, lower heat, cover the pot, and simmer *very slowly* (the broth should be barely shimmering over the beans) until the beans are just tender. Do not overcook. The beans should be cooked but still firm. When cooked, most of the liquid will have cooked off. Cool them in the remaining liquid. Drain and discard the garlic. Add the tuna, oil, lemon juice, half of the parsley, salt, and pepper. Mix carefully but well. Taste for seasoning, adding more oil, lemon juice, salt, and pepper, if desired. Spoon on lettuce leaves and sprinkle with additional parsley. Serve with some good, crusty bread. *Serves 6 to 8.*

BULGUR GARDEN SALAD
(Tabbouleh)

■ ■ ■

Middle Eastern dishes (Armenian, Lebanese, Syrian) are becoming very popular in American cuisine. Here's one that took off in California and swept across the country to the East Coast.

1 CUP BULGUR (FINE CRACKED WHEAT)
2 BUNCHES SCALLIONS (GREEN ONIONS), WHITE PART ONLY, CHOPPED (ABOUT 1 CUP)
1 BUNCH BROADLEAF PARSLEY, CHOPPED (ABOUT 1 CUP)
10 FRESH MINT LEAVES, CHOPPED
4 LARGE, RIPE, FIRM TOMATOES, SKINNED, SEEDED, AND CHOPPED

⅓ CUP LEMON JUICE
⅓ CUP OLIVE OIL
SALT AND PEPPER TO TASTE
LETTUCE LEAVES FROM THE HEART OF A HEAD OF ROMAINE OR BOSTON LETTUCE, OR TENDER CABBAGE, OR GRAPE LEAVES

SOAK THE BULGUR in cold water to cover for 10 minutes. Drain and squeeze very dry with your hands. In a large bowl, combine and blend well the wheat, scallions, parsley, mint, tomatoes, lemon juice, olive oil, salt, and pepper. Taste for seasoning. Serve with the leaves, using them as a scoop, as the Middle Easterners do, or simply serve it on lettuce leaves and eat with a fork. *Serves 6.*

CAESAR SALAD
■■■

Here's a famous "American" salad with both French and Italian touches.

1 HEAD ROMAINE LETTUCE
1 HEAD BOSTON LETTUCE
SALT
1 LARGE GARLIC CLOVE
½ TEASPOON DRIED MUSTARD
3 TABLESPOONS LEMON JUICE
FRESHLY GROUND BLACK PEPPER
⅓ CUP OLIVE OIL
1 EGG, COOKED IN BOILING
   WATER FOR 30 SECONDS

½ CUP GRATED ASIAGO OR
   PARMESAN CHEESE
ONE 2-OUNCE CAN FLAT
   ANCHOVY FILLETS,
   DRAINED
12 CHAPONS (SEE BELOW), OR
   1 CUP GARLIC CROUTONS

DISCARD OUTERMOST leaves from both heads of lettuce. Wash and dry lettuce leaves and chill to crisp. Then break into bite-sized pieces. Lightly sprinkle the bottom of a wooden salad bowl with salt. Vigorously rub the bowl with the garlic and salt. Discard the garlic. Add the mustard, lemon juice, and pepper and blend well. Add the oil and blend. Add the lettuce. Break the egg on top. Sprinkle on the cheese and add the anchovies. Mix all well with wooden salad utensils until all trace of the egg has disappeared. Taste for seasoning, adding more lemon juice or whatever other seasoning your taste demands. Just before serving (so they won't become soggy) add the chapons or croutons. Toss. *Serves 6.*

Chapons

Chapons are slices from the heel of French bread, about 1-inch in diameter, rubbed well with garlic. Added to the salad they give a pleasant garlic flavor and are especially tasty after being mixed with the dressing.

COLE SLAW
■■■

1 LARGE (ABOUT 2 POUNDS), FIRM HEAD CABBAGE, QUARTERED, TOUGH CORE REMOVED AND DISCARDED AND CABBAGE FINELY SHREDDED OR GRATED
1 SMALL CARROT, SCRAPED AND GRATED
2 TEASPOONS CARAWAY SEED
1 TEASPOON CELERY SEED
1 SMALL ONION, MINCED
¾ CUP MAYONNAISE
¾ CUP SOUR CREAM
1 TABLESPOON LEMON JUICE
1 TEASPOON SUGAR
SALT TO TASTE
⅛ TEASPOON CAYENNE PEPPER, OR TO TASTE

IN A BOWL blend all ingredients except the cabbage and carrot and chill. Place the cabbage and carrot in a large serving bowl. Add the chilled dressing and mix well. Serve immediately. *Serves 6 to 8.*

Note: If desired, chopped cucumber or pineapple can be added. Or the cabbage can be mixed with your favorite vinaigrette sauce.

CUCUMBERS STUFFED
WITH FETA CHEESE

■ ■ ■

Here's a classic example of the immigrant's touch with a popular American vegetable. The simple addition of the Greek cheese lifts this into a unique offering.

4 SMALL OR MEDIUM
   CUCUMBERS, CUT IN HALF
   LENGTHWISE AND SEEDS
   SCOOPED OUT TO MAKE A
   CUCUMBER BOAT
1 CUP CRUMBLED FETA CHEESE

2 TABLESPOONS MAYONNAISE
4 DROPS WORCESTERSHIRE
   SAUCE
CHOPPED PARSLEY
LETTUCE LEAVES

IN A BOWL blend feta, mayonnaise, and Worcestershire with a fork into a coarse mixture. Divide the cheese mixture evenly among the cucumber halves and smooth over the hollowed area. Set on lettuce leaves and sprinkle with parsley. *Serves 4.*

Note: For canapés, cut the cucumbers crosswise into 3/8-inch-thick slices. Remove the seedy center and fill with the cheese mixture. Serve on rounds of buttered bread and sprinkle parsley on top.

GREEK SALAD
■■■

1/4 CUP LEMON JUICE
1/2 CUP OLIVE OIL
1/2 TEASPOON DRIED OREGANO
SALT AND PEPPER TO TASTE
1 HEAD ROMAINE LETTUCE,
    OR 1 LARGE HEAD BIBB
    OR BOSTON
1 HEAD CHICORY OR
    ESCAROLE
2 CUCUMBERS, PEELED, CUT
    LENGTHWISE, SEEDS RE-
    MOVED, AND SLICED
1 BUNCH RADISHES, SLICED

6 SCALLIONS (GREEN ONIONS),
    WHITE PART ONLY, CUT
    INTO 1/2-INCH PIECES
3/4 CUP CRUMBLED FETA
    CHEESE
3 RIPE, FIRM TOMATOES,
    PEELED AND CUT INTO
    1/2-INCH SLICES
18 PITTED BLACK OLIVES (THE
    PLUMP, PURPLISH GREEK
    ONES)
1 TABLESPOON CHOPPED
    FRESH MINT (OR PARSLEY)

IN A BOWL blend lemon juice, oil, oregano, salt, and pepper and set aside. Discard outermost leaves on both heads of lettuce. Wash and dry the lettuce leaves thoroughly. Chill to crisp. Tear the lettuce leaves into bite-sized pieces into a salad bowl. Add the cucumbers, radishes, scallions, and feta cheese. Pour on half of the salad dressing and mix thoroughly. Arrange the tomato slices overlapping on top of the greens around the edge of the bowl and the olives in the center. Dribble the remaining salad dressing over the tomatoes and sprinkle with the mint (or parsley). *Serves 6.*

GREEN BEAN SALAD

■ ■ ■

½ CUP OLIVE OIL
3 TABLESPOONS LEMON JUICE
SALT AND PEPPER TO TASTE
1 POUND FRESH TENDER
    GREEN BEANS, COOKED IN
    UNSALTED BOILING WATER
    UNTIL CRISP-TENDER AND
    WELL DRAINED

1 MEDIUM-SIZED RED ITALIAN
    ONION, THINLY SLICED
1 TABLESPOON CHOPPED
    PARSLEY
4 FRESH MINT LEAVES,
    CHOPPED

IN A BOWL blend oil, lemon juice, salt, and pepper into a sauce. While the beans are still warm, mix them with half of the sauce. Add the onion, parsley, and mint and mix. Taste for seasoning, adding more sauce, if desired. Chill before serving. *Serves 4.*

Note: Almond slivers, crisped in butter, add a special crunch to the salad.

SCANDINAVIAN HERRING SALAD
■■■

¾ CUP MAYONNAISE
¾ CUP SOUR CREAM
1 TEASPOON PREPARED
  MUSTARD
1 TEASPOON SUGAR
TWO 12-OUNCE JARS MARI-
  NATED HERRING, DRAINED
  AND CUT INTO ½-INCH
  CUBES
1½ CUPS CUBED COOKED
  POTATOES
1½ CUPS CUBED COOKED
  BEETS
2 TART APPLES, PEELED,
  CORED, AND CUBED

2 HARD-COOKED EGGS, CUBED
2 HARD-COOKED EGGS, FINELY
  CHOPPED, KEEPING THE
  WHITES AND YOLKS SEPA-
  RATE (FOR GARNISH)
1 TABLESPOON MINCED ONION
1 TABLESPOON CAPERS, RINSED
  AND DRIED ON PAPER
  TOWEL
1 SMALL DILL PICKLE, MINCED
LETTUCE LEAVES
3 TABLESPOONS FINELY
  CHOPPED PARSLEY

IN A BOWL blend mayonnaise, sour cream, mustard, and
sugar into a salad dressing. In a large bowl, combine and
blend well but carefully the herring, potatoes, beets, apples, cubed eggs, onions, capers, pickle, and half the salad
dressing. Taste and add more dressing according to taste
(serve what is not used at the table). Arrange the salad on
lettuce leaves on a serving dish and garnish the top with a
line of chopped egg white, a line of chopped egg yolk, and
a line of parsley. *Serves 6 to 8.*

NIÇOISE SALAD

■■■

This popular "American" salad originated in the coastal region around Nice, France. Oddly enough, many of the top professional chefs in that region are Italian, so there are obvious Italianate touches—anchovies, tomatoes, tuna—as well as French—mustard, eggs, vinegar, olives, and tarragon.

¼ CUP WINE VINEGAR
¾ CUP OLIVE OIL
SALT AND PEPPER TO TASTE
½ TEASPOON SUGAR
½ TEASPOON DIJON MUSTARD OR OTHER GOOD PREPARED MUSTARD
1 LARGE HEAD BIBB OR BOSTON LETTUCE, WASHED, DRIED, AND CHILLED TO CRISP
3 MEDIUM-SIZED NEW POTATOES, BOILED IN THEIR SKINS UNTIL TENDER, COOLED, PEELED, AND CUT INTO ¼-INCH SLICES
½ POUND FRESH, TENDER STRING BEANS, COOKED IN BOILING, SALTED WATER UNTIL CRISP-TENDER, COOLED, AND CUT INTO BITE-SIZED PIECES

ONE 7-OUNCE CAN "SOLID" TUNA, DRAINED AND BROKEN INTO SMALL CHUNKS
3 RIPE, FIRM TOMATOES, PEELED AND EACH CUT INTO 6 WEDGES
1 MEDIUM-SIZED RED ONION, SLICES SEPARATED INTO RINGS
1 TABLESPOON CAPERS, RINSED IN WATER AND DRIED
½ CUP PITTED BLACK OLIVES (THE PLUMP, PURPLISH GREEK ONES)
2 HARD-COOKED EGGS, QUARTERED
6 ANCHOVY FILLETS, DRAINED
1 TABLESPOON FINELY CHOPPED FRESH TARRAGON (OR PARSLEY)

IN A BOWL blend vinegar, oil, salt, pepper, sugar, and mustard into a salad dressing. Line a salad bowl with the lettuce leaves. In a large bowl, combine and mix well but carefully the potatoes, string beans, tuna, 2 tomatoes, onion, capers, and half the salad dressing. Taste and add more salad dressing according to taste. Spoon mixture into the salad bowl onto the lettuce. Garnish with the remaining tomato, black olives, egg quarters, and anchovies. Sprinkle with the tarragon. *Serves 4 to 6.*

AUSTRIAN HOT POTATO SALAD
■ ■ ■

7 MEDIUM-SIZED WHITE POTATOES, COOKED IN THEIR SKINS IN BOILING WATER UNTIL JUST TENDER (DO NOT OVERCOOK)

6 SLICES BACON, DICED AND COOKED UNTIL GOLDEN BROWN AND CRISP, DRAINED ON PAPER TOWEL (RESERVE THE BACON FAT)

1 MEDIUM-SIZED ONION, FINELY CHOPPED

¼ CUP CIDER OR WHITE VINEGAR

¼ CUP CHICKEN BROTH

½ TEASPOON SUGAR

SALT AND PEPPER TO TASTE

2 TABLESPOONS FINELY CHOPPED PARSLEY

COOL AND PEEL the potatoes. Cut them into halves lengthwise and then into ¼-inch slices. Cook the onion in the bacon fat until soft (do not brown). Stir in the vinegar, broth, sugar, salt, and pepper and cook, stirring, about 1 minute to blend thoroughly. Add the bacon and heat through. Pour the hot bacon sauce mixture over the potatoes and mix gently until well blended. Serve immediately with parsley sprinkled on top. *Serves 4 to 6.*

GERMAN WILTED SPINACH SALAD

■ ■ ■

1½ POUNDS FRESH TENDER
   SPINACH
1 MEDIUM-SIZED RED ONION,
   THINLY SLICED
¼ CUP OLIVE OIL
¼ CUP CIDER VINEGAR
½ TEASPOON SUGAR
8 SLICES BACON, COOKED
   UNTIL GOLDEN AND CRISP,
   DRAINED ON PAPER TOWELS,
   AND BROKEN INTO SMALL
   PIECES

SALT AND PEPPER TO TASTE
1 HARD-COOKED EGG, SLICED
   (USE AN EGG SLICER FOR
   UNIFORM SLICES)

REMOVE THE STEMS and any discolored edges from the spinach leaves. Wash the spinach and dry thoroughly. Tear the spinach into bite-sized pieces into a salad bowl. Add the sliced onion. Heat the oil in a saucepan, just until hot. Remove from heat and stir in the vinegar, sugar, and bacon. Pour over the spinach and onion in the salad bowl, add salt and pepper, and toss. Garnish with the egg slices. *Serves 4.*

WALDORF SALAD

■■■

This salad owes its birth to no one from the Old World. It was born at New York City's famous Waldorf-Astoria Hotel. Some say that Oscar of the Waldorf suggested it; others that it came about by a lucky accident. Either way, it's a unique American original.

4 LARGE, FIRM, TART APPLES, CORED AND CUBED (DO NOT PEEL UNLESS SKIN SEEMS VERY TOUGH)
JUICE OF HALF A LEMON
1 CUP CUBED CELERY (USE THE TENDER, INNER RIBS, SCRAPED)
½ CUP COARSELY CHOPPED WALNUTS
¾ CUP MAYONNAISE
BOSTON LETTUCE LEAVES

COMBINE THE SALAD just before serving. In a bowl toss apples with the lemon juice. Add the celery, walnuts, and mayonnaise. Line a salad bowl with lettuce leaves and spoon the salad into it. Or serve on lettuce leaves on individual plates. *Serves 6.*

Chapter 2

SOUP

So powerful is the appeal of soup that Americans dip their spoons into ten million bowls yearly, nine out of ten families serving it at least once every three days.

The majority of us probably don't realize that soup is as healthful a meal as it is appetite-satisfying. For example, ten ounces of vegetable, vegetable-beef, or chicken noodle soup give more vitamin A than two heads of lettuce, twelve ears of corn, four tomatoes, or nine eggs, and calorie for calorie more protein and thiamin than peanut butter or rye bread. A single serving of tomato soup has as much vitamin C as half a grapefruit.

Some believe that soup is our oldest food. Historians and archeologists have uncovered evidence of a carbonized hippopotamus tusk in a cooking pot which they dug up in the Fayum basin in Egypt, dated about 6000 B.C.

The oldest cookbook on record is Chinese, dating back 4,700 years. Compiled by the Emperor Shen Hung from the work of three famed Cantonese chefs, it included several soups; the star is a soup of pigeon's eggs, "Golden moons on a silver sea."

Melting pot cookery in America had no greater common denominator than soup, which has always been popular all over the world, not only because it is easy to make and tastes so good but because it can transform leftovers and inexpensive ingredients into imaginative meals.

The word for all soups probably evolved from the German *sop*, the bread over which broth, pottage, or hot liquid was poured. "Soup" may also have come from the sound of sipping or slurping hot liquid.

However it originated, by the Middle Ages every nation had its own word for the favored food: *chupe, soop, sopa, sope, soepe, suppa, soppe, soep, suppe, soppa, sopero, soupe, zuppa, zup.*

The evening meal came from "sup," which traditionally meant to sit down and have a bowl of soup. The word was finally lengthened to "supper," always a simple offering, often soup. In France for many years the importance of soup was clearly spelled out: the evening meal called *la soupe.*

In the United States the tempting call "Soup's on" still means that family and/or guests are invited to sit for supper or dinner. Soup leads the way, as it always has.

UKRAINIAN BARLEY SOUP

■■■

2 POUNDS SHIN BEEF, ON THE BONE
1 ONION STUCK WITH 2 WHOLE CLOVES
1 CELERY RIB, SLICED
1 CARROT, SLICED
2 TEASPOONS SALT
1 TEASPOON PEPPER

3 QUARTS WATER
1 CUP BARLEY
½ POUND MUSHROOMS, THINLY SLICED
3 TABLESPOONS BUTTER
1 TABLESPOON LEMON JUICE
CHOPPED PARSLEY

IN A SOUP pot, place the beef, onion, celery, carrot, salt, pepper, and water. Bring to a boil, cover the pot, lower the heat, and simmer for 2 hours, or until the beef is tender, skimming the top as necessary. Remove the beef and cool. Dice the meat, discard the bone and set meat aside. Strain the liquid, discarding the vegetables, and return it to the pot. Add the barley and cook 30 minutes, or until tender. Meanwhile, cook the mushrooms in the butter with the lemon juice for 2 minutes. Add the mushrooms (and their liquid) and the meat to the soup pot. Simmer 10 minutes. Taste for seasoning. Serve sprinkled with parsley. *Serves 6.*

WESTERN BLACK BEAN SOUP
■■■

2 CUPS DRIED BLACK BEANS, PICKED OVER AND SOAKED FOR 4 HOURS, THEN DRAINED

1 HAM BONE WITH MEAT OR A SMOKED HAM HOCK

2 MEDIUM-SIZED ONIONS, CHOPPED

1 ONION STUCK WITH 3 WHOLE CLOVES

2 CELERY RIBS, SCRAPED AND CHOPPED

2 CARROTS, SCRAPED AND CHOPPED

PINCH EACH MACE AND THYME

1½ QUARTS WATER

1 QUART CHICKEN BROTH (CANNED OR HOMEMADE)

SALT AND PEPPER TO TASTE

2 HARD-COOKED EGGS, CHOPPED

¼ CUP NEW YORK STATE OR CALIFORNIA DRY SHERRY

1 LEMON, THINLY SLICED, SEEDS REMOVED

PLACE THE BEANS in a large soup pot. Add the ham bone or hock, chopped onions, onion with cloves, celery, carrots, mace, thyme, water, and chicken broth. Bring to a boil and, partially covered (a wooden spoon laid across the pot with a cover propped against it does the job), simmer for 1½ hours, or until the beans can easily be mashed against the side of the pot with a spoon. Remove the bone or hock. Remove the meat and cut into small pieces. Reserve it. Remove and discard the onion with the cloves. Run the soup through a food mill, blender, or food processor to purée. If too thick, stir in some chicken broth to obtain consistency desired. Return soup to the pot, taste for seasoning, adding salt and pepper. Just before serving, bring to a simmer, stirring in the meat, chopped eggs, and sherry, and float one or two lemon slices on each serving. *Serves 6.*

ENGLISH BRUSSELS SPROUTS SOUP

■■■

2 CUPS FRESH BRUSSELS
   SPROUTS
3 TABLESPOONS BUTTER
6 SCALLIONS (GREEN ONIONS),
   WHITE PART ONLY, THINLY
   SLICED

3 TABLESPOONS FLOUR
5 CUPS CHICKEN BROTH
SALT AND PEPPER TO TASTE
½ CUP HEAVY CREAM
½ CUP SOUR CREAM

TRIM THE OUTSIDE leaves from the Brussels sprouts and cook the sprouts in boiling salted water until tender. Drain and reserve. Chop up 3 Brussels sprouts for garnish. In a saucepan, over low heat, melt the butter and sauté the scallions until tender. Stir in the flour, blending well. Gradually stir in 2 cups of chicken broth, stirring, as it simmers, into a smooth, medium-thick mixture. Stir in the remaining broth and Brussels sprouts and simmer, covered, 5 minutes. Cool slightly. Put into blender and purée. Season with salt and pepper. Place in pot and heat to a simmer. Stir in the cream and sour cream and bring to a simmer again. Do not boil. Serve piping hot, garnished with the chopped Brussels sprouts. *Serves 6.*

COUNTRY CABBAGE SOUP
■■■

When we say "country," we also mean "countries," for this is a favorite of Russians, Poles, indeed most of the Slavic and Baltic countries, even the French, Spanish, and Italians— and of course, the Americans whose parents came from those countries. It's a simple rural classic.

ABOUT 7C BROTH (SEE BELOW)
2 PARSNIPS, CUT INTO ½-INCH CUBES
2 CARROTS, SCRAPED AND CUT INTO ¼-INCH CUBES
2 CELERY RIBS, SCRAPED AND CUT INTO ¼-INCH CUBES
3 LEEKS, CUT INTO ½-INCH SLICES, USING ABOUT 2 INCHES OF THE GREEN PART.

2 TOMATOES, PEELED, SEEDED, AND CHOPPED
3 CUPS COARSELY GRATED CABBAGE (NOT THE CORE)
RESERVED BEEF CUBES FROM BROTH (SEE BELOW)
1 CUP SOUR CREAM

PLACE ALL INGREDIENTS except sour cream and beef cubes into the pot with the broth and simmer until the vegetables are tender. Add the beef and continue simmering until the beef is heated through. Taste for seasoning. Serve and pass the sour cream at the table. *Serves 6 to 8.*

Note: This soup can be prepared in a simplified "American" way: Use leftover beef—roast beef, pot roast, steak, or any other leftover beef—and cut into small cubes. Make a rich broth by dissolving 4 Knorr beef bouillon cubes in 7 cups of boiling water, then proceed as directed in making the soup.

Broth

2 POUNDS BEEF SHANKS, CUT
   INTO 2-INCH PIECES
1 LARGE ONION, QUARTERED
1 LARGE CARROT, QUARTERED
2 CELERY RIBS, QUARTERED
2 GARLIC CLOVES, HALVED

2 WHOLE CLOVES
6 WHOLE PEPPERCORNS
1 TABLESPOON SALT
1 BAY LEAF
4 QUARTS WATER

Place all ingredients into a large pot and bring to a boil. Lower heat and, partially covered, simmer 1½ hours, or until the beef is tender but not falling apart. Skim the top as necessary. Remove beef, cool, cut into small bite-sized cubes, and set aside. Continue simmering the broth, uncovered, for 2 hours, or until reduced by half its original volume (about 7 cups of rich broth). Strain, discarding vegetables and spices. Return broth to pot.

AMERICAN CARROT-POTATO SOUP
■ ■ ■

4 TABLESPOONS BUTTER
2 MEDIUM-SIZED ONIONS,
  MINCED
1 TABLESPOON FLOUR
4 CUPS CHICKEN BROTH
1 CUP MILK
SALT AND PEPPER TO TASTE

½ TEASPOON DRIED TARRAGON
7 MEDIUM-SIZED CARROTS,
  SCRAPED AND GRATED
2 MEDIUM-SIZED IDAHO
  POTATOES, PEELED, BOILED,
  AND MASHED
1 CUP HEAVY CREAM

IN A POT large enough to hold all ingredients, over medium
heat, melt the butter and sauté the onions until soft.
Sprinkle in the flour and cook, stirring, 1 minute. Gradually add the chicken broth, stirring. Stir in the milk, salt,
pepper, tarragon, carrots, and mashed potatoes. Blend,
bring to a boil, reduce heat to low, and simmer, uncovered, stirring occasionally, for 30 minutes. Add the heavy
cream, stirring until the soup is well blended and hot.
Taste for seasoning. Serve in hot bowls. *Serves 6.*

NEW YORK STATE
CHEESE-POTATO SOUP
■ ■ ■

New York State is proud of its Cheddar cheese, and justly so. The manufacturing know-how for Cheddar cheese came first to the state with English settlers. In fact, the entire world trade, prices, and supply in Cheddar cheese was determined by a group of Cheddar cheese producers in a small town in upstate New York. The cheese is noted for its bite, authority, and creaminess.

2 TABLESPOONS BUTTER
2 MEDIUM-SIZED ONIONS, CHOPPED
4 CUPS CHICKEN BROTH
2 LARGE RUSSET POTATOES, PEELED AND CUT INTO 6 PIECES EACH
1 CUP MEDIUM CREAM OR HALF AND HALF

1 TEASPOON SALT
½ TEASPOON PEPPER
2 CUPS GRATED, VERY SHARP NEW YORK STATE CHEDDAR CHEESE
1 TABLESPOON CHOPPED CHIVES

In a pot, over medium heat, melt the butter and cook the onions until soft. Do not brown. Add the chicken broth and the potatoes and cook, covered, for 30 minutes, or until the potatoes are tender. Remove from the heat and purée in a food processor or blender. Return to the pot, and over medium heat stir in the cream, salt, pepper, and cheese, stirring until the soup is hot and well blended and the cheese is melted. Serve with the chives sprinkled on top. *Serves 6.*

LOUISIANA CHICKEN GUMBO SOUP
■■■

The Spaniards brought hot spices, ollas, rice dishes; the Africans tropical fruit dishes and peppery stews; the native Choctaw Indians made the early gumbos and had interesting ways with seafood; the French introduced the haute cuisine of Paris and Versailles and also the peasant food of provincial France. Out of all this came a most unusual cookery: Creole. There is no mumbo about this gumbo. It is a remarkable combination of poultry, seafood, spices, vegetables, and rice and exists in no other place on earth except Louisiana.

4 TABLESPOONS BACON FAT (OR BUTTER)
ONE 4-POUND CHICKEN, CUT UP
4 QUARTS WATER
ONE 1-POUND CAN TOMATOES (WITH THEIR LIQUID), BROKEN UP
⅛ TEASPOON DRIED THYME
½ TEASPOON CAYENNE, OR TO TASTE
⅛ TEASPOON HOT RED PEPPER FLAKES, OR TO TASTE
1 TEASPOON SALT
1 LARGE ONION, CHOPPED
1 LARGE GARLIC CLOVE, CHOPPED
1 SMALL GREEN PEPPER, CORED, SEEDED, AND CHOPPED
1 SMALL RED PEPPER, CORED, SEEDED, AND CHOPPED
1 CUP FRESH OKRA, TRIMMED, CUT INTO ½-INCH SLICES
1 PINT SMALL OYSTERS
18 (ABOUT ½ POUND MEDIUM) SHRIMP, SHELLED AND DEVEINED
½ TEASPOON TABASCO SAUCE, OR TO TASTE
1½ CUPS COOKED LONG-GRAIN RICE

IN A LARGE soup pot, heat half of the bacon fat and brown the chicken pieces evenly. Add the water, tomatoes, thyme, cayenne, hot pepper flakes, and salt and cook, covered, 35 minutes, or until the chicken is very tender. Take the chicken from the liquid, cool, and remove the meat from the bones. Return the skin and bones to the pot, chop the chicken meat and reserve. Simmer the liquid in the pot, uncovered, and reduce to 2½ to 3 quarts. Strain the liquid, set it aside, and discard what is in the strainer. Heat the remaining bacon fat in the pot and cook the onion, garlic, and green and red peppers until soft. Do not brown. Pour in the strained broth, add the okra, and simmer 15 minutes. Add the oysters and shrimp and cook about 5 minutes, or just until the edges of the oysters curl and the shrimp have barely turned pink and are firm. Stir in the chicken meat, Tabasco, and rice. Heat through. Taste for seasoning, adding more salt, cayenne, etc., if needed. *Serves 6.*

BULGARIAN CREAM OF CUCUMBER SOUP
(Hot or Cold)

■ ■ ■

2 TABLESPOONS BUTTER

1 BUNCH SCALLIONS (GREEN ONIONS), TRIMMED AND SLICED, USING ALL BUT THE LAST INCH OF THE GREEN PART

1 CELERY RIB, SCRAPED AND SLICED

3 CUCUMBERS (PEEL IF WAXED), CUT INTO HALVES LENGTHWISE, SEEDS REMOVED, AND SLICED

1 MEDIUM POTATO, CUBED

1 TABLESPOON FLOUR

3 CUPS RICH CHICKEN BROTH

SALT AND PEPPER TO TASTE

¾ CUP HEAVY CREAM

¼ CUP SOUR CREAM

2 TABLESPOONS CHOPPED FRESH DILL

IN A LARGE saucepan, over medium heat, melt the butter. Add the scallions and cook until soft. Do not brown. Add the celery, cucumbers, and potato and cook 1 minute, stirring to coat with butter. Sprinkle with the flour and stir to blend. Stir in the broth. Bring to a boil, lower heat, cover, and simmer until the vegetables can be mashed against the side of the pot. Taste and season with salt and pepper. Cool slightly and purée in a blender or processor.

Before serving stir in the heavy cream. Serve cold with a dollop of sour cream and some dill atop the sour cream. To serve hot, heat just to the boiling point after the cream has been added. Top with sour cream and dill. *Serves 4.*

GAZPACHO
■ ■ ■

This is one of Spain's contributions to America's melting pot cuisine. It is an extremely popular soup in the United States today, with a number of different versions, including an especially spicy "white" variety. This, however, is the original and classic. In Spain, it's the national soup, as popular as onion soup in France.

5 LARGE RIPE TOMATOES, PEELED, SEEDED, AND COARSELY CHOPPED
1 MEDIUM-SIZED WHITE ONION, COARSELY CHOPPED
1 GARLIC CLOVE, HALVED
3 CUPS COLD BEEF BOUILLON
2 TABLESPOONS OLIVE OIL
2 TABLESPOONS WINE VINEGAR
1 TEASPOON SALT
¼ TEASPOON BLACK PEPPER
¼ TEASPOON PAPRIKA

4 OUNCES DRY SHERRY
½ CUP FINE BREAD CRUMBS
1 CUP PEELED, SEEDED, AND FINELY CHOPPED CUCUMBER
1 CUP CORED, SEEDED, AND FINELY CHOPPED GREEN PEPPER
1 CUP FINELY CHOPPED WHITE ONION
GARLIC CROUTONS

IN A BOWL combine tomatoes, coarsely chopped onion, garlic, bouillon, oil, vinegar, salt, pepper, and paprika. Refrigerate for 2 hours. Pour into a blender container and blend for 1½ minutes. Pour into a bowl and stir in the sherry and bread crumbs. Ladle the soup into chilled soup bowls; add one ice cube to each. Place the chopped cucumbers, peppers, onions, and croutons in separate bowls on the table and encourage your guests to add their own choice of garnishes to the soup. *Serves 6.*

MINESTRONE

■ ■ ■

There's no doubt about who originated this soup. From the name to the flavor, it's an Italian poem.

½ CUP DRIED CHICKPEAS
½ CUP DRIED WHITE KIDNEY BEANS
3 TABLESPOONS OLIVE OIL
1 MEDIUM-SIZED ONION, CHOPPED
1 GARLIC CLOVE, MINCED
1 CUP CHOPPED CABBAGE (NOT THE CORE)
3 CELERY RIBS, SCRAPED AND COARSELY CHOPPED
1 CARROT, SCRAPED AND COARSELY CHOPPED
½ POUND STRING BEANS, CUT INTO ½-INCH PIECES

1 MEDIUM-SIZED POTATO, DICED
ONE 1-POUND CAN TOMATOES (INCLUDING LIQUID), BROKEN UP
2 QUARTS CHICKEN BROTH
½ CUP DITALINI (SHORT TUBULAR PASTA) OR ANY OTHER SMALL SOUP PASTA
SALT AND PEPPER TO TASTE
⅛ TEASPOON HOT DRIED RED PEPPER FLAKES (OPTIONAL)
½ CUP GRATED ASIAGO OR PARMESAN CHEESE

SOAK CHICKPEAS AND kidney beans in water to cover for 5 hours, then drain. Cook the chickpeas and beans in 2 quarts of salted water 1 hour, or until tender (do not overcook, as they will cook a few minutes more later), and drain. In a large pot, over medium heat, heat the olive oil and cook the onions and garlic until soft. Do not brown. Add the cabbage, celery, carrot, string beans, and potato and cook 1 minute, stirring. Add the tomatoes and chicken broth and simmer 30 minutes, until the vegetables are tender. Add the cooked chickpeas and beans and the pasta and cook 10 minutes, or until the pasta is *al dente* (slightly chewy). Season with salt and pepper. Stir in the red pepper flakes, if desired. Serve hot with a spoonful of the cheese sprinkled over each serving. *Serves 6 to 8.*

GREEK LEMON SOUP

■ ■ ■

6 CUPS CHICKEN BROTH
5 TABLESPOONS UNCOOKED
   LONG-GRAIN RICE

3 EGGS
4 TABLESPOONS LEMON JUICE
SALT TO TASTE

In a pot, bring broth to a boil. Stir in the rice; simmer until the rice is tender, about 15 minutes. Remove from heat and let set for 5 minutes. Beat together the eggs and lemon juice and stir the mixture into the soup. Add salt and reheat just to a simmer. Serve immediately in hot soup bowls. *Serves 4 to 6.*

GERMAN LENTIL SOUP

■ ■ ■

1 CUP DRIED LENTILS
2 TABLESPOONS BUTTER
5 SLICES LEAN, THICK-CUT
  BACON, DICED
1 MEDIUM-SIZED ONION,
  THINLY SLICED
1 MEDIUM-SIZED CARROT,
  SCRAPED AND THINLY
  SLICED
1 CELERY RIB, SCRAPED AND
  THINLY SLICED
1 HAM BONE OR SMOKED HAM
  HOCK

6 CUPS BEEF BROTH (CANNED
  IS FINE)
2 MEDIUM-SIZED POTATOES,
  CUT INTO ½-INCH CUBES
1 BAY LEAF
⅛ TEASPOON DRIED MARJORAM
SALT AND PEPPER TO TASTE
2 KNOCKWURST, SKINNED AND
  CUT INTO ¼-INCH SLICES
1 CUP MEDIUM CREAM OR HALF
  AND HALF

Pɪᴄᴋ ᴏᴠᴇʀ ᴛʜᴇ lentils and rinse them in several changes of
water. Cover well with water and soak 5 hours. Over
medium heat, melt the butter in a pot large enough to
hold all ingredients. Add the bacon and onion and cook
until onion is soft. Add the carrot, celery, ham bone, lentils
with the water they soaked in, and beef broth. Cover the
pot and simmer for 1 hour. Add the potatoes, bay leaf, and
marjoram. Simmer, covered, for 30 minutes, or until the
potatoes and lentils are tender. Season with salt and pepper. Add the knockwurst slices and simmer, uncovered,
for 10 minutes. Stir in the cream and heat just to a boil.
Remove bay leaf. Serve. *Serves 6 to 8.*

Note: If preferred, the soup can be puréed in a blender
container or food processor, but instead of dicing the
bacon, cut it into large pieces so they can be removed before
puréeing along with the ham bone and bay leaf. After
puréeing add the sausage slices and cream and heat just
to a boil.

POLISH MUSHROOM SOUP
■ ■ ■

3 TABLESPOONS BUTTER
1 MEDIUM-SIZED ONION,
  FINELY CHOPPED
¾ POUND FRESH MUSHROOMS,
  CLEANED, TRIMMED, AND
  FINELY CHOPPED
SALT TO TASTE
2 TABLESPOONS FLOUR

½ TEASPOON PAPRIKA
4 CUPS CHICKEN BROTH
1 BAY LEAF
2 EGG YOLKS
1 CUP SOUR CREAM AT ROOM
  TEMPERATURE
FRESH CHOPPED DILL

IN A LARGE saucepan, over medium heat, melt the butter and cook the onion until soft. Do not brown. Add the mushrooms and cook 2 minutes, stirring. Do not brown. Season with salt. Sprinkle on the flour and paprika and cook 1 minute, stirring to blend well. Slowly stir in the broth, add the bay leaf, and simmer, covered, for 30 minutes. Remove from heat. Discard the bay leaf. With a whisk, beat together the egg yolks and sour cream and mix well with the broth–mushroom mixture. Heat 1 minute. Do not boil. Serve immediately, sprinkling dill on top of each serving. *Serves 4 to 6.*

FRENCH ONION SOUP

■ ■ ■

This is the French revolution—in soup. It has conquered everyone.

5 TABLESPOONS BUTTER
3 CUPS THINLY SLICED ONIONS
6 CUPS RICH BEEF OR CHICKEN BROTH
SALT AND PEPPER TO TASTE
6 THICK (½- TO 1-INCH) SLICES FRENCH BREAD, FRIED IN BUTTER AND DRAINED ON A PAPER TOWEL

½ CUP GRATED GRUYÈRE CHEESE
½ CUP GRATED PARMESAN CHEESE
2 TABLESPOONS CHOPPED PARSLEY

IN A LARGE deep saucepan, over medium heat, melt 4 tablespoons of the butter. Add the onions and cook until tender and golden in color. Do not brown. Pour in the broth and simmer 30 minutes. Taste and season with salt and pepper. Lay the slices of bread on a baking sheet. Sprinkle with the combined cheeses, dot with remaining butter, and place under a broiler until cheese has melted and is golden. Ladle the hot soup into hot bowls. Sprinkle with the parsley and place a slice of the hot, cheesed bread on the top. Serve immediately. *Serves 6.*

Note: The bread can be put on the soup in individual ovenproof bowls, then browned under the broiler, but removing 6 hot bowls from the broiler can be tricky. It works just as well the other way providing everything is very hot.

VIRGINIA OYSTER SOUP

■ ■ ■

In Virginia, where some of the world's best oysters are found, the people are oyster purists. No spices, herbs, tomatoes, or other hearty seasonings. The delicate flavor of the oysters, carefully undercooked, is always sought, no matter what recipe is used.

1 PINT FRESH OYSTERS
   (PREFERABLY CHINCOTEAGUE)
4 TABLESPOONS BUTTER
1 QUART MILK

1½ TEASPOONS SALT
½ TEASPOON PEPPER
PAPRIKA

IN A LARGE pot, over low heat, cook the oysters in their liquor for 3 minutes, or just until the edges begin to curl. Quickly stir in the butter, milk, salt, and pepper. Heat to a near boil. Serve immediately with paprika sprinkled on top each serving. *Serves 4.*

PASTA E FAGIOLI
■ ■ ■

This national meatless dish of Italy, usually served on Friday, was brought to the United States by early immigrants and quickly became a favorite of many of us, regardless of nationality.

1 POUND PEA BEANS, PICKED OVER, SOAKED IN COLD WATER TO COVER FOR 5 HOURS, AND DRAINED

CHICKEN BROTH TO COVER THE BEANS BY 2 INCHES

2 TEASPOONS SALT

½ TEASPOON PEPPER

2 GARLIC CLOVES, CHOPPED

ONE 1-POUND CAN ITALIAN PLUM TOMATOES, PUT THROUGH A FOOD MILL

CELERY LEAVES FROM 3 RIBS

1 CARROT, QUARTERED

1 MEDIUM-SIZED ONION, QUARTERED

1 BAY LEAF

2 CLOVES

2 CUPS DITALINI (A SHORT TUBULAR PASTA), COOKED IN BOILING, SALTED WATER UNTIL *AL DENTE* (SLIGHTLY CHEWY), AND DRAINED

1 CUP GRATED ASIAGO OR PARMESAN CHEESE

IN A LARGE pot, bring the beans, broth, salt, pepper, and garlic to a boil. Reduce the heat and simmer for 10 minutes. Stir in the tomatoes. Tie celery leaves, carrot, onion, bay leaf, and cloves in a cheesecloth, add to pot, cover, and stirring occasionally, simmer for 1 hour, or until the beans are tender. Remove and discard the cheesecloth bag, stir in the pasta, and cook, uncovered, until the pasta is just heated through. If the dish is too thick for your taste, add a little chicken broth to obtain the consistency that pleases you. Sprinkle each serving with grated cheese. Plenty of warm buttered Italian bread and cold white wine are classic accompaniments. *Serves 6 to 8.*

DUTCH SPLIT PEA SOUP

■■■

A ham bone isn't essential for a good split pea soup, but it does make the soup sing.

2 CUPS GREEN SPLIT PEAS, PICKED OVER AND WASHED IN SEVERAL CHANGES OF WATER
½ CUP DICED SALT PORK
1 LARGE LEEK, CHOPPED, USING ALL THE WHITE PART AND THE LIGHT GREEN
1 MEDIUM-SIZED ONION, CHOPPED
1 CELERY RIB, SCRAPED AND CHOPPED
1 MEDIUM-SIZED CARROT, SCRAPED AND CHOPPED
1 GARLIC CLOVE, MASHED

PINCH DRIED THYME
1 BAY LEAF
2 SPRIGS PARSLEY
6 CUPS CHICKEN BROTH (HOMEMADE OR CANNED)
1 HAM BONE WITH SOME MEAT ON IT (IF AVAILABLE)
SALT AND PEPPER TO TASTE
2 TABLESPOONS BUTTER
½ CUP HEAVY CREAM
SLICES OF A NARROW COOKED SAUSAGE SUCH AS KIELBASA OR FRANKFURTERS (IF YOU DO NOT HAVE A HAM BONE WITH MEAT)

IN A LARGE pot, cover the peas with water and bring to a boil. Remove from the heat and let stand 1 hour. Meanwhile, cook the salt pork in a frypan until golden brown. Remove with a slotted spoon and discard. Add the leek, onion, celery, and carrot to the fat in the frypan and cook until they are soft. Do not brown. Tie the garlic, thyme, bay leaf, and parsley together in a cheesecloth bag. Drain the peas, return them to the pot, and add the broth, vegetables, cheesecloth bag, and ham bone. Bring to a boil, lower heat, and simmer 1 to 1½ hours, or until the peas can be mashed against the side of the pot. Remove and discard the cheesecloth bag. Remove the ham bone, take the meat from it, cut it up, and reserve. Push the soup through a sieve or food mill. Return to the pot. Taste and season with salt and pepper. Just before serving, add the butter and cream and stir until the butter has melted. Serve hot garnished with the bits of ham, or if you did not use a ham bone, garnish with the slices of sausage. *Serves 4 to 6.*

PISTOU
■■■

This lusty French peasant meal-in-one supper soup comes with a guarantee to make your taste buds tango.

1 POUND PEA BEANS, PICKED OVER, SOAKED 5 HOURS IN COLD WATER TO COVER, AND DRAINED

3 QUARTS WATER

4 MEDIUM-SIZED LEEKS, WHITE PART ONLY, FINELY DICED

3 LARGE, RIPE TOMATOES, PEELED, SEEDED, AND CHOPPED

3 SMALL LEAVES FRESH SAGE

1½ TEASPOONS SALT

½ TEASPOON PEPPER

½ POUND FRESH YELLOW STRING BEANS, CUT INTO ½-INCH PIECES

4 NEW POTATOES, PEELED, CUT INTO ½-INCH CUBES

4 SMALL ZUCCHINI, CUT INTO CUBES SLIGHTLY LARGER THAN THE POTATOES

4 OUNCES VERMICELLI, BROKEN UP

PISTOU (SEE BELOW)

IN A LARGE pot, bring the beans and 3 quarts of water to a boil. Reduce heat to low and simmer, partially covered, for 40 minutes. Add the leeks, tomatoes, sage, salt, and pepper. Simmer for half an hour, stirring constantly. Add the string beans, potatoes, and zucchini and simmer, uncovered, 15 minutes, or until the vegetables are barely tender. Stir in the vermicelli and cook 5 minutes, or until the pasta is cooked. Just before serving, stir in the Pistou, blending it well with the vegetables and pasta. Taste for seasoning and add salt and pepper if needed. *Serves 6 to 8.*

Pistou

½ CUP OLIVE OIL
¾ CUP GRATED SHARP CHEESE

5 GARLIC CLOVES
6 LARGE, FRESH BASIL LEAVES

Place all ingredients in a blender container and blend into a smooth paste.

PENNSYLVANIA PUMPKIN SOUP
■ ■ ■

3 TABLESPOONS BUTTER
1 MEDIUM-SIZED ONION,
　CHOPPED
1 GARLIC CLOVE, MINCED
SALT TO TASTE
½ TEASPOON GROUND ALLSPICE
5 CUPS CHICKEN BROTH
2 CUPS CUBED, FRESH PUMPKIN
　(½-INCH CUBES)

2 MEDIUM-SIZED POTATOES,
　CUT INTO ½-INCH CUBES
⅛ TEASPOON HOT RED PEPPER
　FLAKES
2 CUPS CUBED COOKED
　CHICKEN (½-INCH CUBES)
2 TABLESPOONS CHOPPED
　PARSLEY

In a large pot, over medium heat, melt the butter. Add the onion and garlic and cook 2 minutes. Stir in the salt, allspice, chicken broth, pumpkin, potatoes, and red pepper flakes. Bring to a boil, then simmer for 15 minutes, or until the pumpkin and potatoes are tender. Taste for seasoning. Stir in the chicken and simmer until heated through. Sprinkle parsley on top of each serving. *Serves 6.*

TOMATO EGGDROP SOUP
■■■

We have a substantial population of Chinese Americans making their influence on our cooking strongly felt.

2 QUARTS RICH CHICKEN
  BROTH
ONE 1-POUND CAN STEWED
  TOMATOES, CHOPPED INTO
  SMALL PIECES
2 TABLESPOONS CORNSTARCH

¼ CUP COLD WATER
3 EGGS, BEATEN
6 SMALL TENDER SCALLIONS
  (GREEN ONIONS), CHOPPED
  (USE THE WHOLE SCALLION)
SALT TO TASTE

IN A LARGE pot, bring the broth to a boil; stir in the tomatoes. Blend together the cornstarch and cold water, and when the soup comes to the boil again, blend in the dissolved cornstarch. Reduce to a simmer and cook, stirring, until the soup thickens. Then gradually stir in the beaten eggs. Remove from the heat. Season with salt. Serve immediately in warm soup bowls with the raw chopped scallions scattered on top. *Serves 6.*

Chapter 3

EGGS

Perhaps many of us inherited our respect for eggs. Each of us in the American family eats 273 yearly, and one leading fast-food chain sells one million every morning.

Our forebears who came here brought the egg-eating habit with them, always aware that the egg was the most economical food that they could accomplish the most with. They used it with the same respect they showed for costlier meat. Eggs were a meal, not just a coupling with bacon for breakfast, and egg meals were imaginative, flavorful, and often dramatic.

It is doubtful whether many of our ancestors knew what a powerhouse of nutrition eggs are. Like many of us, few realized that some nutritionists consider eggs our most nourishing food.

Coming from that shell is one of the purest and most perfectly packaged of all foods, with no chemicals or preservatives added, untouched by human hands until cracked for cooking, and containing a remarkable variety of vitamins and nutrients.

Actually, eggs are a complete food, with all of the essential amino acids, those building blocks necessary for growth that are not produced by the body. Amazingly, in that little shell are *all of the vitamins except one*, C. Also the rare "sunshine" vitamin D, a very valuable growth vitamin, in eggs is second only to that in fish liver oil. Eggs also have thirteen minerals, including the most important—iron, magnesium and phosphorus.

Besides all this, eggs are so versatile that in 1919 Chef Adolphe Meyer wrote a cookbook, *Eggs in a Thousand Ways.*

In fact, eggs are so important that it would be difficult to cook without them. They are used as lightening, thickening, binding, and enriching agents. They are needed for cutlets, fritters, custards, mayonnaise; important for garnishes, salads, dressings, sauces, and soups, for clarifying liquids, and for baking all kinds of desserts.

Italian *zabaglione*, French soufflés, even American baked Alaska would be impossible without eggs. They can be scrambled, fried, boiled, poached, baked—also used in main dishes such as omelets and the Italian *frittatas*, or flat omelets.

One French chef succinctly summed up the egg's value. "The egg," he wrote, "is the cement that holds all the castle of cookery together."

Jack's Scotch grandmother put it a little differently. "Without the egg ," she said, "I'd close my kitchen."

So would we.

CREPES

■ ■ ■

Makes about twenty-four 6-inch crepes:

1 CUP LIGHT CREAM
1 CUP WATER
4 EGGS
1 TEASPOON SALT
2 CUPS SIFTED ALL-PURPOSE
   FLOUR (MEASURED AFTER
   SIFTING)

3½ TABLESPOONS MELTED
   UNSALTED BUTTER

PLACE ALL INGREDIENTS except the melted butter in a blender jar. Blend at highest speed, covered, for 1½ minutes. Scrape the flour sticking to the sides down into the batter. Add the melted butter, cover, and blend for another half minute. Put the batter (right in the blender jar) into the refrigerator to rest for 3 hours. The batter should be the consistency of medium cream. If heavier, the crepes will be heavy. If batter seems too thick, add a small amount of milk. After the resting period, remove the batter from the refrigerator and blend again for a few seconds. Heat a 6-inch crepe pan (or frypan), grease lightly with oil. Spoon 2 tablespoons of the batter into the hot pan and immediately tip the pan back and forth to spread the batter evenly and thinly. If this amount doesn't cover the bottom of the pan after tipping, add a little more batter to the next one. Cook until the bottom is golden brown and the edge is dry and lacy; turn to brown the other side. Stack on a plate to keep moist. The first side of the crepe to brown will be browner than the other side. Lay the crepe to be stuffed with the lighter-colored side up, so when it is rolled the darker side will show.

Note: Depending on what the crepe is being stuffed with, instead of the water you can use other liquids to give the crepe flavor—clam juice, broth, tomato juice.

EGGS BENEDICT IN CREPES

■ ■ ■

FOUR 6-INCH CREPES (SEE P. 51)
BLENDER HOLLANDAISE SAUCE
(SEE P. 58)
4 LARGE, THIN SLICES COOKED
HAM AS NEAR THE SIZE OF
THE CREPES AS POSSIBLE (OR
USE 2 SMALLER SLICES)

8 POACHED EGGS, WELL
DRAINED AND KEPT VERY
WARM

MAKE A RECIPE of crepes. Those you do not use for this recipe can be frozen to be used later. Make a recipe of Blender Hollandaise Sauce. What do you not use for this recipe can be frozen to be used later.

Have all ingredients as warm as possible before assembling. Arrange the slice (or slices) of ham on the crepes. Lay the eggs as close to one end of the crepe as possible. Spoon some sauce over the eggs. Bring the other end of the crepe up and carefully tuck it under the opposite end where the eggs are. Top the crepe with a tablespoon or two of the Hollandaise. Run each crepe under the broiler for a minute before serving. *Serves 4.*

Note: Another delicious adaptation of popular Eggs Benedict (an American creation) is to substitute slices of smoked turkey breast for the usual ham.

POACHED EGGS À LA MARYLAND
■■■

4 TABLESPOONS BUTTER
SIX ½-INCH SLICES FIRM WHITE
  BREAD
6 JUMBO EGGS
2 TEASPOONS WHITE VINEGAR
2 LARGE, RIPE, FIRM TOMATOES,
  PEELED AND EACH CUT
  INTO THREE ½-INCH SLICES
  FROM THE CENTER, AT ROOM
  TEMPERATURE

SALT AND PEPPER TO TASTE
BLENDER HOLLANDAISE SAUCE
  (SEE P. 58), WARM
2 TABLESPOONS CHOPPED
  CHIVES

OVER MEDIUM HEAT, melt half of the butter in a frypan and "fry" 3 slices of the bread until golden on both sides. Repeat with remaining 3 slices of bread. If necessary, add more butter. Keep warm. Poach the eggs in simmering water to which 2 teaspoons of white vinegar have been added, until cooked to taste. Remove with a slotted spoon and drain briefly on paper towels. Place a slice of the fried bread on a plate, lay a slice of tomato on it, sprinkle with salt and pepper. Set an egg on each slice of tomato. Top with a tablespoon of the Blender Hollandaise Sauce and sprinkle with chives. *Serves 6.*

FRITTATAS

■■■

Mention omelets and they are immediately associated with French cookery and seem complicated. They aren't. A friend, Howard Helmer, has removed all the mystique from them (as you will see in his recipe for a 40-Second Omelet in this chapter). Actually, the Italians are masters of a flat omelet or egg cake called a frittata *and were whipping them out long before the French created their rolled versions. The Italian flat omelets also have a nice golden crust, which makes them the tastiest, and they are almost as easy as cracking an egg. Like all omelets,* frittatas *make a delicious first course or a unique luncheon or supper dish.*

With Mushrooms

7 EGGS
¼ CUP FRESHLY GRATED
  ASIAGO OR PARMESAN
  CHEESE
SALT AND PEPPER TO TASTE
⅛ TEASPOON NUTMEG
2 TABLESPOONS BUTTER

2 TABLESPOONS OLIVE OIL
2 SCALLIONS (GREEN ONIONS),
  CHOPPED, USING ALL BUT
  THE LAST INCH OF THE DARK
  GREEN TAIL
¼ POUND MUSHROOMS,
  THINLY SLICED

Beat eggs, cheese, salt, pepper, and nutmeg together in a bowl. In an 8- or 9-inch frypan, over medium heat, heat the butter and oil. Add the scallions and cook 2 minutes. Add the mushrooms and cook until the scallions are soft and the mushrooms limp. If too much liquid collects from the mushrooms, turn the heat high and cook off the liquid, but take the pan off the heat as soon as the liquid has evaporated so the scallions do not brown. Pour the egg mixture into the frypan and stir just enough to mix with the scallions and mushrooms. Cook over medium-low heat without stirring until the bottom is golden and set. The top will still be moist. If the *frittata* seems to be sticking, loosen the sides and bottom with a spatula. Place a plate, larger than the frypan, inverted, over the pan and flip the *frittata* over onto the plate (the golden side will be up). Slip it back into the frypan, golden side up. Cook until the bottom is golden. Serve right from the pan in wedges. *Serves 3.*

Note: Instead of turning it out onto the plate then returning it to the frypan, you can finish the *frittata* in a 450° oven until the top is set.

With Onion

Cook 2 medium-sized onions, thinly sliced, and 1 garlic clove, minced, in the butter and oil until soft. Add the beaten egg mixture and proceed as above.

With Asparagus

Peel stems of ½ pound of asparagus and cook in boiling salted water until tender-crisp. Cut into 1-inch pieces. Carefully stir into the egg mixture and cook in the butter and olive oil as above.

With Other Cooked Vegetables

Chopped, cooked broccoli, peas (do not chop), zucchini, or other vegetables can be substituted for the asparagus.

With Italian Sausage

Cut 3 lean, hot or sweet Italian sausage links into thin slices. Cook in the butter and oil until cooked through. Add the egg mixture (omitting the nutmeg and cheese) and add a pinch of dried thyme. Cook as above.

With Other Meat or Seafood

Cooked ham can be substituted for the sausage, as can cooked crabmeat or uncooked, cut-up shrimp.

HAM PUDDING

■ ■ ■

3 EGGS, WELL BEATEN IN A
  LARGE BOWL
1 CUP MILK
2 TABLESPOONS MELTED
  BUTTER

1¼ CUPS SIFTED ALL-PURPOSE
  FLOUR, SIFTED WITH ½
  TEASPOON SALT
3 CUPS CUBED COOKED HAM
PEPPER TO TASTE

ADD THE MILK and butter to the egg bowl and beat. Add the
flour and salt and beat with an electric beater until well
blended. Butter an 8-inch baking dish suitable for serving.
Arrange the ham in an even layer on the bottom. Sprinkle
with pepper. Carefully pour the batter over the ham. Bake
in a preheated 425° oven for 15 minutes. Lower oven heat
to 350° and bake another 15 minutes, or until topping is
set, puffed, and golden crisp. *Serves 4.*

HAM AND CHEESE SOUFFLÉ
■■■

Here's an elegant way to serve ham and eggs.

3 TABLESPOONS BUTTER
3 TABLESPOONS FLOUR
1 CUP MILK
6 TABLESPOONS GRATED
   PARMESAN CHEESE
½ CUP GRATED CHEDDAR
   CHEESE

½ CUP COOKED GROUND HAM
3 EGG YOLKS, BEATEN
⅛ TEASPOON CAYENNE, OR TO
   TASTE
SALT TO TASTE
4 EGG WHITES, STIFFLY BEATEN

BUTTER A 7-INCH soufflé dish, sprinkle bottom and sides with 2 tablespoons of the Parmesan. Shake out any excess. In a saucepan, over medium heat, melt the butter. Stir in the flour, stirring into a smooth paste. Gradually pour in the milk, stirring into a smooth, thick sauce. Remove from the heat, add the cheeses, and stir until melted. Add the ham and beaten egg yolks, cayenne, and salt. Blend well. Fold in the egg whites, carefully but thoroughly. Pour into the prepared soufflé dish, and bake in a preheated 375° oven 40 minutes, or until puffed, set, and golden. Serve with a good sharp mustard, *Serves 4.*

BLENDER HOLLANDAISE SAUCE
■■■

Makes about 1½ cups:

6 EGG YOLKS
¼ CUP FRESHLY SQUEEZED, STRAINED LEMON JUICE
¾ TEASPOON SALT
¼ TEASPOON CAYENNE
½ POUND BUTTER, MELTED, BUT NOT HOT

PUT THE EGG yolks, lemon juice, salt, and cayenne in a blender jar. Turn blender to high, then turn right off. Turn the blender on high again and slowly pour in the butter. Taste for seasoning. Blend for another second. Keep warm over warm water. This can be frozen and reheated over warm water.

HOWARD HELMER'S 40-SECOND OMELET
■ ■ ■

Don't combine mixtures, make one omelet at a time.

Howard Helmer is the world's champion omelet maker, teaching over one million people how to expertly make one in 40 seconds, so a few quotes from him are in order. He knows what he is talking about, holding the record in The Guinness Book of World Records *for tossing 217 omelets in 30 minutes.*

He advises: "Forget the special 'seasoned' pan. Forget what you've heard about shaking the pan, and 'rolling' the omelet. Forget 'omelet mystique.' Think of what an omelet really is: a pocket waiting to be filled, a sandwich waiting to be spread."

Howard doesn't "roll" omelets, he folds them. This means the filling doesn't have to be diced or finely chopped, as a folded omelet accepts bulk—whole asparagus spears, potato slices, rosettes of broccoli and many other combinations, from hearty slices of breast of chicken, even to pink strips of sirloin.

AN 8- OR 10-INCH SILVERSTONE NONSTICK FRYPAN WITH SLOPING SIDES	2 EGGS 2 TABLESPOONS WATER 1 TABLESPOON BUTTER

PLACE THE EGGS and water in a small bowl and briefly beat. Over medium-high heat, heat the pan just to the brink of smoking. Melt the butter and pour the beaten egg in. Immediately the egg will burst into bubbles. Those bubbles are the water in the egg evaporating, leaving air pockets in the omelet, which makes it light and fluffy. With a spatula, lift the cooked egg around the edges of the pan, allowing the uncooked egg to flow underneath and quickly cook. Don't overcook! While it is still light and fluffy and not very runny on top, it's time to fill and fold it. Turn the handle of the pan so it is pointed at your stomach. Fillings should be chopped, sliced, and cooked first (before you start to cook the eggs). Filling goes on the left side of the omelet. Now insert a spatula under the right side of the omelet and fold it, lifting the unfilled side over the filled side. Now you are ready to take the omelet out of the pan. The handle of the pan should now be pointed at your right hand. A warm plate should be ready to the left of the pan. Hold the plate in your left hand, take the handle of the pan in your right, and simply invert the pan so the omelet flips out on the plate upside down. *Serves 1.*

Note: For those interested in going onward and upward with omelets, Howard Helmer, the champ, has written a nifty book, *The 40-Second Omelet Guaranteed,* both amusing and authoritative, published by Atheneum in New York, which costs about the price of an omelet.

PENNSYLVANIA DUTCH RED EGGS
■■■

1 POUND FRESH SMALL
  BEETS, PEELED
½ CUP CIDER VINEGAR
2 TABLESPOONS SUGAR

½ TEASPOON COLEMAN'S
  DRIED MUSTARD
6 HARD-COOKED EGGS, SHELLED

IN A SAUCEPAN, cook the beets in boiling, salted water to cover, until very tender (about 30 minutes). With a slotted spoon transfer the beets to a bowl. Add the vinegar, sugar, and mustard to the beet water and simmer, stirring, until the sugar has dissolved. Pour over the beets and cool. Add the eggs to the bowl, pushing them down into the liquid with the beets. Cover tightly with plastic wrap and refrigerate overnight. Before serving, drain. Slice the beets and quarter the eggs. Serve on lettuce leaves with the eggs surrounding the sliced beets. *Serves 6.*

Note: Canned beets (a 1-pound can) can be used, using the liquid in the can for the marinade. However, fresh beets are better.

PORTUGUESE POACHED EGGS
■■■

All immigrants considered inexpensive, vitamin-rich eggs as important as meat. Sometimes they made a meal just from the eggs, and sometimes they varied the recipe by adding meat, as the Portuguese did in this tasty dish.

2 TABLESPOONS BUTTER
2 MEDIUM-SIZED ONIONS, CHOPPED
1 CUP BEEF BROTH
2 CUPS SHELLED SMALL PEAS, COOKED, BUT STILL FIRM (OR A 10- OUNCE PACKAGE OF FROZEN SMALL PEAS, DEFROSTED BUT NOT COOKED)

2 LARGE, RIPE, FIRM TOMATOES, PEELED, SEEDED, AND CHOPPED
6 SMALL, SMOKED GARLIC SAUSAGES, SUCH AS SPANISH CHORIZO, CUT INTO ¼-INCH ROUNDS
SALT AND PEPPER TO TASTE
6 JUMBO EGGS

IN A LARGE frypan, over medium heat, melt the butter. Add the onions and cook until soft. Do not brown. Stir in the beef broth, peas, and tomatoes. Stud the sausage rounds around the pan. Bring the sauce to a boil, partially cover the pan, reduce the heat, and simmer for 12 minutes. Taste for seasoning, adding salt and pepper. One at a time, break the eggs into a small saucer and slide into the sauce. Cover the pan and simmer for 5 minutes, or until the whites are set and the eggs poached to personal preference. Serve each egg on a bed of the sauce. *Serves 6.*

SPANISH BASQUE PIPERADE

■■■

5 TABLESPOONS BUTTER
2 TABLESPOONS OLIVE OIL
½ A SWEET GREEN PEPPER, SEEDS AND CORE REMOVED, THINLY SLICED
½ A SWEET RED PEPPER, SEEDS AND CORE REMOVED, THINLY SLICED
1 GARLIC CLOVE, MINCED
1 MEDIUM-SIZED WHITE ONION, THINLY SLICED
2 MEDIUM-SIZED RIPE, FIRM TOMATOES, SKINNED, SEEEDED, AND COARSELY CHOPPED

SALT AND PEPPER TO TASTE
1 TEASPOON CHOPPED FRESH THYME, OR ⅓ TEASPOON DRIED
1 CUP CUBED (¼ -INCH) PROSCIUTTO OR OTHER COOKED HAM
8 EGGS, BEATEN
3 ANCHOVY FILLETS, DRAINED AND CUT INTO SMALL PIECES
2 TABLESPOONS CHOPPED PARSLEY

In a large frypan over medium heat, heat the butter and oil. Add the green and red peppers, garlic, and onion and cook until the vegetables are soft. Do not brown. Add the tomatoes, season with salt and pepper. Add the thyme and cook until most of the liquid has evaporated and the sauce has thickened. Stir in the ham. Mix the anchovies with the beaten eggs. Add to the pan and cook, stirring, until firm but still moist. Stop stirring and allow the bottom to set. Turn out, like a cake, onto a hot, round serving dish and sprinkle with the parsley. *Serves 4.*

TEX-MEX SCRAMBLED EGGS

■■■

4 TABLESPOONS BUTTER
1 MEDIUM-SIZED ONION,
　FINELY CHOPPED
2 MEDIUM-SIZED RIPE,
　FIRM TOMATOES, PEELED,
　SEEDED, AND CHOPPED

1 TABLESPOON CHILI POWDER
12 EGGS
1/4 CUP HEAVY CREAM
SALT AND PEPPER TO TASTE
2 TABLESPOONS CHOPPED
　PARSLEY

IN A LARGE frypan, over medium heat, melt the butter. Add the onion and cook until soft. Do not brown. Stir in the tomatoes and the chili powder and cook until all of the liquid from the tomatoes has evaporated. Beat eggs with heavy cream and stir in. Cook, stirring, to cook the eggs evenly. Season with salt and pepper. The eggs should be slightly moist and have the texture of scrambled eggs. Stir in the parsley. *Serves 4 to 6.*

Chapter 4

FISH AND SHELLFISH

America may be the richest country on earth in its abundance and variety of seafood. Our Maine lobster is famous worldwide, and no one can equal our shad and shad roe, shrimp, scallops, trout, bass, clams, crabs, mussels, and oysters.

In fact, this wealth of seafood may be this country's greatest contribution to what is currently being called "America's new cuisine."

Actually, there is just about nothing new on earth, especially in cookery. No matter what we attempt, someone has been there before us. Of course, individual touches of creativity and imagination give old dishes new looks and tastes, but that's always been the case.

For example, take the American dish, Lobster Newburg. It is said to have been created by the chef at Manhattan's famous Delmonico's in honor of a patron named Wenburg. Lobster Wenburg. But when the owner of the restaurant and Mr. Wenburg had a falling out, the name was changed by reversing the first three letters of Wenburg's name, thus Newburg. The sauce itself, of butter, flour, cream, lemon juice, and egg yolks, is standard French, with the American additions of cayenne, paprika, and sherry—and, of course, lobster, a food we have a lock on.

California's Fisherman's Wharf's famous *cioppino* is believed to have been named as the result of a habit of needy people who lived near there going from fisherman's boat to boat lugging buckets and asking fishermen to generously "chip in" to help those doing the asking have free fish stew for supper.

That handout stew finally had an "o" added to the "chip in," becoming "chipino," and could contain anything from crabs to squid. The present spelling evolved to make the word as Italian as the fishermen who made the stew possible. This fish stew may be considered American, but it is very closely related to *zuppa di pesce*, brought here by Italian immigrants.

We expect, however, that one of the best ways to prepare our delicate rainbow trout is absolutely American, as it goes back to one of the basic foods of the real Americans, American Indians. Corn, maize, whatever it is called, when used as cornmeal, makes an effective and tasty protective covering for frying or sautéing fish, keeping it moist and flavorsome.

Our various seafood chowders are also supposed to be American, and some of the ways of handling them certainly are. But the word "chowder" came from the French *la chaudière* and a ceremony that originated in the coastal villages of France centuries ago. When the fishing fleets reached port, each fisherman tossed a share of his catch into a large kettle, called *la chaudière*, which was bubbling with a combination of water, wine, and various seasonings. The entire community joined in eating the fish stew feast in thanksgiving for the safe return of the fishermen.

The ceremony was brought to Canada by French immigrants, then drifted down the coast to Maine and finally to the rest of New England. But about the only thanks involved today are to the canny American cooks who have concocted various chowders, using everything from clams to shrimp, heavy cream to tomatoes, even salt pork, which is certainly a New England touch. Few of us today will go so far as the lucky folk in Maine, who have chowders consisting solely of lobster, with a few touches of seasonings.

Fish with spinach is a popular American dish, but that combination originated in Florence, Italy, centuries ago, where many foods are given the attractive and tasty touch of spinach, thus earning the name "Florentine."

Pickled shrimp and crab salad are most definitely American, as are crab cakes and clam fritters.

But let's keep it uncomplicated and just consider that the American family has the best seafood in the world, no matter where the recipes originated.

BROILED BLUEFISH WITH LEMON-BUTTER-CAPER SAUCE

■ ■ ■

6 SMALL BLUEFISH FILLETS,
   OR LARGER FILLETS CUT INTO
   6 SERVING PIECES
¼ POUND SOFT BUTTER
SALT AND PEPPER

6 TABLESPOONS BUTTER
5 TABLESPOONS LEMON JUICE
3 TABLESPOONS CAPERS,
   RINSED IN WATER AND
   DRAINED

ARRANGE THE FILLETS side by side, in a buttered shallow baking dish just large enough to hold them snugly in a single layer. Spread the fillets with the soft butter and sprinkle with salt and pepper. Broil 10 minutes, or until the fish flakes easily with a fork but is still moist. Heat together the butter, lemon juice, and capers and serve the sauce at the table to be spooned over the broiled fillets. *Serves 6.*

DANISH FISH PUDDING

(with Mushroom Sauce)

■ ■ ■

2 POUNDS RAW COD OR HADDOCK
4 TABLESPOONS SOFT BUTTER
1 TEASPOON ANCHOVY PASTE
1 TEASPOON SALT
¼ TEASPOON PEPPER
GOOD PINCH CAYENNE, OR TO TASTE
4 EGG YOLKS
3 TABLESPOONS FLOUR
1 CUP LIGHT CREAM
1 CUP HEAVY CREAM, BEATEN
4 EGG WHITES, STIFFLY BEATEN
FINE BREAD CRUMBS
PARSLEY
MUSHROOM SAUCE (SEE BELOW)

PUT THE FISH through the fine blade of a meat chopper twice (or use a food processor, but do not purée the fish). In a bowl, combine and blend well the fish, butter, anchovy paste, salt, pepper, and cayenne. In another bowl, beat the egg yolks, flour, and light cream together to blend well. Beat the egg yolk mixture, a small amount at a time, into the fish mixture. Gently fold in the heavy cream and egg whites until well blended. Butter a 2-quart, deep baking dish, then dust with breadcrumbs. Invert the dish to allow excess crumbs to drop out. Pour the fish mixture into the baking dish, place in a pan of hot water, and bake in a preheated 350° oven for 1 to 1½ hours, or until a knife blade inserted just off center comes out clean. Let set for several minutes, then turn out onto a hot serving dish (or serve right from the baking dish). Garnish with the parsley and serve with a bowl of Mushroom Sauce. *Serves 6.*

Sauce

7 TABLESPOONS BUTTER
4 SHALLOTS (OR 1 SMALL
   WHITE ONION), MINCED
¼ POUND SMALL MUSHROOMS,
   THINLY SLICED

SALT AND PEPPER TO TASTE
3 TABLESPOONS FLOUR
2 CUPS CHICKEN BROTH
½ CUP HEAVY CREAM

In a frypan, over medium heat, melt 2 tablespoons of the butter, add the shallots, and cook until soft. Do not brown. Add 2 more tablespoons of butter and the mushrooms and cook 2 minutes. The mushrooms should be firm. Season with salt and pepper. In a saucepan, melt the remaining butter over medium heat. Stir in the flour and cook, stirring into a smooth paste. Gradually add the chicken broth and cook, stirring into a smooth, medium-thick sauce. Stir in the cream, add the shallots and mushrooms, and simmer until the sauce is again medium-thick. Taste for seasoning.

FISH FILLETS WITH SPINACH
■■■

TWO 10-OUNCE PACKAGES
FRESH SPINACH, OR TWO
10-OUNCE PACKAGES FRO-
ZEN LEAF SPINACH,
DEFROSTED
2½ POUNDS FILLETS OF SOLE
OR FLOUNDER, CUT INTO
SERVING PIECES
5 SHALLOTS (OR 1 WHITE
ONION), MINCED
3 TABLESPOONS CHOPPED
PARSLEY
SALT AND PEPPER

1 TABLESPOON LEMON JUICE
1½ CUPS (OR JUST ENOUGH
BARELY TO COVER THE
FISH) DRY WHITE WINE
8 TABLESPOONS BUTTER
3 TABLESPOONS FLOUR
2 CUPS LIGHT CREAM OR HALF
AND HALF
12 MEDIUM-SIZED MUSHROOM
CAPS
3 TABLESPOONS GRATED
ASIAGO OR PARMESAN
CHEESE

IF USING FRESH spinach, remove the stems and cook in a large amount of boiling water just until wilted (about 2 minutes). Remove with a large fork and drain well.

Butter 2 shallow baking dishes, each large enough to hold the fish in one layer. One should be a stove-top-to-oven dish. Lay the fillets in the stove-top-to-oven dish. Sprinkle the shallots and parsley around the edge of the fish. Sprinkle with salt and pepper and lemon juice. Pour in the wine and dot the fish with 2 tablespoons of butter. Cover with foil, bring to a boil on top of the stove, then place in a preheated 400° oven for 10 minutes, or until the fish is white and barely flakes with a fork (if it flakes too easily, it will be overcooked) and is still moist. Line the bottom of the second baking dish with the spinach and sprinkle with salt and pepper. Carefully transfer the fish, laying them on the spinach in a single layer. Reduce the wine, in the dish in which the fish cooked, to about ½ cup. Strain and reserve. In a saucepan, over medium heat, melt 3 tablespoons of the butter and blend in the flour, cooking and stirring into a smooth paste. Gradually add the reduced wine and the cream, stirring into a smooth, medium-thick sauce. Season with salt and pepper. Cook the mushrooms in 3 tablespoons of butter, until slightly browned but still firm. Pour the wine sauce over the fish. Sprinkle with the cheese. Place in a preheated 400° oven until the sauce bubbles, then under the broiler until the top is golden. Garnish with the mushrooms. *Serves 6.*

FISKESUPPE

(Scandinavian Fish Stew)

■ ■ ■

TRIMMINGS FROM A COD OR OTHER WHITE FISH (TAIL, HEAD, FINS, BONES) (SEE NOTE)

2 MEDIUM-SIZED ONIONS, CHOPPED

2 MEDIUM-SIZED CARROTS, SCRAPED AND CHOPPED

3 MEDIUM-SIZED POTATOES, CHOPPED

SALT AND PEPPER

1 SMALL BAY LEAF

2 CELERY RIBS (WITH LEAVES), SCRAPED AND CHOPPED

3 QUARTS WATER

¾ CUP OF ¼-INCH CUBES OF TURNIPS

¾ CUP OF ¼-INCH CUBES OF CARROTS

¾ CUP OF FINELY CHOPPED ONIONS

2 POUNDS COD (OR OTHER WHITE FISH) FILLETS, IN LARGE PIECES

2 EGG YOLKS

SALT AND PEPPER TO TASTE

SOUR CREAM

IN A LARGE soup pot, combine fish trimmings, chopped onions, chopped carrots, potatoes, 1 teaspoon salt, ½ teaspoon pepper, bay leaf, celery, and water. Bring to a boil, lower heat, and simmer, partially covered for 45 minutes. Strain the liquid. Discard the fish parts. Push the vegetables through the strainer and return the liquid and strained vegetables to the pot. Over high heat, reduce to about 8 cups. Add the turnips, cubed carrots, and finely chopped onions to the reduced stock. Simmer, uncovered, for 10 minutes. Add the fish and simmer 8 minutes or until it flakes with a fork. With a slotted spoon remove the fish and keep it warm. In a bowl beat the egg yolks with half a cup of the hot soup. Remove pot from the heat and add the egg yolk–soup mixture, vigorously stirring until well blended. Cut the fish into ½-inch cubes and stir them into the soup. Taste for seasoning, adding salt and pepper, if needed. Return to the heat just to heat through. Do not bring to a boil. Serve in deep bowls with a dollop of sour cream on top. Some dark, buttered bread and cold beer make this a supper-in-a-soup-bowl. Serves 6.

Note: If no fish trimmings are available, buy an additional half-pound of fish and use that, cut up.

HADDOCK FILLETS WITH HERB TOPPING
■■■

4 TABLESPOONS OLIVE OIL
1 MEDIUM-SIZED ONION,
   FINELY CHOPPED
1 GARLIC CLOVE, MINCED
2 CUPS BREAD CRUMBS, MADE
   FROM DAY-OLD OR 2-DAY-
   OLD BREAD
¼ CUP CHOPPED WALNUT
   MEATS
1 TABLESPOON RAISINS,
   "PLUMPED" IN WHITE
   VERMOUTH, DRAINED, AND
   CHOPPED

¼ CUP CHOPPED PARSLEY
2 FRESH BASIL LEAVES,
   CHOPPED, OR ½ TEA-
   SPOON DRIED
¼ TEASPOON DRIED OREGANO
1 LARGE RIPE TOMATO, PEELED,
   SEEDED AND FINELY
   CHOPPED
SALT AND PEPPER TO TASTE
3 POUNDS HADDOCK (OR OTHER
   WHITE FISH) FILLETS
1 CUP DRY WHITE WINE

In a frypan, over medium heat, heat 2 tablespoons of olive oil; add the onion and garlic and cook until soft. Do not brown. In a bowl, with a fork, combine and mix well the onion, garlic, remaining oil, bread crumbs, walnut meats, raisins, parsley, basil, oregano, tomato, salt, and pepper. If mixture seems dry, sprinkle on additional oil and mix. Lay the fillets in a buttered, shallow baking dish just large enough to hold them snugly in one layer. Sprinkle with salt and pepper and cover evenly with the topping. Pour the wine around the edge of the dish to a depth of ¼ inch. Bake, uncovered, in a preheated 350° oven for 30 minutes, or until the fish flakes easily with a fork but is still moist. *Serves 6.*

MIKE MADIGAN'S POOR MAN'S LOBSTER

■ ■ ■

ABOUT 1 QUART WATER,
   DEPENDING ON THE AMOUNT
   OF FISH BEING COOKED
1 ONION, SLICED
6 WHOLE BLACK PEPPERCORNS
2 WHOLE ALLSPICE
3 TABLESPOONS LEMON JUICE
1 BAY LEAF

1 TEASPOON SALT
½ CUP DRY WHITE WINE
2 POUNDS VERY FRESH WHITE
   FISH FILLETS (SMALL-
   MOUTH BASS IF YOU CAN
   CATCH IT), CUT INTO
   BITE-SIZED PIECES
MELTED BUTTER

COMBINE ALL INGREDIENTS except the fish and butter in a pan (you'll need enough water just to cover the fish pieces, so the amount of water may be varied if you are using more fish and feeding more people). Simmer the ingredients together for 20 minutes. Cook the fish in the poaching liquid for 3 minutes. Remove with a slotted spoon. Serve each person a small bowl of hot melted butter in which to dip the pieces of fish. *Serves 4.*

NEW ENGLAND FISH CHOWDER
■ ■ ■

Fish chowder can be varied. In some areas of the country white wine is added and sometimes tomato, but the classic New England fish chowder always includes salt pork, onions, potatoes, milk and/or cream, and of course, the fish.

3 POUNDS WHOLE COD, HADDOCK, OR OTHER WHITE FISH
1/4 TEASPOON DRIED THYME
1 BAY LEAF
1 TEASPOON SALT
1/4 TEASPOON PEPPER
2 CUPS WATER
ONE 2-INCH CUBE SALT PORK, CUT INTO 1/4 -INCH CUBES

1 LARGE ONION, COARSELY CHOPPED
2 CELERY RIBS, SCRAPED AND COARSELY CHOPPED
2 LARGE POTATOES, CUT INTO 1/2-INCH CUBES
2 CUPS HEAVY CREAM, SCALDED
2 CUPS MILK, SCALDED
3 TABLESPOONS BUTTER

Cut off the head and tail of the fish and fillet the fish, saving the back bone. Cut fillets into 2-inch pieces. In a large pot, combine the head, tail, bones, thyme, bay leaf, salt and pepper, and 2 cups of water and simmer for 20 minutes. Strain and reserve the liquid and discard the head, tail, and other solids. In a heavy large deep pot, over medium heat, cook the salt pork until golden and crisp. Add the onion and celery and cook just until the onion is soft. Add the potatoes and 1½ cups of hot water and simmer for 10 minutes, uncovered. Add the pieces of fish and simmer 10 minutes, or until the fish flakes easily with a fork and the potatoes are tender. If the liquid cooks off, add a small amount of hot water. Add the fish broth, cream, and milk and bring to a simmer. Taste for seasoning. Just before serving, stir in the butter. *Serves 6.*

Note: If whole fish are not available, substitute clam broth for the fish broth and 2 pounds of fish fillets, cut up.

SHAD ROE VERONIQUE

■■■

6 MEDIUM TO LARGE SHAD
  ROE
1½ CUPS DRY WHITE WINE
WATER
10 TABLESPOONS BUTTER
SALT AND PEPPER
TWO 8½-OUNCE CANS SEED-
  LESS WHITE GRAPES,
  DRAINED (OR USE FRESH
  WHITE SEEDLESS GRAPES,
  POACHED IN A MEDIUM
  SUGAR SYRUP FOR 5
  MINUTES, AND DRAINED)

3 TABLESPOONS FLOUR
1 CUP MILK
1½ CUPS CREAM
¼ CUP DRY SHERRY

In a large frypan, arrange the roe in a single layer and pour in the white wine and enough water barely to cover. Bring to a simmer and simmer for 10 minutes, or until firm. Drain and cool. You may remove the membrane or not. If you remove it, do so carefully so roe will not separate. Discard the wine and water. Melt 6 tablespoons of butter in the frypan over medium heat and, handling very carefully, cook the roe on both sides to brown evenly. Sprinkle with salt and pepper. Carefully transfer the roe to a shallow, buttered baking dish just large enough to hold the roe in one layer. Sprinkle the grapes over and around the roe. In a saucepan over medium heat, melt the remaining 4 tablespoons of butter. Stir in the flour and cook, stirring into a smooth paste. Gradually add the milk, cream, and sherry, stirring constantly into a smooth, medium-thick sauce. Season with salt and pepper. Spoon the sauce over the roe and grapes. Place in a preheated 400° oven until the sauce is bubbling, then under the broiler until golden. *Serves 6.*

SHAD TOPPED WITH ROE

■ ■ ■

1 PAIR SHAD ROE
1 CUP DRY WHITE WINE
WATER
6 TABLESPOONS BUTTER
4 SHALLOTS (OR 1 SMALL
  WHITE ONION), MINCED
2 TABLESPOONS FLOUR
1½ CUPS HEAVY CREAM

2 EGG YOLKS
3 TABLESPOONS DRY WHITE
  WINE
SALT AND PEPPER TO TASTE
1 TABLESPOON MINCED CHIVES
1 SHAD (WEIGHING 3 POUNDS
  AFTER BONING)
½ CUP BREAD CRUMBS

PLACE THE ROE, 1 cup of wine, and enough water just to cover in a small frypan. Bring to a boil, then simmer for 10 minutes. Drain and discard wine and water. Remove the membrane from the roe and mash the roe. In a frypan, or saucepan, over medium heat, melt 3 tablespoons of butter. Add the shallots and cook until soft. Do not brown. Stir in the flour, the roe, and the cream and bring to a simmer, blending well. Remove from the heat. Beat egg yolks with the 3 tablespoons of wine and stir in. Season with salt and pepper. Blend in the chives and, over low heat, cook, stirring until thickened. Do not allow to boil. Place the shad, open, skin side down, in a shallow, buttered baking dish. Dot with the remaining butter, sprinkle with salt and pepper, and bake in a preheated 350° oven for 10 minutes, or until the shad flakes with a fork but is still moist. Spread roe mixture over the shad, then sprinkle with the bread crumbs. Brown under the broiler and serve. *Serves 6.*

SOLE FILLETS WITH SHRIMP QUENELLES STUFFING

■ ■ ■

ONE 10-OUNCE PACKAGE
FRESH SPINACH, OR ONE
10-OUNCE PACKAGE OF FRO-
ZEN, CHOPPED SPINACH,
DEFROSTED
12 MEDIUM-SIZED MUSHROOMS
4 TABLESPOONS OF BUTTER
2 TEASPOONS OF LEMON JUICE
6 FILLETS OF SOLE, EACH
WEIGHING ABOUT 6
OUNCES
½ POUND OF SHRIMP, SHELLED
AND DEVEINED
1 EGG WHITE

½ TEASPOON SALT
PINCH EACH OF NUTMEG AND
CAYENNE
½ CUP OF WELL CHILLED
HEAVY CREAM
1 CUP OF DRY WHITE WINE
1 TABLESPOON OF CHOPPED
PARSLEY
3 SHALLOTS (OR 1 SMALL WHITE
ONION), FINELY CHOPPED
1 CUP HEAVY CREAM AT ROOM
TEMPERATURE
1 EGG YOLK, BEATEN
SALT AND PEPPER TO TASTE

PUSH FRESH SPINACH down into boiling water and cook about 2 minutes, or until limp. Drain. Cool and squeeze out all liquid with your hands. If using frozen spinach, do not cook, but squeeze out liquid. Purée spinach in a processor or blender. Set aside. Remove stems from the mushrooms, chop them and set them aside. In a frypan, heat 2 tablespoons of butter and 1 teaspoon of lemon juice and cook the mushroom caps for 2 minutes. Remove with a slotted spoon and set aside. Reserve liquid they cooked in. Between sheets of waxed paper, carefully flatten the fillets with the side of a cleaver or broad-bladed knife, being careful not to put any holes in them.

In a food chopper (using the finest blade), food processor or blender, puree the shrimp. (If using a food chopper, run the shrimp through twice.) Transfer to a bowl set in ice and with a wooden spoon work into a smooth paste. Thoroughly blend in the egg white, remaining lemon juice, ½ teaspoon of salt, nutmeg and cayenne. Very gradually (a teaspoonful at a time) add the chilled cream, incorporating each addition before adding more. The mixture should be the consistency of firm whipped cream. Refrigerate 2 hours or more.

Divide the mixture among the fillets and spread smoothly over each. Roll lengthwise starting at the narrow end. Secure with toothpicks or cord. In a deep frypan, just large enough to hold the rolls in one layer, heat the wine, remaining butter, parsley, shallots, mushroom stems and the liquid the mushrooms cooked in. When the liquid is simmering, add the rolled fillets, cover and cook 8 minutes (turning at 4 minutes) or until the filling has set and the fish flakes with a fork. To test filling, insert a fork or skewer. If it comes out clean, it is ready.

Remove the rolls and keep warm. Strain the liquid into a saucepan and reduce it to about ¼ cup. Add the cup of room temperature cream. Lower heat. Heat to a simmer. Mix ¼ cup of the hot liquid with the egg yolk and return it to the pan, stirring. Cook, stirring constantly, until the sauce has slightly thickened. Do not boil or the egg will curdle. Stir in the spinach purée. Taste for seasoning, then add salt and pepper. Heat through without boiling.

Arrange the rolls on a serving dish and spoon the sauce over them. Garnish with the mushroom caps. Serves 6.

COLD POACHED BROOK TROUT

■ ■ ■

2 CUPS DRY WHITE WINE
1 CUP WATER
1 TABLESPOON FRESH CHOPPED
   TARRAGON, OR 1 TEA-
   SPOON DRY TARRAGON
2 TABLESPOONS CHOPPED
   PARSLEY
1 TEASPOON SALT
4 PEPPERCORNS
SIX 10-OUNCE (APPROXIMATELY)
   BROOK TROUT, DRESSED
   (CAN BE BOUGHT FROZEN, 2
   IN EACH PACKAGE), IF
   FROZEN, DEFROST

3 TABLESPOONS (3 ENVELOPES)
   PLAIN GELATIN, SOAKED IN
   ½ CUP COLD WATER
SIX ¾-INCH SLICES RIPE,
   FIRM TOMATOES, SKINS
   REMOVED
6 HEAPING TABLESPOONS
   WHIPPED CREAM
1½ TABLESPOONS FRESHLY
   GRATED HORSERADISH OR
   WELL-DRAINED COMMERCIAL
   HORSERADISH

COMBINE THE WINE, water, tarragon, parsley, salt, and peppercorns in a deep frypan large enough to hold 2 or 3 trout at a time, laid side by side. Bring to a boil and simmer for 10 minutes. Add 2 or 3 of the trout and over low heat cook for about 5 minutes, or until the fish flakes easily with a fork, but are still moist. Do not overcook. Carefully (a long, broad spatula is good for this) transfer the trout to a wire rack to drain. Cook the remaining trout and cool. Strain the liquid in which the fish cooked. Warm the gelatin over hot water until it becomes liquid and clear, then stir it into the strained, hot liquid. Pour into a shallow casserole (a Pyrex works well) and refrigerate to set. Arrange the trout side by side on a flat serving dish and refrigerate. When the gelatin has set firmly, chop it into small cubes and scatter the cubes over the cold trout on the serving dish. Mix the whipped cream and horseradish and mound each slice of tomato with the mixture. Serve the trout with the tomato–horseradish garnish. *Serves 6.*

RAINBOW TROUT IN CORNMEAL
■ ■ ■

4 RAINBOW TROUT (ABOUT
   10 OUNCES EACH), CLEANED,
   WITH HEADS ON (AVAILABLE
   FRESH OR FROZEN IN MOST
   SUPERMARKETS), WASHED
   IN COLD WATER, DRIED WITH
   PAPER TOWEL; IF FROZEN,
   DEFROST FIRST

SALT TO TASTE
2 EGGS, BEATEN
ABOUT 1½ CUPS CORNMEAL
3 TABLESPOONS BUTTER
1 TABLESPOON OLIVE OIL

SRINKLE TROUT WITH salt. Dip into the egg, then into the cornmeal, coating well. In a frypan, over medium heat, heat the butter and oil and brown the trout, turning several times to avoid overbrowning. Fish should be golden brown and coating should be crisp. Some peel the cornmeal off and eat the moist tender trout, but the cornmeal itself is also delicious. *Serves 4.*

CIOPPINO
■■■

⅓ CUP OLIVE OIL

1 LARGE ONION, FINELY CHOPPED

1 LARGE GARLIC CLOVE, MINCED

1 SMALL GREEN PEPPER, SEEDED, DERIBBED, AND CHOPPED

2 CELERY RIBS, SCRAPED AND CHOPPED

4 RIPE, FIRM TOMATOES, PEELED, SEEDED, AND CHOPPED, OR ONE 1-POUND CAN TOMATOES (PREFERABLY BELL-SHAPED), DRAINED AND CHOPPED

2 TABLESPOONS TOMATO PASTE

2 CUPS DRY WHITE WINE

½ TEASPOON EACH DRIED BASIL AND OREGANO

SALT AND PEPPER TO TASTE

TWO 1½-POUND LOBSTERS CUT INTO SERVING PIECES, OR 2 LARGE CRABS

1½ POUNDS HALIBUT, COD, OR OTHER FIRM, WHITE FISH, CUT INTO SERVING PIECES

2 DOZEN MUSSELS, OR 1 DOZEN MUSSELS AND 1 DOZEN CLAMS, WELL SCRUBBED (SEE NOTE)

24 SHRIMP, SHELLED AND DEVEINED

½ CUP CHOPPED PARSLEY

IN A LARGE soup pot or casserole, heat the oil over medium heat. Add the onion, garlic, green pepper, and celery and cook until soft. Do not brown. Add the tomatoes, tomato paste, wine, basil, oregano, salt, and pepper. Bring to a boil. Cover and simmer for 15 minutes. Add the lobster or crab and cook, covered, 5 minutes. Add the fish and the mussels and clams and cook 5 minutes. Add the shrimp and cook three minutes, or until the shrimp just turn pink and the mussels and clams are firm but not tough. Serve in deep, large soup bowls with parsley sprinkled over each bowl and plenty of crusty bread. Supply bowls for discarded shells . *Serves 6.*

Note: Clams and mussels will be tough if overcooked.

NEW ENGLAND CLAM PIE

(with variation)

■■■

4 TABLESPOONS BUTTER
2 MEDIUM-SIZED ONIONS,
    CHOPPED
3 TABLESPOONS FLOUR
TWO 6½-OUNCE CANS MINCED
    CLAMS, DRAINED, LIQUID
    RESERVED
1 CUP CLAM BROTH
½ CUP HEAVY CREAM
1 MEDIUM-SIZED CARROT,
    SCRAPED, CUBED, AND
    COOKED

1 CELERY RIB, SCRAPED,
    CHOPPED, AND COOKED
¼ CUP CHOPPED PARSLEY
3 HARD-COOKED EGGS,
    COARSELY CHOPPED
SALT AND PEPPER TO TASTE
PASTRY (SEE BELOW)

In a frypan, over medium heat, melt the butter. Add the onions and cook until soft. Do not brown. Stir in the flour and blend well with the onion and butter. Gradually add the liquid from the canned clams, the clam broth, and the heavy cream, cooking and stirring into a smooth, medium-thick sauce. Stir in the clams, carrot, celery, parsley, and eggs. Spoon into a 9-inch pie dish. Roll out the dough one inch in diameter larger all around than the pie dish. Moisten the edge of the pie dish, cover with the dough. Fold the overhang under, press against the moist rim of the dish, and flute. Bake in a preheated 450° oven for 20 minutes, or until golden brown. *Serves 4.*

Variation: Instead of the pastry, top the clam mixture in the pie dish with an even layer of seasoned mashed potatoes (about 1½ to 2 cups) and brown in the 450° oven.

Pastry

For a single-crust, 9-inch pie shell, or to top a pie:

1½ CUPS ALL-PURPOSE FLOUR
1 TEASPOON SALT
¼ CUP BUTTER

¼ CUP CRISCO OR OTHER
  VEGETABLE SHORTENING
3 TABLESPOONS COLD WATER

In a bowl, with a pastry mixer, mix the flour and salt, butter, and Crisco until it has the texture of coarse meal. Add the water and mix with a fork just long enough for it to hold together. Roll into a ball, wrap in waxed paper, and refrigerate until ready to roll out.

NORTH CAROLINA CLAM FRITTERS
■ ■ ■

2 EGG YOLKS, WELL BEATEN
2 CUPS MINCED CLAMS, FRESH
  OR CANNED
1 CUP VERY FINE CRACKER
  CRUMBS

1 TEASPOON SALT
PINCH CAYENNE PEPPER, OR TO
  TASTE
2 EGG WHITES, STIFFLY BEATEN
VEGETABLE OIL

ADD THE CLAMS, cracker crumbs, salt, and cayenne to the beaten egg yolks. Fold in the egg whites. Drop from a spoon into the hot oil (about ½-inch deep), not too close together, as they will expand. As you cook the fritters, drain them on paper towels and keep warm in a 250° oven. *Serves 4.*

CAROLINA CRAB SALAD

■ ■ ■

1 POUND FRESH-COOKED
   CRABMEAT, WELL PICKED
   OVER TO REMOVE ANY
   SHELL OR CARTILAGE (CAN-
   NED CRAB CAN BE USED)
2 HARD-COOKED EGGS,
   COARSELY CHOPPED
4 SMALL SCALLIONS (GREEN
   ONIONS), CHOPPED (WHITE
   PART ONLY)

1 CELERY RIB, SCRAPED AND
   CHOPPED
2 TABLESPOONS CHOPPED
   SWEET PICKLE
SALT TO TASTE
½ CUP MAYONNAISE
BOSTON LETTUCE LEAVES

IN A BOWL, combine everything except lettuce, blending well but carefully. Refrigerate for 2 hours. Spoon onto lettuce leaves and serve. *Serves 4.*

GEORGIA GUEST CRAB SURPRISE

■ ■ ■

1½ POUNDS CRABMEAT,
   WELL PICKED OVER TO
   REMOVE ANY BITS OF
   SHELL AND CARTILAGE
2 EGGS, BEATEN
1 CUP LIGHT CREAM
4 TABLESPOONS MELTED
   BUTTER

⅛ TEASPOON CAYENNE PEPPER,
   OR TO TASTE
1 TEASPOON WORCESTERSHIRE
   SAUCE
SALT TO TASTE
1½ CUPS BREAD CRUMBS

IN A LARGE bowl, combine and blend well the crabmeat,
eggs, cream, butter, cayenne, Worcestershire, salt, and 1
cup of the bread crumbs. Spoon into a buttered soufflé
dish, sprinkle with the remaining bread crumbs, and dot
with butter. Cook, uncovered, in a preheated 350° oven
for half an hour, or until set and golden brown. *Serves 4.*

MARYLAND CRAB CAKES

■■■

7 TABLESPOONS BUTTER
1 MEDIUM-SIZED ONION, FINELY CHOPPED
2 EGGS
1 TEASPOON SALT
1 TEASPOON DRY MUSTARD
1 TEASPOON WORCESTERSHIRE SAUCE
1 DASH TABASCO SAUCE
2 TABLESPOONS FINELY CHOPPED PARSLEY

1½ CUPS SOFT BREAD CRUMBS
1½ POUNDS FRESH, COOKED CRABMEAT, PICKED OVER TO REMOVE ANY BITS OF SHELL OR CARTILAGE
HEAVY CREAM
FLOUR (OR FINE DRIED BREAD CRUMBS
2 TABLESPOONS OLIVE OIL

IN A FRYPAN, over medium heat, melt 3 tablespoons of butter. Add the onion and cook until soft. Do not brown. Beat eggs, salt, mustard, Worcestershire, Tabasco, and parsley together in a large bowl to blend well. Stir the soft bread crumbs and the crabmeat into the onions, and as soon as it is well mixed, transfer to the bowl with the egg mixture and stir with a fork to blend well. Add just enough heavy cream to hold mixture together. Shape into 2-inch balls, then slightly flatten into thick cakes. Dredge with the flour. In a frypan, heat 2 tablespoons of butter and 1 tablespoon of oil. Add a few cakes (do not crowd) and brown evenly on both sides. Transfer the browned cakes to a hot serving dish and keep warm while you brown the remaining cakes in the remaining butter and oil. Serve with lemon wedges or tartar sauce. *Serves 6.*

STUFFED GREEK EGGPLANT, NEW ENGLAND STYLE

■ ■ ■

2 MEDIUM-SIZED FIRM
  EGGPLANTS
3 TABLESPOONS BUTTER
1 TABLESPOON OLIVE OIL
4 SCALLIONS (GREEN ONIONS),
  FINELY CHOPPED
2 TENDER CELERY RIBS, SCRAPED
  AND FINELY CHOPPED
1 MEDIUM-SIZED RIPE TOMATO,
  PEELED, SEEDED, AND
  CHOPPED

SALT AND PEPPER TO TASTE
3 TABLESPOONS MINCED
  PARSLEY
2 CUPS SLIGHTLY UNDERCOOKED
  CRABMEAT OR SHRIMP
4 TABLESPOONS FRESH BREAD
  CRUMBS
4 TABLESPOONS GRATED
  ASIAGO OR PARMESAN
  CHEESE

CUT THE EGGPLANT in half lengthwise. Make some slashes
in the pulp and bake in a preheated 350° oven for 20
minutes, or until tender. Scoop out the pulp, leaving a
shell ¼ inch thick, and chop the pulp. In a frypan, heat the
butter and oil over medium heat and cook the scallions
and celery until soft. Do not brown. Add the tomato and
eggplant pulp and cook until liquid cooks off. Sprinkle
with salt and pepper. Add the parsley and crabmeat or
shrimp and stir over heat until heated through. Mound the
mixture in the eggplant shells, dividing it equally. Sprinkle
with the bread crumbs and grated cheese. Place in a shallow
baking dish. Pour ½ inch of boiling water around the eggplant
and bake in a preheated 375° oven for 20 minutes, or
until browned. *Serves 4.*

LOBSTER NEWBURG

■ ■ ■

5 TABLESPOONS BUTTER
3 CUPS SLIGHTLY UNDERCOOKED
   LOBSTER, CUT INTO BITE-
   SIZED PIECES
¼ CUP DRY SHERRY
1½ CUPS HEAVY CREAM
3 EGG YOLKS
SALT TO TASTE

⅛ TEASPOON CAYENNE, OR TO
   TASTE
1 TEASPOON LEMON JUICE
6 FROZEN PEPPERIDGE FARM
   PATTY SHELLS, COOKED
   ACCORDING TO PACKAGE
   DIRECTIONS
PAPRIKA

IN A LARGE saucepan, over medium heat, melt the butter. Stir in the lobster; cook, stirring, 40 seconds. Add the sherry and 1 cup of the cream, blend well, bring to a boil, and immediately lower heat so the sauce is at a bare simmer. Stirring, cook 1 minute. Beat the egg yolks with the remaining half-cup of cream. Add 3 tablespoons of the hot lobster sauce, blending well, then stir this into the lobster pan. Stirring, cook 30 seconds, or until the sauce begins to thicken. Do not allow to boil as it will curdle. Blend in the salt, cayenne, and lemon juice. Spoon into the patty shells, sprinkle lightly with paprika, and serve immediately. *Serves 6.*

CAPE COD SCALLOPS

■■■

1 CUP CLAM BROTH
1 CUP DRY WHITE WINE
1½ POUNDS SCALLOPS (IF BAY
   SCALLOPS, LEAVE THEM
   WHOLE; IF SEA SCALLOPS,
   CUT INTO HALVES)
4 TABLESPOONS BUTTER
6 GREEN ONIONS (SCALLIONS),
   FINELY CHOPPED, USING
   ALL BUT THE LAST INCH OF
   THE DARK GREEN PART
1 TEASPOON CHOPPED FRESH
   TARRAGON OR ⅓ TEASPOON
   DRIED

3 TABLESPOONS FLOUR
1 CUP HEAVY CREAM
SALT TO TASTE
¼ TEASPOON CAYENNE PEPPER,
   OR TO TASTE
6 THICK SLICES OF BREAD,
   FRIED IN BUTTER UNTIL
   GOLDEN ON BOTH SIDES
CHOPPED PARSLEY

IN A SAUCEPAN, heat the broth and wine. Add the scallops
and simmer, uncovered, just until firm, but still tender
(about 5 minutes). Do not overcook or they will toughen.
Drain, reduce liquid to 1½ cups. Hold the scallops in a
warm place. In a saucepan or deep frypan, heat the butter
over medium heat. Add the green onions and tarragon
and cook until the onions are soft. Do not brown. Sprinkle
in the flour and blend well. Gradually add the reduced
liquid and, stirring constantly, cook into a smooth, thickened sauce. Stir in the heavy cream. Taste for seasoning,
adding the salt and cayenne. Add scallops and heat through.
Serve on the fried bread, sprinkle with parsley. *Serves 6.*

BEER-BATTER-FRIED SHRIMP

■■■

This was created by the late master chef Albert Stockli, who introduced it to our mentor, Antoine Gilly, one of the four greatest French chefs, who, in turn, passed it on to us.

36 MEDIUM-SIZED SHRIMP,
SHELLED (LEAVE THE TAILS
ON), SLIT ALONG THE
BACK, DARK VEIN REMOVED,
THEN WASHED AND DRIED
WITH PAPER TOWELS

JUICE OF 3 LEMONS
OIL FOR DEEP FRYING
FLOUR FOR DREDGING SHRIMP
BEER BATTER (SEE BELOW)

PLACE THE SHRIMP on a large platter, keeping them at room temperature until time for frying. Sprinkle them liberally with lemon juice. Heat enough oil in a deep fryer to fully cover the shrimp, for cooking them a batch at a time. Dredge the shrimp with the flour so they are well coated. Holding shrimp by the tail, dip them into the beer batter, again coating well. The double coating ensures that they will be moist and full of flavor. When the oil has reached 375° (bread dropped into it will brown almost immediately), carefully drop the shrimp in, one by one, and cook until they are golden brown and crisp. Drain on paper towels and serve immediately with a plum sauce (available bottled) or with ¾ cup of orange marmalade blended with 2 teaspoons of horseradish. *Serves 6.*

Beer Batter

TWO 12-OUNCE CANS BEER
2 CUPS ALL-PURPOSE FLOUR

1½ TABLESPOONS SALT
1 TABLESPOON PAPRIKA

Pour the beer into a large mixing bowl. Sift the flour, salt, and paprika into the beer, blending into a light, frothy batter. We use a wire whisk for better blending. The batter keeps a week in the refrigerator.

GEORGIA PICKLED SHRIMP

■■■

2 POUNDS RAW SOUTHERN
  SHRIMP (THE SMALL, SWEET
  VARIETY), SHELLED AND
  DEVEINED, BUT LEAVE TAIL
  ON
3 SMALL ONIONS, SLICED INTO
  THIN RINGS

1½ CUPS PEANUT OIL
1½ CUPS WHITE VINEGAR
½ CUP SUGAR
1½ TEASPOONS CRUSHED
  CELERY SEED

IN A POT of boiling, salted water, place the shrimp and cook
for 2 minutes, or until the shrimp just turn pink. Drain
and immediately rinse with very cold water. Refrigerate
until thoroughly chilled. In a container or dish that can be
tightly sealed, alternate layers of shrimp and onions. Blend
the oil, vinegar, sugar, and celery seed and pour over all.
Seal tightly and refrigerate for 8 hours. Remove shrimp
from marinade to serve. *Serves 4 to 6.*

SHRIMP JAMBALAYA
■■■

This dish, famous around New Orleans, came into being when white Creole mistresses gave cooking instructions they had learned in France, or from their French parents, to their Negro cooks, who, in turn, added their own touches. Thus, Creole cookery was born.

3 TABLESPOONS BUTTER

1 TABLESPOON OLIVE OIL

2 MEDIUM-SIZED WHITE ONIONS, FINELY CHOPPED

1 GARLIC CLOVE, MINCED

1 CELERY RIB, SCRAPED AND FINELY CHOPPED

½ CUP SEEDED, DERIBBED, AND FINELY CHOPPED GREEN PEPPER

2 CUPS CHICKEN BROTH (CANNED IS GOOD)

ONE 1-POUND CAN TOMATOES, CHOPPED (USE ALL LIQUID)

¼ TEASPOON DRIED THYME

¼ TEASPOON HOT RED PEPPER FLAKES, OR TO TASTE, CRUSHED

SALT TO TASTE

1 CUP UNCOOKED LONG-GRAIN RICE

2 CUPS COOKED CUBED HAM (NO FAT)

3 GREEN ONIONS (SCALLIONS), THINLY SLICED, INCLUDING MOST OF THE GREEN PART

1½ POUNDS MEDIUM-SIZED SHRIMP, SHELLED AND DEVEINED

In à large, heavy-bottomed pot, over medium heat, heat the butter and oil. Add the white onions, garlic, celery, and half of the green pepper and cook until the onions are soft. Do not brown. Stir in the chicken broth, tomatoes and their liquid, thyme, red pepper flakes, and salt. Bring to a boil. Stir in the rice. Lower heat, cover, and simmer 10 to 15 minutes, or until the rice is still quite *al dente* (slightly chewy). Stir in the ham and remaining green pepper and the green onions. Simmer for 10 minutes, or until the rice is tender. Add the shrimp and cook 5 minutes, or just until they turn pink. (Do not overcook the shrimp or they will toughen.) Taste for seasoning. *Serves 4 to 6.*

Chapter 5

POULTRY

Mention poultry and most Americans immediately think of chicken, and many with ethnic backgrounds also quickly associate the word with favorite ways their mothers and grandmothers prepared it. Oddly enough, even though it seems that chicken has been here forever and is as American as apples and cornmeal, we were late in adding it to our food supply.

The chicken is a direct descendent of Asia's wild red jungle fowl, and we were slow to realize the possibilities of the domesticated bird. At our first poultry exhibition in Boston in 1849, no American bird took any prize or was even mentioned; winners were from China, India, Britain, and Germany. Since then, however, we've surged to the forefront of all breeders and eaters of chicken, five U.S. companies producing 90 percent of the breeding chickens for the entire world. Americans eat 10.6 *billion* pounds of chicken a year. It is one of our best-liked foods, also heading the recipe list of most countries and coming to market in America in over thirty ways.

But recently there's been a revolution in the markets. The new supermarket superstar is truly American, born here and brought to its peak of perfection here—the turkey.

Even our turkey had to make a round trip to Europe before we discovered how valuable it was. Taken from Mexico to Spain by early Spanish explorers, the domestic turkey returned here to the New World with the colonists in the 1600s and was eventually crossbred with our native wild turkeys to produce the remarkable bird that we have today.

What about the current revolution? Right now the turkey is such a smashing success in supermarkets that it dominates not only the poultry but the meat sections and is offered in a dazzling display of seventy varieties. This "everything" turkey duplicates nearly every cut of meat and has been so successful that the pork producers protested, launching a legal battle to prevent about 30 million pounds of turkey "ham" from being sold yearly. They lost.

The winners were our pocketbooks and palates. Tailored for taste, but also for the most value for our shopping dollar of any meat (costing less now than even fifteen years ago), turkey in any form has the bonus of fewer calories than other meats and poultry. It supplies high quality protein (only some fish are higher), generous amounts of B vitamins, calcium, riboflavin, iron, and niacin. And although it may be the largest of all poultry, through continued superior breeding it is getting leaner, while chicken is getting fatter. In fact, turkey is the lowest in fat and cholesterol of all popular meats.

Shoppers today can buy inexpensive turkey steaks, turkey wings, legs, thighs, breasts, cutlets, cubes for shish kebab, turkey hamburger. Today we annually buy 652 million pounds of whole turkey and turkey parts, and 884 million pounds of "deli" turkey, ham, hotdogs, bologna, and so on.

But the important development is the marketing breakthrough that has made it possible to buy fresh turkey almost any way we want it.

This is not meant to downgrade chicken. Just half a chicken breast supplies 61.1 percent of the protein needed daily. Chicken contains vitamin A, niacin, calcium, and all the essential amino acids, the building blocks necessary for growth and general good health.

Chicken and turkey also are low in sodium and, being short-fibered, are the most easily digested of all meats. Both also are probably our most versatile and economical buy.

There are chicken devotees and turkey fans, and now, with all the variety available, both can shop happily, healthfully, and inexpensively for this palatable pair, which represents the most popular food around these days.

ALSATIAN CHICKEN WITH WINEKRAUT
■■■

In Europe the classic bird was partridge, pheasant, or even guinea hen, but in the United States immigrants from the Alsace used inexpensive chicken, creating a New World taste delight from an Old World recipe.

3 TABLESPOONS COOKING
    OIL
ONE 4- TO 4½-POUND CHICKEN,
    TRUSSED
SALT AND PEPPER
2 MEDIUM-SIZED YELLOW
    ONIONS, CHOPPED

2 GARLIC CLOVES, FINELY
    CHOPPED
ONE 1-POUND, 11-OUNCE CAN
    SAUERKRAUT, DRAINED
1 HEAPING TEASPOON CARA-
    WAY SEEDS
2 CUPS DRY WHITE WINE

IN A STOVE-top-to-oven casserole large enough to hold all ingredients, over medium heat, heat the oil. Season the chicken liberally with salt and pepper and evenly brown it. Remove the chicken. Stir the onions and garlic well into the oil and browned particles in the casserole, sautéing over medium heat until they are soft but not brown. Stir in the drained sauerkraut, mixing well with the onions and garlic. Sprinkle in the caraway seeds, blending well. Simmer the sauerkraut for 10 minutes. Pour in the white wine, blending it with the sauerkraut. Return the chicken to the pot and cover it with sauerkraut. Cover the casserole and cook in a preheated 350° oven 1 hour, or until the chicken is fork-tender. Carve the bird and serve on beds of "winekraut." Hashed brown potatoes or Potatoes Roesti (see p. 203) are an excellent accompaniment. *Serves 4.*

ARROZ CON POLLO

■■■

4 TABLESPOONS OLIVE OIL
ONE 4½-POUND CHICKEN CUT
　INTO SERVING PIECES
　(SAVE THE BACK AND WING
　TIPS FOR BROTH)
3 HOT ITALIAN SAUSAGE LINKS,
　CUT INTO ½-INCH SLICES
1 LARGE ONION, CHOPPED
1 GARLIC CLOVE, MINCED
2 CUPS LONG-GRAIN RICE
3 CUPS CHICKEN BROTH
　(CANNED OR HOMEMADE)
2 CUPS CANNED TOMATOES,
　BROKEN UP (USE YOUR
　HANDS)

½ TEASPOON SAFFRON
SALT AND PEPPER TO TASTE
1 SWEET RED PEPPER, SEEDS
　AND WHITE RIBS REMOVED
　AND DISCARDED, CUT INTO
　2- BY-½-INCH STRIPS
ONE 10-OUNCE PACKAGE FRO-
　ZEN "TINY" PEAS, COOKED
　ACCORDING TO PACKAGE
　DIRECTIONS, BUT ADDING
　A SCANT TEASPOON OF
　SUGAR TO THE WATER

HEAT 3 TABLESPOONS OF the oil in a stove-top-to-oven casse-role and evenly brown the chicken pieces. Transfer the chicken to another dish. Add the sausage pieces to the casserole and brown the slices on both sides. Transfer to the dish with the chicken. Add the onion, garlic, and rice to the casserole (adding more oil if needed) and cook, stirring, until the onion is soft. Pour in the broth. Stir in the tomatoes, saffron, and sausage. Add the chicken, push-ing the pieces down into the rice. Bring to a boil on top of the stove. Cover tightly and cook in a preheated 350° oven for 45 minutes, or until the chicken is tender and the liquid has been absorbed by the rice. If the liquid is absorbed before rice is tender, add a small amount of hot broth. Or if the rice is tender and there is still plenty of liquid, remove the top of the casserole to cook off liquid. Taste for season-ing, adding salt and pepper, if needed (the broth may have supplied enough salt). In small frypan, cook red pepper in 1 tablespoon of oil until crisp-tender. Just before serving stir the peas and red pepper strips into the casserole. *Serves 6.*

BELGIAN BRAISED CHICKEN WITH CREAM-WINE-MUSHROOM SAUCE

■ ■ ■

6 TABLESPOONS BUTTER

2 TABLESPOONS OLIVE OIL

ONE 4- TO 4½-POUND CHICKEN, CUT INTO SERVING PIECES

12 SMALL WHITE ONIONS, ROOT ENDS SCORED

SALT AND PEPPER TO TASTE

¾ CUP CHICKEN BROTH (HOMEMADE OR CANNED)

3 SCALLIONS (GREEN ONIONS), FINELY CHOPPED, WHITE PART ONLY

¾ CUP DRY WHITE WINE

¾ CUP HEAVY CREAM

1 TABLESPOON CALVADOS OR APPLEJACK BRANDY

½ POUND MUSHROOMS (IF SMALL, HALVE, IF MEDIUM, QUARTER)

2 TABLESPOONS CHOPPED PARSLEY

OVER MEDIUM HEAT, in a stove-top-to-oven casserole, heat 3 tablespoons of the butter and the oil. Add the chicken and brown on one side. Add the onions, brown them, and turn the chicken to brown it evenly. Sprinkle with salt and pepper. Pour in the broth, bring to a boil, cover the pot, and cook in a preheated 350° oven for 35 minutes, or until the chicken and onions are tender. Transfer the chicken and onions to a hot serving dish to keep warm. Spoon off excess fat. Add the scallions to the pot and cook until tender. Add the wine and reduce by half. Stir in the cream and Calvados and cook five minutes, or until the sauce has thickened. Cook the mushrooms in 3 tablespoons of butter until brown but still quite crisp. Add the mushrooms to the casserole and heat through. Taste for seasoning. Spoon the sauce over the chicken and onions and sprinkle with parsley. *Serves 4.*

CHICKEN CACCIATORE
WITH RED WINE AND TOMATO

■ ■ ■

2 TABLESPOONS OLIVE OIL
4 TABLESPOONS BUTTER
ONE 4-POUND CHICKEN, CUT
  INTO SERVING PIECES
SALT AND PEPPER TO TASTE
1 MEDIUM-SIZED ONION,
  CHOPPED
1 GARLIC CLOVE, MINCED
3/4 CUP DRY RED WINE
2 OUNCES BRANDY
1 CUP CHICKEN BROTH
3 LARGE, RIPE TOMATOES,
  PEELED, SEEDED, AND
  FINELY CHOPPED, OR ONE
  1-POUND CAN TOMATOES
  WITH THEIR LIQUID, CHOPPED

1/2 TEASPOON DRIED OREGANO
1 TABLESPOON CHOPPED
  FRESH BASIL, OR 1
  TEASPOON DRIED
1/2 POUND FRESH MUSHROOMS,
  SLICED

IN A LARGE, deep frypan, over medium heat, heat the oil
and 2 tablespoons of butter. Add the chicken and evenly
brown, sprinkling with salt and pepper (add more butter
and oil if needed). Transfer to a bowl and keep warm. Add
the onion and garlic to the frypan and cook until soft.
Remove with a slotted spoon and add to the chicken bowl.
Pour off any fat remaining in the frypan. Pour in the wine
and brandy. Simmer, scraping the bottom of the pan to
loosen the brown particles and reduce the liquid by half.
Pour in the broth. Add the tomatoes, oregano, and basil
and simmer, covered, 10 minutes. Return the chicken
and onion to the frypan and cook, covered for 20 minutes.
Remove cover and cook until chicken is tender and sauce
has thickened. Sauté mushrooms in 2 tablespoons of butter until browned but firm, add to casserole, and cook long
enough to heat them thoroughly. Serve with Polenta (see
p. 185), rice, or pasta, spooning sauce over them. *Serves 4.*

WHITE CHICKEN CACCIATORE
■■■

3 TABLESPOONS OLIVE OIL
ONE 4-POUND CHICKEN, CUT
   INTO SERVING PIECES
SALT AND PEPPER TO TASTE
3 MEDIUM-SIZED WHITE
   ONIONS, CHOPPED
1 GARLIC CLOVE, MINCED
2 CELERY RIBS, SCRAPED AND
   CHOPPED

1 BAY LEAF
¼ TEASPOON DRIED OREGANO
½ CUP DRY VERMOUTH
1½ CUPS DRY WHITE WINE
6 PLUMP BLACK OLIVES
   (ITALIAN OR GREEK),
   PITTED AND QUARTERED
2 TABLESPOONS CHOPPED
   PARSLEY

IN A LARGE, deep frypan, over medium heat, heat the oil. Add the chicken and brown evenly, sprinkling with salt and pepper and adding more oil, if needed. Transfer the chicken to a warm bowl. If there is more than 2 tablespoons of fat in the frypan, pour off all but that amount. If the chicken has absorbed the oil, pour in 2 tablespoonsful. Add the onion, garlic, and celery and cook until soft. Do not brown. Add the bay leaf, oregano, and half of the vermouth and wine. Simmer, scraping the bottom of the pan to release the brown particles. Return the chicken to the pan. Pour in the remaining vermouth and wine and simmer, covered, for 20 minutes. Remove the cover and cook until the chicken is tender. Transfer the chicken to a hot serving dish. Add the olives to the sauce and simmer 2 or 3 minutes. Taste for seasoning. Serve the sauce spooned over the chicken. Sprinkle the parsley on top. *Serves 4.*

CHICKEN HASH, FRENCH STYLE

■■■

1½ CUPS HEAVY CREAM
MEAT FROM 1 WHOLE CHICKEN
   BREAST, COOKED AND
   CUBED
SALT TO TASTE
PINCH CAYENNE PEPPER, OR TO
   TASTE

PINCH NUTMEG
4 TABLESPOONS BUTTER
1 EGG YOLK
2 TABLESPOONS DRY SHERRY

IN A SAUCEPAN, bring the cream to a boil. Lower heat. Add the chicken, salt, cayenne, and nutmeg and simmer for 5 minutes. Knead the butter and egg yolk together with a fork. Off heat, stir the butter egg yolk mixture into the chicken–cream mixture. When well blended, stir in the sherry. Return to low heat and, without boiling, heat until the hash thickens. This may be served on dry toast or in patty shells and, if desired, topped with a poached egg which, in turn, must be topped with a tablespoon of Hollandaise sauce (see p. 58). *Serves 4.*

CHICKEN EMPANADA
■ ■ ■

From Jack's Spanish neighbor in upstate New York.

Bread Dough

1 PACKAGE DRY ACTIVE
   YEAST
½ TEASPOON SUGAR
¼ CUP WARM WATER (ABOUT
   105°—IF TOO HOT IT
   CAN KILL THE ACTION OF
   THE YEAST)

ABOUT 3 CUPS FLOUR
1 TEASPOON SALT
½ CUP WARM MILK

Combine in a measuring cup the yeast, sugar, and warm water and stir to dissolve. Place in a warm, draft-free place (a slightly warmed oven, turned off, is a good place) for 7 minutes, or until bubbling and doubled in volume. Sift 2½ cups of flour and the salt into a large bowl. Make a well in the center and pour in the yeast mixture and the milk. Stir, mixing well, adding more flour, small amounts at a time, if necessary, to make a slightly firm dough that can be gathered into a ball. Transfer to a lightly floured board and knead 10 minutes. Place in a buttered bowl, turn over to evenly grease the dough. Cover and place in a warm, draft-free place (as you did the yeast) and allow to rise to double in volume, about 1½ hours. Punch down and allow to rise again until doubled in volume, about 45 minutes.

Filling

3-POUND CHICKEN, CUT UP

1 ONION, STUCK WITH 2 WHOLE CLOVES

1 CARROT, CUT IN CHUNKS

1 CELERY RIB, CUT IN CHUNKS

2 TABLESPOONS OLIVE OIL

1 TABLESPOON BUTTER

1 MEDIUM-SIZED ONION, FINELY CHOPPED

1 GARLIC CLOVE, MINCED

1 SMALL SWEET RED PEPPER, SEEDS AND WHITE RIBS REMOVED, FINELY CHOPPED

1 SMALL SWEET GREEN PEPPER, SEEDS AND WHITE RIBS REMOVED, FINELY CHOPPED

SALT AND PEPPER TO TASTE

½ CUP FINELY CUBED COOKED HAM

3 MEDIUM-SIZED, RIPE TOMA-TOES, SKINNED, SEEDED, AND FINELY CHOPPED

Combine chicken, onion, carrot, celery, and water to cover in a deep saucepan and simmer, covered, 30 minutes, or until chicken is tender. Cool the chicken, remove meat from the bones (discarding skin and bones), and cut into small cubes. In a frypan, over medium heat, heat the oil and butter. Add the chopped onion, garlic, and peppers and cook until soft. Do not brown. Season with salt and pepper. Stir in the ham and tomatoes and simmer, uncovered, until the watery content of the tomatoes has cooked off. It should be a thick mixture. Stir in chicken. Cook 2 minutes. Cool. Divide the dough into 2 parts. Roll each into a 12-inch circle about ¼ inch thick. Place one circle on a lightly greased baking sheet. Spoon on the filling to within 1 inch of the edge of the dough. Moisten the edge of the dough with a little water. Place the second circle over the filling. Press the edges of the dough together, sealing and flute, or use the tines of a fork to seal in the filling. Let rise in a warm place for 20 minutes. Brush with an egg wash made of 1 egg beaten with 1 tablespoon of water. Bake in a preheated 375° oven for 45 minutes, or until golden brown. Serve hot, but allow to set a few minutes before cutting. *Serves 6.*

CHICKEN PAPRIKAS

■ ■ ■

2 TABLESPOONS BUTTER
2 TABLESPOONS LARD OR
  CRISCO
ONE 3½- TO 4-POUND
  CHICKEN, CUT INTO SERV-
  ING PIECES
SALT TO TASTE
2 MEDIUM-SIZED ONIONS,
  CHOPPED
1 GARLIC CLOVE, MINCED
1 TABLESPOON SWEET
  HUNGARIAN PAPRIKA

PINCH OF CAYENNE, OR TO
  TASTE (OPTIONAL)
1 CUP CHICKEN BROTH
  (HOMEMADE OR CANNED,
  OR USE 1 KNORR CHICKEN
  BOUILLON CUBE DIS-
  SOLVED IN 1 CUP HOT
  WATER)
1 TABLESPOON TOMATO PURÉE
1 TABLESPOON FLOUR
1½ CUPS SOUR CREAM

IN A LARGE, deep frypan, heat the butter and lard over medium heat. Add the chicken pieces, sprinkle with salt and evenly brown. Transfer them to a bowl. Pour off all but 2 tablespoons of fat, or if the fat has been absorbed by the chicken, add 2 tablespoons of butter. Add the onions and garlic and cook until soft, but do not brown. Sprinkle with the paprika and cayenne and stir to blend with the onion. Add the chicken broth and tomato purée and stir, scraping the bottom of the pan to release the brown particles. Return the chicken to the frypan and simmer, covered, for 40 minutes, or until tender. Transfer the chicken to a hot bowl and keep warm. Blend together the flour and sour cream until smooth, stir into the liquid in the frypan, and simmer for 5 minutes, or until slightly thickened. Return the chicken to the pan and simmer for 5 minutes. Taste for seasoning. Once the sour cream has been added, the dish should not cook too long. *Serves 4.*

CHICKEN PIE WITH SWEET POTATO BISCUIT TOPPING

■ ■ ■

Although we're of the school that does not agree with the current fad that is trying to prove that there is pure American cooking (most recipes used in the United States owe their origin to European immigrants), chicken pies, such as this one with a Southern accent, could be the exception that proves the rule.

ONE 3½-POUND CHICKEN
1 CARROT, CUT UP
1 ONION STUCK WITH 2 WHOLE
   CLOVES
1 CELERY RIB, CUT UP
¼ TEASPOON DRIED THYME
2 TEASPOONS SALT
½ TEASPOON PEPPER

3 TABLESPOONS BUTTER
3 TABLESPOONS FLOUR
1½ CUPS CHICKEN BROTH
   (FROM POACHING THE
   BIRD)
½ CUP HEAVY CREAM
1 CUP COOKED PEAS
BISCUITS (SEE BELOW)

PUT THE CHICKEN, carrot, onion, celery, thyme, salt, and pepper into a large pot. Cover with water, bring to a boil, lower heat, and simmer, partially covered, until the chicken is tender (about 1 hour). Remove chicken (reserve broth) and cool. Take the meat from the bones, discarding skin and bones. Cut meat into bite-sized pieces. Strain the broth and, over medium heat, reduce to about 2 cups. In a saucepan, over medium heat, melt the butter. Stir in the flour and cook, stirring into a smooth paste. Gradually add the broth and cook, stirring into a medium-thick sauce. Stir in the cream. Taste for seasoning. Place the chicken and peas in a shallow baking dish. Pour the sauce over them. Sauce and chicken should be hot before the biscuits are placed on top. *Serves 4.*

Biscuits

Makes sixteen or more 1½- to 2-inch biscuits:

1 CUP MASHED COOKED
   SWEET POTATO
¼ CUP MELTED BUTTER
½ CUP MILK
1 TEASPOON GRATED ORANGE
   RIND

1 CUP ALL-PURPOSE FLOUR
1 TABLESPOON BAKING POWDER
1 TEASPOON SALT
2 TEASPOONS SUGAR

Blend sweet potato, melted butter, milk, and orange rind
in a large bowl. Sift together the flour, baking powder, salt,
and sugar and stir into the sweet potato mixture. Turn onto
a floured board, turning to flour entire surface. Roll or
flatten into a ½-inch-thick sheet. Cut with a floured 1½- or
2-inch biscuit cutter and arrange on top of the *hot* chicken
pie barely touching each other. (If there are extra biscuits,
bake them on a separate sheet.) Bake in a preheated
450° oven for 12 to 15 minutes, or until the biscuits are
raised and golden.

CHICKEN SALAD

■■■

3 LARGE WHOLE CHICKEN
   BREASTS
1 ONION, STUCK WITH 2
   WHOLE CLOVES
LEAVES FROM 3 CELERY RIBS
1 CARROT, CUT UP
1 BAY LEAF
1 TEASPOON SALT
¼ TEASPOON PEPPER
3 TENDER CELERY RIBS,
   SCRAPED AND THINLY SLICED
12 CHERRY TOMATOES, HALVED
   AND DRAINED IF THEY
   SEEM TO HAVE A LOT OF
   LIQUID

½ CUP TOASTED CASHEWS
¾ CUP SOUR CREAM
¾ CUP MAYONNAISE
1 TEASPOON MINCED ONION
1 TABLESPOON LEMON JUICE
SALT AND PEPPER TO TASTE
BOSTON OR BIBB LETTUCE
   LEAVES
GARNISH: ARTICHOKE HEARTS,
   OLIVES, QUARTERED HARD-
   COOKED EGGS, CAPERS,
   PIMENTO STRIPS, ETC.

SIMMER THE CHICKEN breasts in water to barely cover with the onion, celery leaves, carrot, bay leaf, salt, and pepper, covered, until tender (about 40 minutes). When cool enough to handle, remove and discard the skin and bones and cut the meat into ½-inch cubes. In a bowl, combine the chicken with the sliced celery, tomatoes, and cashews. Blend sour cream, mayonnaise, minced onion, lemon juice, salt, and pepper to taste into a sauce and add half the mixture to the chicken, mixing gently but well. Taste and add more sauce according to taste. Arrange on lettuce leaves on a serving dish and garnish. Serve any remaining sauce at the table. *Serves 6.*

EASTERN SHORE CHICKEN
WITH OYSTERS

■ ■ ■

4 TABLESPOONS BUTTER
ONE 3½-POUND CHICKEN, CUT
   UP (SAVE THE BACK AND
   WING TIPS TO MAKE BROTH)
¾ CUP MILK

1 PINT OYSTERS, DRAINED
1 CUP HOT HEAVY CREAM
SALT AND PEPPER TO TASTE
1 TABLESPOON FLOUR

OVER MEDIUM HEAT, in a stove-top-to-oven casserole just large enough to hold the chicken in one layer, heat 3 tablespoons of the butter. Add the chicken pieces and evenly brown them. Pour in the milk, heat to a simmer, cover, and bake in a preheated 375° oven until just fork tender (about 30 minutes). Add the oysters, setting them between the chicken pieces. Pour in the cream, sprinkle with salt and pepper, and bake until the oysters puff and their edges curl. Transfer the chicken and oysters to a hot serving dish and keep warm. Knead 1 tablespoon of butter with the flour, add to the liquid in the pan, and simmer on top of the stove, stirring, until thickened. Taste for seasoning. Spoon the sauce over the chicken and oysters and serve. *Serves 4.*

•••

FARMER'S CHICKEN STEW
WITH DUMPLINGS

■ ■ ■

ONE 4-POUND CHICKEN, CUT
   INTO SERVING PIECES (SAVE
   THE WING TIPS AND BACK
   FOR MAKING BROTH)
1 ONION, STUCK WITH 2
   WHOLE CLOVES
1 CELERY RIB, SCRAPED AND
   CUT UP
1 CARROT, SCRAPED AND CUT
   UP

1 BAY LEAF
1 TEASPOON SALT
½ TEASPOON PEPPER
2½ CUPS CHICKEN BROTH
   (CANNED IS GOOD, OR
   USE 2 KNORR CHICKEN
   BOUILLON CUBES DIS-
   SOLVED IN 2½ CUPS WATER)
GRAVY (SEE BELOW)
DUMPLINGS (SEE BELOW)

PLACE THE CHICKEN in a heavy pot and add the onion, celery, carrot, bay leaf, salt, pepper, and broth. Bring to a boil, lower heat, cover pot, and simmer until tender (about 45 minutes), skimming the top when necessary. Remove the chicken from the pot and keep warm (a 200° oven is good for this). Strain the broth and reserve it for the gravy.

To serve, arrange the chicken in the center of a large hot serving dish and surround with the dumplings. Serve with the gravy spooned over. *Serves 4.*

Gravy

3 TABLESPOONS BUTTER
3 TABLESPOONS FLOUR
STRAINED BROTH FROM COOK-
   ING THE CHICKEN

SALT AND PEPPER TO TASTE

In a pot that is large enough to cook the dumplings (recipe follows) and can be covered tightly, melt the butter over medium heat. Stir in the flour, stirring into a smooth paste. Gradually add the broth and cook, stirring into a smooth, slightly thickened sauce. Taste and season.

Dumplings

2 CUPS FLOUR
1 TABLESPOON BAKING POWDER
1½ TEASPOONS SALT
1 TABLESPOON MELTED BUTTER

2 EGGS
½ CUP MILK
ADDITIONAL MILK

Sift flour, baking powder, and salt together in a bowl. Add butter and blend. Mix eggs and half cup of milk just to blend and stir in. With a spoon, beat in just enough additional milk to make a soft dough. Heat the gravy to a simmer. Drop the dumpling dough by tablespoonfuls onto the gravy, barely touching each other, cover tightly, and simmer for 15 minutes, or until they are puffed and a toothpick inserted comes out clean.

Note: Commercial biscuit mix can be used. Follow package directions for making dumplings.

MARYLAND FRIED CHICKEN

■ ■ ■

2 SMALL FRYING CHICKENS
   (ABOUT 2½ POUNDS EACH),
   CUT INTO SERVING PIECES
   (SAVE THE WING TIPS AND
   BACKS FOR MAKING BROTH)
1 CUP FLOUR

1 TEASPOON SALT
½ TEASPOON PEPPER
VEGETABLE OIL
2 TABLESPOONS BUTTER
1½ CUPS MILK
SALT AND PEPPER TO TASTE

SHAKE FLOUR, SALT and pepper in a clean bag. Add the chicken and shake to lightly coat. Pour about half an inch of oil in a large, deep frypan. Heat on medium-high heat, add the chicken (just enough pieces to fit comfortably in the pan at one time), and cook, covered, until golden brown, turning once to brown evenly (about 6 minutes). Hold cooked pieces in a dish or bowl until all have been browned. Pour off the oil, add about ⅛ inch of water, return all chicken to the pan, cover, and steam over medium heat until tender. Add small amounts of hot water if liquid cooks off. Transfer the chicken to a hot serving dish and keep warm (a 200° oven is a good place for this). Pour off any fat left in the pan. Add the butter and scrape up all the crispy brown bits covering the bottom of the pan. Add 2 tablespoons of the seasoned flour and blend with the butter. Gradually add the milk and, stirring constantly, cook into a thickened gravy. Taste and season with salt and pepper. Strain the sauce and serve in a gravy boat, to be spooned over the chicken. *Serves 4.*

SOUTHERN BRUNSWICK STEW

■■■

Originally, Brunswick stew was made with squirrels, as there were more squirrels around than chickens. But today we seem to have a greater taste for chicken than squirrel.

ONE 3½- TO 4-POUND CHICKEN, CUT INTO SERVING PIECES, WASHED, AND WELL DRIED

SALT AND PEPPER

4 TABLESPOONS BUTTER

1 MEDIUM-SIZED ONION, CHOPPED

1 SMALL GREEN PEPPER, SEEDED, TRIMMED, AND CHOPPED

3 CUPS WATER

3 MEDIUM-SIZED RIPE TOMATOES, PEELED, SEEDED, AND EACH CUT INTO 6 PIECES (OR ONE 1-POUND CAN OF TOMATOES WITH THEIR LIQUID)

2 TEASPOONS WORCESTERSHIRE SAUCE

¼ TEASPOON CAYENNE PEPPER, OR TO TASTE

2 CUPS FRESH LIMA BEANS, OR ONE 10-OUNCE PACKAGE FROZEN, DEFROSTED

2 CUPS FRESH CORN KERNELS, CUT FROM THE COB, OR ONE 10-OUNCE PACKAGE FROZEN, DEFROSTED

½ CUP COARSE TOASTED BREAD CRUMBS

LIGHTLY SALT AND pepper the chicken pieces. In a frypan over medium heat, melt the butter and evenly brown the chicken. Transfer the chicken to a stew pot large enough to hold all ingredients. Add the onion and green pepper to the frypan and cook (add more butter, if needed) until soft. Do not brown. Transfer to the stew pot. Add the water, tomatoes, Worcestershire sauce, and cayenne. Cover and simmer for 30 minutes, or until the chicken is almost tender. Add the limas and corn and cook 15 minutes, or until the chicken and vegetables are tender. Taste for seasoning. Stir in the crumbs just before serving. The chicken meat may be removed from the bone, if desired. And if the stew is slightly overcooked, it will only add to its flavor. *Serves 4.*

SOUTHERN SMOTHERED CHICKEN

■ ■ ■

ONE 4-POUND CHICKEN
½ POUND BACON, CUT INTO
  THIN STRIPS
1 LEMON, THINLY SLICED
1 CUP CHICKEN BROTH
  (CANNED OR HOMEMADE)
2 CARROTS, SCRAPED AND
  THINLY SLICED

2 MEDIUM-SIZED ONIONS,
  THINLY SLICED
¼ TEASPOON DRIED THYME
1 TABLESPOON CHOPPED
  PARSLEY
1 BAY LEAF
SALT AND PEPPER TO TASTE

TRUSS THE CHICKEN. In a pot just large enough to hold the chicken snugly, place half of the bacon in a layer, cover with the lemon slices, then with the rest of the bacon. Pour ½ cup of chicken broth over this. Layer the carrots and onions over the bacon and lemon slices; sprinkle with the thyme and parsley and add the bay leaf. Place the chicken on top, cover tightly and cook in a preheated 375° oven for 1 hour, or until the chicken is tender. Remove and detruss the bird. Cut into serving pieces and place on a warm platter. Add the remaining broth to the liquid in the pot, bring to a boil. Taste for seasoning. Discard the bay leaf. Spoon the hot sauce over the chicken. *Serves 4.*

GERMAN BABY CHICKENS
■■■

If you are lucky and know a farmer who raises chickens, perhaps you can buy 6-week-old chickens (Stubenkuken) for this favorite German dish. Otherwise, use Cornish hens, the smallest you can find.

2 TABLESPOONS BUTTER
½ POUND *LEAN* GROUND PORK
SALT AND PEPPER TO TASTE
PINCH POWDERED GINGER, OR
   TO TASTE
1 MEDIUM-SIZED TART APPLE,
   PEELED, CORED, AND
   DICED

1 TABLESPOON CHOPPED
   WHITE RAISINS
2 OUNCES MADEIRA WINE
4 BABY ("SQUAB" CHICKENS) OR
   SMALL CORNISH HENS
4 SLICES BACON, CHOPPED
1 CUP CHICKEN BROTH

IN A SAUCEPAN, over medium heat, melt the butter and sauté the pork, seasoning with salt, pepper, and ginger, for 5 minutes, or until it starts to brown. Remove from heat. Stir in the apple, raisins, and wine, blending. Stuff the chickens with the apple–raisin mixture. Truss them and season well with salt and pepper. In a casserole or pot that will snugly hold all of the birds, over medium heat, sauté the bacon until brown and most of the fat is rendered. With a slotted spoon remove the bacon pieces and discard. Evenly brown the chickens in the bacon fat. Pour in the chicken broth, cover pot tightly, lower heat, and simmer for 35 minutes, or until the chickens are tender. Skim off the fat and spoon some of the hot liquid the chickens braised in over the birds as they are served. *Serves 4.*

CREOLE SQUABS (OR GAME HENS)

■■■

Squabs are difficult to find in markets. If you have a neighbor who has a barn and a young son who can climb, perhaps he can find a nest with the young pigeons in it. But, since that is unlikely, use game hens. They do not have the rich flavor of the squab, being white meat (squab are dark meat), but cooked in this manner game hens have a new authority.

4 SQUABS OR 4 SMALL GAME HENS, EACH WEIGHING 1¼ POUNDS OR LESS, WASHED AND WELL DRIED
SALT AND PEPPER
3 TABLESPOONS BUTTER
2 TABLESPOONS OLIVE OIL
1 LARGE ONION, FINELY CHOPPED
2 CELERY RIBS, SCRAPED AND CHOPPED
1 GARLIC CLOVE, MINCED
1 CARROT, SCRAPED AND CHOPPED
3 TABLESPOONS FLOUR
3 CUPS CHICKEN BROTH (OR USE 2 KNORR CHICKEN BOUILLON CUBES DISSOLVED IN 3 CUPS HOT WATER)
½ CUP DRY RED WINE
½ TEASPOON CAYENNE, OR TO TASTE
3 SMALL LEEKS, WHITE PART ONLY, CUT INTO ½-INCH PIECES
1 CUP (SHELLED) FRESH PEAS, OR 1 CUP FROZEN, DEFROSTED
3 TABLESPOONS CHOPPED PARSLEY

SALT AND PEPPER the insides of the birds and truss (the needle-and-cord method is the best see our section on "Needle Trussing" in *The Chicken and the Egg Cookbook* [Bantam Books, p. 66]). In a stove-top-to-oven casserole just large enough to hold the birds snugly, heat the butter and oil over medium heat. Evenly brown the birds in the fat, being careful not to break the skin. Remove from the casserole. Add the onion, celery, garlic, and carrot to the pot and simmer, adding more butter and oil, if needed, for 10 minutes, or until the vegetables are soft. Do not brown.

Sprinkle the vegetables with the flour and stir to mix well. Gradually pour the broth and wine into the pot, stirring steadily until all has been added and the sauce has slightly thickened. Season with salt and the cayenne. Mix in the leeks. Return the birds to the pot, spoon the sauce over them, and cook in a preheated 350° oven, covered, for 45 minutes, or until tender, turning the birds every 15 minutes and spooning sauce over them. Add the peas the last 15 minutes of cooking. Sprinkle with the parsley and serve from the casserole with some small, new, boiled, parsleyed potatoes. *Serves 4.*

BREAST OF TURKEY SCALOPPINE
■■■

Turkey was popular in Italy before it was here, so Italian cooks' ways with it are many and unique. They cover the breast with ham and cheese and bake it, and they adopt techniques they use with veal, as with this recipe. Today many of us, whether we have Italian forebears or not, use this somewhat Americanized version.

SIX ½-INCH-THICK SLICES UNCOOKED TURKEY BREAST, EACH LARGE ENOUGH FOR 1 SERVING
SALT AND PEPPER TO TASTE
FLOUR
2 EGGS, BEATEN IN A SHALLOW BOWL

FINE DRIED BREAD CRUMBS
6 TABLESPOONS BUTTER
2 TABLESPOONS OLIVE OIL
1 JUICY LEMON, HALVED
3 TABLESPOONS CHOPPED PARSLEY
2 LEMONS, EACH CUT INTO 3 WEDGES

SALT AND PEPPER the turkey slices. Lightly dredge with flour, shaking off any excess. Dip in the beaten eggs, then dredge in bread crumbs to coat. (If you run out of egg, beat another.) In a large frypan, over medium heat, heat half of the butter and oil. Controlling the heat so as not to burn the butter, brown 3 turkey slices on one side for 4 minutes. Turn and brown other side to cook thoroughly for about 4 minutes. When cooked they will be fairly firm. Transfer to a hot serving dish and keep warm. Heat the remaining butter and oil in the frypan and repeat procedure with the remaining slices. Pour the butter in the pan over the breasts. Squeeze lemon juice from the halved lemon over and sprinkle with parsley. Garnish each serving with a lemon wedge. *Serves 6.*

TURKEY HASH
■■■

3 TABLESPOONS BUTTER
1 MEDIUM-SIZED ONION, FINELY CHOPPED
1 CELERY RIB, SCRAPED AND FINELY CHOPPED
3 CUPS COOKED CUBED TURKEY MEAT, WHITE OR DARK
2 MEDIUM-SIZED POTATOES, BOILED, COOLED, AND CUBED
SALT AND PEPPER TO TASTE
½ CUP TURKEY OR CHICKEN GRAVY (HOMEMADE OR COMMERCIAL) AND ½ CUP HEAVY CREAM (OR OMIT THE GRAVY AND USE ¾ CUP HEAVY CREAM)
2 TABLESPOONS CHOPPED PARSLEY
3 TABLESPOONS GRATED CHEDDAR CHEESE

IN A FRYPAN that can go under a broiler, melt the butter over medium heat. Add the onion and celery and cook until soft. Do not brown. Add the turkey, potato, salt, and pepper. Add the gravy and cream (or just the cream) and mix gently but well. Simmer for a few minutes to thicken. Add the parsley and gently mix. Sprinkle the cheese on top and place under the broiler until the cheese has melted and is golden. *Serves 4.*

It is rapidly being discovered that turkey can successfully be substituted for most other meats, and with a substantial saving. It's become the American family food friend. Here are a couple of recipes from the National Turkey Federation that prove the point—Hawaiian Simmered Turkey and Turkey Stew Italian Style.

HAWAIIAN SIMMERED TURKEY

■ ■ ■

2 POUNDS TURKEY BREAST
5 OUNCES WHITE OR CIDER
   VINEGAR
6 TABLESPOONS SOY SAUCE
½ CUP BROWN SUGAR
½ TEASPOON POWDERED
   GINGER, OR 2 SLICES,
   FRESH, PEELED GINGER
   CHOPPED

2 TABLESPOONS CORNSTARCH
   DISSOLVED IN 2 TABLE-
   SPOONS WATER

USE HALF OR whole deboned turkey breast and adjust ingredient quantities in proportion to weight. If using whole breast, tie into a roll with string.

Place breast in Dutch oven or other wide pot. Combine vinegar, soy sauce, brown sugar, and ginger, blend, and pour over the turkey. Cover and simmer until tender, about 15 to 20 minutes per pound, turning several times and basting during cooking. Transfer to platter. Keep warm in a 200° oven. Add dissolved cornstarch to the pan juices. Cook, stirring until bubbly. Taste and season with salt and pepper as needed. Remove string, if necessary, and slice into thick slices. Spoon sauce over slices to serve. *Serves 4 to 6.*

TURKEY STEW ITALIAN STYLE
■■■

½ CUP FLOUR
3 TEASPOONS SALT
½ TEASPOON PEPPER
3 POUNDS TURKEY BREAST, CUT
　INTO 1½-INCH CUBES
3 TABLESPOONS OLIVE OIL
3½ TABLESPOONS BUTTER
1 CUP SLICED ONIONS
2 GARLIC CLOVES, PRESSED
4 OUNCES TOMATO PURÉE
1 TEASPOON FRESH CHOPPED
　BASIL LEAVES
1 TEASPOON FRESH CHOPPED
　THYME LEAVES
1 BAY LEAF
A FEW PARSLEY STEMS

1 CUP CELERY, CUT INTO
　2-INCH PIECES
1 BAG FROZEN BABY CARROTS,
　OR FRESH, CUT INTO
　1-INCH PIECES (IF USING
　FRESH, STEAM OR BLANCH
　IN SALTED BOILING WATER
　UNTIL NOT QUITE DONE
　AND COOL UNDER RUNNING
　COLD WATER)
1½ CUPS DRY WHITE WINE
½ CUP WATER
2 TABLESPOONS FRESH
　CHOPPED PARSLEY
½ TABLESPOON GRATED LEMON
　RIND

Mix FLOUR, SALT, and pepper. Dredge the turkey cubes with the flour mixture. Shake off excess. Heat the oil and butter in a heavy pot. Brown the meat in the hot fat, processing in batches, if necessary, so that there is only a single layer in the pot. Remove the meat. Add the onion and garlic. Cook, stirring, for 5 minutes. Add the tomato purée, basil, thyme, bay leaf, and parsley stems. Stir and add the celery, carrots, wine, and water. Stir. Then add the turkey. Bring to a boil, cover, and cook over low heat for half an hour, or until the turkey is just tender. Mix together parsley and lemon rind and stir into the stew. Simmer, uncovered, another 5 minutes. Taste for seasoning, adding more salt and pepper, if needed. Serve over rice or pasta, garnished with additional chopped parsley. *Serves 6 to 8.*

RICH TURKEY POT PIE
■■■

5 TABLESPOONS BUTTER
1 LARGE ONION, CHOPPED
½ GREEN PEPPER, SEEDED,
  WHITE RIBS REMOVED,
  AND CHOPPED
1 LARGE CELERY RIB, SCRAPED
  AND CHOPPED
5 TABLESPOONS FLOUR
4 CUPS TURKEY OR CHICKEN
  BROTH
2 TABLESPOONS DRY SHERRY
1 CUP GRATED CHEDDAR,
  GRUYÈRE, OR CHEESE OF
  YOUR CHOICE

SALT AND PEPPER TO TASTE
4 CUPS COOKED, BITE-SIZED
  PIECES OF TURKEY MEAT
ONE 10-OUNCE PACKAGE
  FROZEN TINY PEAS,
  DEFROSTED
8 TO 10 PEPPERIDGE FARM
  PATTY SHELLS, DEFROSTED
1 EGG YOLK MIXED WITH 2
  TABLESPOONS WATER

IN A LARGE frypan, over medium heat, melt the butter. Add the onion, green pepper, and celery and cook until the vegetables are soft. Do not brown. Stir in the flour and cook about 1 minute, stirring to blend well. Gradually pour in the broth, stirring constantly until all has been added and the sauce has thickened. Add the sherry and the cheese, stirring until the cheese has melted. Taste and add salt and pepper. Arrange the turkey pieces on the bottom of a shallow (2 to 3 inches deep) baking dish large enough to hold all ingredients and to fill the dish to within half an inch of the top. Sprinkle with the peas. Spoon on the sauce with the vegetables. On a pastry board, lay the patty shells next to each other, pressing the edges together to form a solid sheet of pastry. Roll out to a size slightly larger than the top of the baking dish. Moisten the edges, cover the pie with the pastry, and press the edges against the rim of the dish. Insert a funnel in the center of the pastry to allow steam to escape. Brush with the egg yolk mixture. Bake in a preheated 425° oven for 25 minutes.

Lower heat to 350° and bake another 30 minutes, or until the pastry has puffed and is golden. *Serves 6.*

Note: If preferred, substitute your favorite pie pastry for the puff pastry.

ROAST AMERICAN TURKEY WITH OYSTER STUFFING

■ ■ ■

Although the Italians and Spaniards were eating turkey long before this country was settled, most of us still consider this dish traditionally American. Oyster stuffing does set the American stamp firmly on this recipe.

6 TABLESPOONS SOFT BUTTER
2 MEDIUM-SIZED ONIONS, CHOPPED
2 CELERY RIBS, SCRAPED AND CHOPPED
3 CUPS DRY BREAD CUBES
2 TEASPOONS BELL'S POULTRY SEASONING
3 TABLESPOONS GRATED ASIAGO OR PARMESAN CHEESE

1 TABLESPOON CHOPPED PARSLEY
⅓ CUP CHICKEN BROTH (OR USE THE TURKEY NECK AND GIBLETS AND MAKE SOME TURKEY BROTH)
1 EGG, BEATEN
SALT AND PEPPER TO TASTE
1 PINT FRESH OYSTERS, WITH THEIR LIQUOR
ONE 12-POUND TURKEY

In a deep saucepan, over medium heat, melt 2 table-spoons of butter and cook the onions and celery for 5 minutes, or until soft. Do not brown. Remove pan from heat. Add the remaining ingredients (except the turkey), blending well. Stuff the bird, truss it, and rub with the remaining butter. Season liberally with salt and pepper. Place the turkey in a roasting pan, breast up, and cook in a preheated 375° oven for 4 hours (20 minutes to a pound), basting well every 20 minutes. Test for doneness by inserting the point of a knife into the thigh. If the juice that runs out is yellow, it is ready, if it is pink, cook a few minutes longer. Let set at least 15 minutes before carving to allow the juices to settle, making carving easier. *Serves 8.*

FRICASSEED TURKEY WINGS

■ ■ ■

4 YOUNG TURKEY WINGS
  (ABOUT 2 POUNDS)
FLOUR
7 TABLESPOONS BUTTER
SALT AND PEPPER TO TASTE
5 CUPS TURKEY OR CHICKEN
  BROTH
1 WHOLE ONION, STUCK WITH
  2 WHOLE CLOVES
1 CELERY RIB, SLICED

1 CARROT, SLICED
1 BAY LEAF
12 SMALL WHITE ONIONS, ROOT
  ENDS SCORED
4 TABLESPOONS FLOUR
½ CUP HEAVY CREAM
1 EGG YOLK
1 TABLESPOON OF LEMON
  JUICE

DREDGE THE WINGS with the flour. In a heavy-bottomed pot or top-of-the-stove casserole just large enough to hold the wings in a single layer, melt 3 tablespoons of the butter over medium heat. Add the wings and brown evenly, seasoning with salt and pepper. Pour in the broth. Add the onion with the cloves, celery, carrot, and bay leaf. Bring to a boil, lower heat, cover, and simmer for 1 hour, or until the wings are tender. Transfer them to a hot, deep serving dish and keep warm. Add the onions to the broth and simmer, covered, for 20 minutes, or until tender. Using a slotted spoon, transfer them to the serving dish (discard the onion with the cloves). Strain the broth, discarding the vegetables. Melt the remaining butter in the pot. Stir in the 4 tablespoons of flour and cook, stirring into a smooth paste. Gradually stir in 3 cups of the strained broth and cook, stirring into a smooth, slightly thickened sauce. Lower heat. Beat heavy cream lightly with egg yolk and add a half-cup of the hot sauce to the cream–egg yolk mixture. Return to the pot and stir until thoroughly incorporated. Heat, stirring, but do not boil. When sauce has thickened, stir in the lemon juice. Taste and season with salt and pepper. Spoon the sauce over the turkey wings and onions in the serving dish. Serve with rice or noodles. *Serves 4.*

Note: Any of the turkey parts now in the markets can be successfully fricasseed—legs, thighs, breasts—the technique certain to make them tender, the sauce keeping them moist and tasty. Fricassee is now thought to be American, but it was originated by the French, foremost in the use of cream, eggs, and lemon with poultry, and first served probably in our South by the Creoles.

DUCKS BRAISED LOUISIANA STYLE
■■■

This is probably more Creole than just Southern. Wild ducks, mallards or canvasbacks, are usually used, but domestic ducklings are excellent. Although this is a Louisiana favorite, the teaming of duck with turnips is definitely French— and definitely delicious.

2 TABLESPOONS BUTTER
2 DUCKLINGS CUT INTO SERVING PIECES
SALT AND PEPPER TO TASTE
2 MEDIUM-SIZED ONIONS, CHOPPED
1 LARGE GARLIC CLOVE, MINCED
½ TEASPOON DRIED THYME
1 TABLESPOON CHOPPED PARSLEY
1 BAY LEAF
6 SMALL TURNIPS, PEELED AND QUARTERED
CHICKEN BROTH, ENOUGH JUST TO COVER THE DUCKS

IN A HEAVY top-of-the-stove casserole or pot large enough to handle the duck pieces, melt the butter over medium heat. Salt and pepper the duck and brown evenly. Remove duck. Add onion and garlic to the pot and cook until soft. Do not brown. Add the thyme, parsley, and bay leaf. Return the duck pieces to the pot and add the turnips. Pour in chicken broth, bring to a boil, lower heat, tightly cover the pot, and simmer for 45 minutes, or until duck is tender. Discard bay leaf and spoon off excess fat. *Serves 6.*

Note: This can be varied by substituting diced carrots and small whole onions for the turnips and adding green peas 15 minutes before the cooking time has elapsed. In the South they also stir in half a cup of Madeira when they add the peas.

Geese, brought from Europe (where they have been a staple for centuries), were served here by the pioneers before turkey became popular. Today, rather than turkey, a good many families with ethnic backgrounds make it their holiday bird. It is different, and remarkably tasty. Here, from the National Goose Council, are three unique recipes—California Charcoal-Grilled Lemon Goose, Roast Goose Hawaiian Style, and New England Maple Syrup-Glazed Goose.

CALIFORNIA CHARCOAL-GRILLED LEMON GOOSE

■ ■ ■

ONE 10- TO 12-POUND
   READY-TO-COOK GOOSE
4 LARGE LEMONS
1 TABLESPOON CORNSTARCH

⅓ CUP SUGAR
1 CUP ORANGE JUICE
GLAZED GRAPES (SEE BELOW)

PREPARE OUTDOOR, COVERED grill using indirect heat method, with drip pan for barbecuing, as manufacturer directs (see below for oven-roasting).

Prepare goose; remove neck, giblets, excess fat, and neck skin (use for soup or some other purpose). Rinse the bird and drain. Fold neck skin to back of bird and secure with a skewer. With the bird breast side up, lift wings up toward neck, then fold under back of bird so they stay flat and balance bird. With string, tie the legs together or tuck into band of skin at tail, if present. Rub outside of bird with salt. Place the goose, breast side up, on grill over drip pan. Insert meat thermometer deep into inside thigh muscle. Cover grill and roast 2½ hours, or until the thermometer registers 180° to 185°, adding more briquettes to each side of the grill at the end of each hour, as manufacturer directs. During the grilling, spoon or siphon off accumulated fat (reserve this for other uses, siphoning it off at half-hour intervals so that the fat doesn't brown too much). If a thermometer is not used, press meaty part of leg with fingers protected by paper towels; it should feel very soft when goose is done. While the goose is grilling prepare a glaze. Cut 3 lemons crosswide into halves. Squeeze juice; reserve shells and juice. Remove crushed pulp and membrane from inside lemon shells by scraping with a spoon. Trim edge of shells in a scalloped design, if desired. With a vegetable peeler, peel strips of rind from the fourth lemon; cut lemon peel julienne. Boil the strips in water to cover for 2 minutes; drain and pat dry. Cut off all white membrane from peeled lemon; slice lemon. In a saucepan, combine the cornstarch and sugar; stir in orange juice. Cook, stirring, until thickened and bubbly; remove from heat. Stir in ¼ cup of lemon juice (use leftover juice in other recipes).

When the goose is cooked, transfer to a large hot serving dish. Brush with some glaze. Garnish the breast of the bird with the lemon slices, parsley, and lemon strips. Serve glaze in a bowl to pass. Garnish with the grape-filled lemon cups. *Serves 6 to 8.*

Glazed Grapes

Wash and pat dry half a pound of red seedless grapes. Cut into small bunches. Brush with some lemon glaze from above. Place the grapes in the lemon cups.

To Roast Goose in Oven

Prepare goose as above. Place on rack in roasting pan. Roast uncovered for 1 hour in preheated 400° oven. Reduce oven to 325° and continue roasting until goose is cooked. Roast a 10- to 12-pound bird a total of 2½ to 3 hours; add ½ hour if stuffed. For smaller goose, roast a total of 1¾ to 2¼ hours.

NEW ENGLAND
MAPLE SYRUP-GLAZED GOOSE
(with Acorn Squash)

■ ■ ■

ONE 10- TO 12-POUND
READY-TO-COOK GOOSE
4 SMALL ACORN SQUASH

½ CUP MAPLE (OR MAPLE-
BLENDED) SYRUP

PREPARE THE BIRD as directed for California Charcoal-Grilled Lemon Goose (see p. 123). Rub outside of bird with salt. Place the goose, breast side up, on rack in roasting pan. Insert meat thermometer into inside thigh muscle. Roast uncovered in a preheated 400° oven for 1 hour. During roasting, spoon or siphon off accumulated fat (reserve this for other uses, siphoning it off at half-hour intervals so that the fat doesn't get too brown). Reduce the oven to 325° and continue roasting 1½ to 2 hours, or until thermometer registers 180° to 185°. If thermometer is not used, press meaty part of leg with fingers protected by paper towels; it should feel very soft when goose is cooked. If goose is stuffed, add about half an hour to roasting time. For an 8- to 10-pound bird, roast a total of 2 to 2½ hours.

About 1 hour before goose is cooked, cut each squash lengthwise into quarters. Remove seeds and arrange quarters in a shallow baking pan, brush with goose drippings, and bake squash along with the goose. About 30 minutes before the goose is cooked, brush it and the squash with syrup several times. When ready, place the bird on a large, hot serving dish and border with the squash. Serve with cranberry sauce. *Serves 6 to 8.*

ROAST GOOSE HAWAIIAN STYLE

■■■

ONE 10- TO 12-POUND   ½ CUP HONEY
   READY-TO-COOK GOOSE   1 TABLESPOON SOY SAUCE
FRIED RICE STUFFING (SEE   1 TEASPOON SALT
   BELOW)   ½ TEASPOON GROUND GINGER

PREPARE BIRD AS directed for California Charcoal-Grilled
Lemon Goose (see p. 123). Rinse bird and drain. To stuff,
fill neck and body cavity loosely with the rice mixture.
(Wrap remaining stuffing in foil and cook along with the
bird.) Fasten neck skin to back with a skewer. Lift wings
up toward neck and fold under back of goose. Tie legs
together or tuck into band of skin at tail, if present. Rub
outside of the bird with salt. Place goose, breast side up,
on rack in roasting pan. Insert meat thermometer deep
into inside thigh muscle. Roast uncovered for 1 hour in a
preheated 400° oven. During roasting, spoon or siphon
off accumulated fat and reserve for other uses (this should
be done at half-hour intervals so that the fat doesn't brown
too much). After roasting for 1 hour, reduce oven to 325°
and continue roasting about 2 to 2½ hours, or until thermometer in thigh registers 180° to 185°. If thermometer
is not used, press meaty part of leg with fingers protected
by paper towels. It should feel very soft. Combine honey,
soy sauce, salt, and ginger in a bowl and blend. Brush
honey–soy sauce mixture on goose 3 times during the last
30 minutes of roasting. *Serves 6 to 8.*

Fried Rice Stuffing

2 CUPS REGULAR LONG-
   GRAIN RICE, COOKED AC-
   CORDING TO PACKAGE
   DIRECTIONS, AND COOLED
½ POUND BACON SLICES

2 EGGS
1 CUP DICED CELERY
1 CUP CHOPPED SCALLIONS
   (GREEN ONIONS)
3 TABLESPOONS SOY SAUCE

In a large saucepan, fry the bacon slices until crisp; drain on paper towel and crumble. Discard all but about ⅓ cup of the bacon drippings. In the drippings fry the eggs until firm, breaking them into small pieces. Add the celery and onions. Stir in the cooked rice and cook, stirring, until well mixed. Stir in the soy sauce. Taste for seasoning and add salt, if needed.

Chapter 6

MEAT

Someone once said that America is not a melting pot but a stew pot into which each immigrant, each newly arrived race and ethnicity, has tossed unique recipes with different aromas, colors, and textures, each nationality contributing food culture, economy, imagination, technique, and even style of serving to what has come to be known as American cooking.

The most popular foods in the United States are red meats, each of us eating about 150 pounds yearly of beef, ham, lamb, pork, and veal. Half of that amount is beef, our favorite by far, with pork the runner-up.

Among the recipes that follow you'll find a variety of unusual pork dishes exemplifying the economic good sense of those who came before us. For example, some of the Old World recipes called for veal. But since veal is the most expensive of meats, pork was often substituted—and the result was an even tastier dish than the original.

The following are what we consider collectors' items from many nations, some with distinctly American touches, a "stew" that we hope is appealing and unique.

BEEF BRAISED IN CIDER

■ ■ ■

This is claimed as an American dish, especially in the South. We suspect that a cook of German heritage was caught short without the beer that is usually used and substituted cider. Thus—American!

2 CUPS CIDER
1 GARLIC CLOVE, MINCED
1 LARGE ONION, CHOPPED
¼ TEASPOON POWDERED
  GINGER
¼ TEASPOON CINNAMON
¼ TEASPOON NUTMEG
3½- TO 4-POUND BOTTOM
  ROUND OF BEEF OR
  CHUCK IN ONE SOLID,
  BONELESS PIECE

SALT AND PEPPER
FLOUR
6 TABLESPOONS BUTTER
1 TABLESPOON OLIVE OIL
3 TABLESPOONS FLOUR

COMBINE CIDER, GARLIC, onion, ginger, cinnamon, and nutmeg in a deep bowl just large enough to snugly hold the beef to marinate. Sprinkle the meat with salt and pepper and slip it into the bowl with the marinade. Cover and marinate for several hours or overnight, turning occasionally. Remove the meat from the marinade (save the marinade), pat it dry with paper towels, sprinkle with salt and pepper, and dredge with flour. In a stove-top-to-oven casserole, over medium heat, heat 3 tablespoons of butter and the olive oil. Add the beef and evenly brown it. Pour in the marinade, bring to a boil on top of the stove, cover, and cook in a preheated 325° oven for 3 hours, or until tender. Transfer the beef to a hot dish to keep warm while you make the sauce. Strain the liquid in which the beef cooked. In a saucepan, over medium heat, heat the 3 remaining tablespoons of butter. Add the flour and stir into a smooth paste. Gradually add the strained liquid and cook, stirring into a smooth sauce. Taste for seasoning. Slice the meat and overlap on a serving dish. Spoon some of the sauce over and serve the remaining at the table. German Potato Pancakes (see p. 200) are a good accompaniment. *Serves 6 to 8.*

BEEF STEW WITH A CRUST
■ ■ ■

2 POUNDS LEAN BEEF (CHUCK, TOP, OR BOTTOM ROUND), CUT INTO 1-INCH CUBES AND DRIED WITH PAPER TOWEL
FLOUR
3 TABLESPOONS BACON FAT OR BUTTER
2 TABLESPOONS OLIVE OIL
SALT AND PEPPER TO TASTE
BEEF BROTH TO COVER (ABOUT 3 CUPS) (HOMEMADE OR CANNED)
1 GARLIC CLOVE, MINCED

BOUQUET GARNI (1 BAY LEAF, 3 PARSLEY SPRIGS, SEVERAL CELERY LEAVES, 2 WHOLE CLOVES, PINCH OF DRIED THYME TIED IN A CHEESECLOTH)
1 CUP ½-INCH-CUBED POTATOES
1 CUP ¼-INCH-CUBED CARROTS
½ CUP CHOPPED ONIONS
½ CUP ½-INCH SLICES OF MUSHROOMS
PASTRY FOR A SINGLE-CRUST, 9-INCH PIE (SEE P. 83)

Dredge the beef cubes lightly with flour. Over medium heat, on a stove-top-to-oven casserole, heat the bacon fat and the oil. Add the beef and evenly brown, sprinkling with salt and pepper. Pour off any fat remaining in the pan. Pour in the beef broth. Stir the pot, scraping to release brown particles adhering to the bottom. Add the garlic and bouquet garni. Bring to a boil on top of the stove, cover, and transfer to a preheated 325° oven. Cook for 1 to 1½ hours, or until the beef is very nearly tender. Check pot from time to time to see if liquid cooks off. If it does, add a small amount of hot broth (or water). Add the potatoes, carrots, and onion and cook until vegetables and meat are tender (about half an hour). Add the mushrooms during the last 5 minutes of cooking. Remove and discard the bouquet garni. Taste for seasoning. Transfer to a deep pie dish large enough to allow the stew to come within a half-inch of the top of the dish. Roll out the dough to a diameter of 1 inch all around larger than the pie dish. Moisten rim of dish. Cover pie, tuck the edge of the dough under to make a thick edge, pinch against the rim of the dish, and flute. Cut 2 or 3 vents in the dough and bake in a preheated 375° oven for 40 minutes, or until the pastry is golden brown and steam is pouring out of the vents. *Serves 4 to 6.*

NEW ENGLAND BOILED DINNER
■■■

4 POUNDS CORNED BEEF BRISKET

1 BAY LEAF

6 PEPPERCORNS

1 ONION, STUCK WITH 3 WHOLE CLOVES

6 SMALL CARROTS, SCRAPED AND HALVED

3 CELERY RIBS, SCRAPED AND HALVED

12 SMALL ONIONS, WHOLE, ROOT ENDS SCORED

1 HEAD GREEN CABBAGE, CUT INTO 6 WEDGES

1 BUTTERNUT SQUASH PEELED, SEEDED, AND CUT INTO CHUNKS

6 MEDIUM-SIZED POTATOES, HALVED

PLACE THE BEEF in a deep pot; cover with water. Add the bay leaf, peppercorns, and onion stuck with cloves. Bring to a boil, lower heat, cover, and simmer for 3 hours, or until almost tender. Skim top as necessary. Add the carrots, celery, small onions, and cabbage; simmer 30 minutes. Add the remaining vegetables and simmer until meat and vegetables are tender. To serve, place the sliced beef in the center of a large, hot serving dish and surround with the vegetables (discard the onion with the cloves). Good accompaniments are horseradish, freshly cooked beets vinaigrette, or mustard pickles. *Serves 6.*

GEORGE HERZ'S GERMAN POT ROAST
■■■

Good friend George Herz, whose parents came from Germany, added his own touch to their traditional pot roast, the blend of tomato and red wine. Many ethnic dishes have become American through this kind of originality, making our cuisine the most unique in the world.

2 TABLESPOONS BUTTER
2 TABLESPOONS OLIVE OIL
3 ½-POUND BONELESS CHUCK
   OR TOP OR BOTTOM
   ROUND ROAST OF BEEF (IN
   ONE SOLID PIECE)
SALT AND PEPPER TO TASTE

FLOUR
ONE 8-OUNCE CAN HUNT'S
   TOMATO SAUCE
4 OUNCES DRY RED WINE
1 CELERY RIB, CUT UP
1 CARROT, CUT UP
1 LARGE ONION, QUARTERED

OVER MEDIUM HEAT, in a stove-top-to-oven casserole just large enough to hold the roast snugly, heat the butter and oil. Sprinkle the beef with salt and pepper and dredge with flour. Add to the pot and brown evenly. Blend the tomato sauce and wine and pour over the meat; add the celery, carrot, and onion, placing them to the side of the beef. Bring to a boil, cover tightly, and cook in a preheated 300° oven for 3 hours, or until fork-tender. Serve with plain, old-timey mashed potatoes topped with a spoonful of the sauce, which you'll also spoon over the sliced beef. *Serves 6.*

GREEK AMERICAN BEEF AND ZUCCHINI CASSEROLE

■ ■ ■

¼ CUP OLIVE OIL

3 ZUCCHINI, EACH ABOUT 4½ INCHES BY 2 INCHES, DICED

SALT AND PEPPER TO TASTE

1 MEDIUM-SIZED ONION, MINCED

1 GARLIC CLOVE, MINCED

1 POUND GROUND, LEAN CHUCK BEEF

4 FRESH MINT LEAVES, CHOPPED

½ TEASPOON CUMIN

¾ CUP GRATED ASIAGO, PARMESAN, OR OTHER GOOD GRATING CHEESE

½ CUP BREAD CRUMBS

¾ CUP TOMATO SAUCE (HOMEMADE IS BEST)

IN A LARGE frypan, heat the oil over medium-high heat and sauté the zucchini until golden. Remove with a slotted spoon, drain on paper towels, and sprinkle with salt and pepper. In the same pan, lowering the heat to medium, cook the onion and garlic until soft. Do not brown. Add the beef, mint, and cumin, season with salt and pepper, and cook, breaking up the meat with a fork, until it loses its pink color. In a large bowl combine and mix the meat mixture, the zucchini, half of the cheese, and all of the bread crumbs. Transfer to a casserole. Evenly spoon the tomato sauce on top; sprinkle with the remaining cheese. Bake, uncovered, in a preheated 350° oven for 30 minutes, or until the top starts to brown. *Serves 4 to 6.*

ITALIAN FOGGIA CHOPPED BEEF ROLL

■ ■ ■

3 POUNDS GROUND ROUND
   OF BEEF, OR A COMBINATION
   OF PORK, BEEF, AND VEAL
1 CUP FINE, DRY BREAD
   CRUMBS
1 MEDIUM-SIZED ONION,
   MINCED
1 GARLIC CLOVE, MINCED
½ TEASPOON DRIED BASIL
½ CUP MINCED PARSLEY
   (BROADLEAF IS BEST)
4 EGGS, BEATEN
½ CUP GRATED ASIAGO OR
   PARMESAN CHEESE
SALT AND PEPPER TO TASTE

OLIVE OIL
THREE 4-INCH-LONG ITALIAN
   SWEET SAUSAGES, BROILED
6 HARD-COOKED EGGS, A THIN
   SLICE CUT FROM EACH
   END
FOUR ½-INCH-THICK, ½-INCH-
   WIDE, LONG STRIPS OF PRO-
   VOLONE CHEESE
3 CUPS TOMATO SAUCE
   (HOMEMADE IS BEST)
1 TEASPOON SUGAR
¼ TEASPOON CINNAMON
½ TEASPOON DRIED OREGANO

IN A LARGE bowl, combine and mix well but lightly (your hands are good for this) the ground meat, bread crumbs, onion, garlic, basil, parsley, eggs, grated cheese, salt, and pepper. Do not mash. Lay, overlapping, two 2-foot-long sheets of waxed paper on a work surface. Oil the paper lightly with olive oil. Place all but ½ cup of the mixture on the paper and flatten into a ½-inch thickness, slightly more rectangular than square. Lengthwise, arrange the sausages, hard-cooked eggs (end to end) and the provolone strips on the meat, each in a straight line so that when the roll is sliced, each slice will show a slice of sausage and a slice of egg. Pick up the end of the waxed paper and, using it to guide and lift the meat, roll it (lengthwise) into a firm cylinder, sealing the sausage, etc., inside. Seal the ends, and if any of the filling has poked through the meat, patch it with the meat you have reserved for that purpose. Slide the roll off of the waxed paper onto an oiled, shallow baking pan. Bake, uncovered, in a preheated 400° oven for 30 minutes, or until it is firm and brown. Spoon off the fat in the pan, mixing 2 tablespoons of it with the tomato sauce. Heat the sauce and pour it over the meat. Blend sugar, cinnamon, and oregano. Lower oven heat to 350°, sprinkle the roll with the cinnamon mixture, and bake 45 minutes, occasionally basting the roll. Transfer the roll to a serving dish and let set for 15 minutes to become firm and slightly cooler for easier slicing. *Serves 6 to 8.*

PFEFFERPOTTHAST

■■■

German folk who came here from the Westphalia area specialized in these ribs for years, knowing that the meat closest to the bone is the tastiest—and usually the cheapest.

4 POUNDS BEEF SHORT RIBS,
   CUT INTO 2-INCH PIECES
SALT AND PEPPER
¼ CUP COOKING OIL
4 MEDIUM-SIZED ONIONS,
   THINLY SLICED
2 GARLIC CLOVES, MINCED
3 CUPS BEEF BROTH

1 BAY LEAF
2 WHOLE CLOVES
½ CUP STALE PUMPERNICKEL
   BREAD CRUMBS
1 TABLESPOON CAPERS, RINSED,
   DRAINED, AND CHOPPED
1 TEASPOON GRATED LEMON
   RIND

SEASON THE RIBS with salt and pepper. In a large, stove-top-to-oven casserole, over medium heat, heat the oil and brown the ribs evenly. Remove the ribs. Add the onions and garlic and cook for 4 minutes, or until soft but not brown. Stir in the beef broth, bay leaf, and cloves, scraping the bottom of the casserole to loosen brown particles. Return the ribs to the casserole, cover, and cook in a preheated 375° oven for 1½ hours, or until fork-tender. Transfer the ribs to a hot serving dish and keep warm. Skim the fat from the liquid in the casserole and discard the bay leaf and cloves. Stir in the bread crumbs, capers, and lemon rind, blending well. Simmer, uncovered, on top of the stove for 5 minutes, or until thickened, stirring often. Spoon the sauce over the short ribs on the serving dish. *Serves 4.*

SAUERBRATEN WITH POTATO DUMPLINGS

■ ■ ■

ONE 3- TO 4-POUND SOLID
   PIECE OF LEAN CHUCK,
   TOP OR BOTTOM ROUND POT
   ROAST
SALT
2 CUPS RED WINE VINEGAR
2 CUPS WATER
½ LEMON, THINLY SLICED
1 LARGE ONION, THINLY SLICED
1 CARROT, THINLY SLICED
1 CELERY RIB, THINLY SLICED
1 GARLIC CLOVE, HALVED
6 PEPPERCORNS
2 BAY LEAVES
3 WHOLE CLOVES
FLOUR
4 TABLESPOONS BUTTER
POTATO DUMPLINGS (SEE
   BELOW)

Rub THE BEEF with salt and place in a deep non-metal bowl. Combine remaining ingredients except flour and butter in a saucepan and heat just to a boil. Pour the hot marinade over the beef, cool, cover, and refrigerate 3 days, turning the meat once a day.

Remove the meat from the marinade (strain and reserve the marinade). Dry the meat well and dredge with flour. In a heavy, stove-top-to-oven casserole, melt the butter. Evenly brown the meat. Pour half of the marinade over, bring to a boil on top of the stove, cover tightly, and cook in a pre-heated 350° oven for 2 hours, or until fork-tender. If liquid cooks off, add more hot marinade to maintain about 2 cups of liquid. Slice the beef and serve with one of the following sauces spooned over the sliced beef and dumplings. *Serves 6.*

Sauce #1: Strain the liquid in the casserole and stir in ¾ cup of crumbled gingersnaps and ½ tablespoon of sugar. Simmer until the sauce thickens. Taste for seasoning.

Sauce #2: Strain the liquid in the casserole and stir in 2 tablespoons of flour mixed with ¼ cup of water. Simmer, stirring, until the sauce thickens. Stir in 1 tablespoon of chopped fresh dill or 1 teaspoon of dried dill weed. Taste for seasoning.

Potato Dumplings

ABOUT 1 CUP ½-INCH BREAD
    CUBES BROWNED IN
    BUTTER
6 MEDIUM-SIZED POTATOES,
    COOKED IN BOILING,
    SALTED WATER UNTIL TEN-
    DER, DRAINED, DRIED
    OVER HEAT, RICED, AND
    COOLED

2 EGGS, BEATEN
SALT TO TASTE
½ CUP FLOUR

Beat the egg into the potatoes, season with salt, and mix
in the flour. Shape into balls the size of walnuts. Push a
bread cube or two into each, sealing it in. Drop, a few at a
time, into simmering, salted water and cook until the
dumplings surface, then cook 4 minutes longer. Remove
with a slotted spoon and thoroughly drain. Split in half
with two forks and serve with one of the above sauces or
melted butter.

SLAVIC STUFFED CABBAGE ON SAUERKRAUT

■■■

The list of ingredients may appear long, but the method is easy, the dish inexpensive and deliciously different—and it can be prepared the day before you want to serve it.

1 LARGE, SOLID HEAD CABBAGE	1½ TEASPOONS SALT
3 TABLESPOONS MINCED BACON	1 TEASPOON PEPPER
2 MEDIUM-SIZED ONIONS, CHOPPED	⅛ TEASPOON DRIED THYME
	1 EGG, BEATEN
1 LARGE GARLIC CLOVE, MINCED	ONE 1-POUND CAN SAUER-KRAUT, DRAINED
1 POUND GROUND CHUCK BEEF	1½ CUPS BEEF BROTH
½ CUP SLIGHTLY UNDERCOOKED LONG-GRAIN RICE	2 TABLESPOONS TOMATO PASTE
	CREAM SAUCE (SEE BELOW) (OPTIONAL)
1 TABLESPOON PAPRIKA	

PLACE THE CABBAGE in a large pot and cover it with boiling water. Simmer for 20 minutes. Remove the cabbage, drain, and cool. Carefully separate all the largest leaves intact and drain them on paper towels. Cut the tough spine out of the outer leaves and cut the leaves through to have 2 smaller leaves from each large one. If the inner leaves are difficult to remove, place the cabbage back into the boiling water to cook a few minutes. In a large frypan, over medium heat, sauté the bacon for 4 minutes. Stir in the onions and garlic and cook for 5 minutes or until soft but not brown. Add the chopped meat, rice, paprika, salt, pepper, and thyme, blending well. Simmer, stirring, for 3 minutes. Taste for seasoning. Remove from heat and cool slightly. Stir in the egg. Spread the cabbage leaves flat, being careful not to tear them. Spoon a tablespoon of the meat mixture (or whatever amount each will hold) onto each leaf, tuck in the sides, and roll tightly into sausage-like bundles. If necessary, toothpicks can be used to se-

• •

cure the rolls. The purpose is to keep the stuffing completely encased in the cabbage leaves. Line the bottom of a large casserole with the drained sauerkraut. Place the stuffed cabbage on top. Blend the broth and tomato paste and pour over the cabbage rolls. Cover the pot, bring to a boil on top of the stove, then cook in a preheated 350° oven for 1 hour. Spoon the sauerkraut onto a large hot serving dish, bedeck with the cabbage rolls, and spoon the cream sauce over the rolls. *Serves 6.*

Cream Sauce

2 TABLESPOONS BUTTER
1½ TABLESPOONS FLOUR

1 CUP LIGHT CREAM OR HALF
   AND HALF
2 TABLESPOONS LEMON JUICE

In a saucepan, over medium heat, melt the butter. Stir in the flour, stirring into a smooth paste. Gradually add the cream, stirring into a smooth sauce. Stir in the lemon juice. Over low heat, simmer 2 or 3 minutes into a smooth sauce.

TEXAS CHILI CON CARNE

■ ■ ■

This was supposed to have originated in Mexico, but over the years it has become so Americanized that most states have their own versions, and many even have annual chili cook-offs.

¼ CUP OLIVE OIL
4 MEDIUM-SIZED ONIONS, CHOPPED
1 SMALL GREEN PEPPER, CORED, SEEDED, AND CHOPPED
1 SMALL RED PEPPER, CORED, SEEDED, AND CHOPPED
4 CELERY RIBS, SCRAPED AND CHOPPED
4 GARLIC CLOVES, MINCED
4 POUNDS GROUND CHUCK BEEF
1 LEVEL TABLESPOON CHILI POWDER

1 TEASPOON BLACK PEPPER
1 TEASPOON SALT
1½ TEASPOONS CUMIN POWDER
1 TEASPOON CELERY SEEDS, CRUSHED
1 TEASPOON PAPRIKA
2 TEASPOONS DRIED OREGANO
ONE 1-POUND, 14-OUNCE CAN TOMATOES, PUT INTO A BLENDER CONTAINER FOR 1 MINUTE TO EVENLY BREAK UP THE TOMATOES
TWO 15-OUNCE CANS RED KIDNEY BEANS

In a large pot, over medium heat, heat the oil and sauté the onions, peppers, celery, and garlic for 5 minutes. Add the meat, breaking it up as it cooks and browning it lightly. Stir in the chili powder, black pepper, salt, cumin, celery seeds, paprika, and oregano, blending. Add the tomatoes, stirring in and blending well. Over low heat, covered, cook, stirring frequently, for 1 hour. Stir in the kidney beans and their liquid and cook for half an hour, stirring frequently. This top-of-the-stove cooking requires stirring to prevent the bottom burning and scorching. *Serves 8 to 10.*

Note: Another Southwest version uses cubed beef and no beans or tomatoes.

DANISH BEEF LIVER
WITH SPINACH SAUCE

■■■

Too few of us realize how good liver is for us, an inexpensive and tasty treasure house of protein, iron, and vitamins. In Europe beef liver is preferred to calf's liver, both for its flavor and low price. Ask for "baby" beef liver, but no matter what you get it will be tasty, tender, and good for you—if cooked properly.

4 SLICES BABY BEEF LIVER, CUT SLIGHTLY LESS THAN ½ INCH THICK, AND TRIMMED

½ CUP FLOUR, SEASONED WITH 1 TEASPOON SALT AND ½ TEASPOON PEPPER

2 SMALL EGGS, BEATEN

BREAD CRUMBS

6 TABLESPOONS BUTTER

3 LARGE SCALLIONS (GREEN ONIONS), WHITE PART ONLY (OR 1 WHITE ONION), MINCED

1½ CUPS BEEF BROTH

JUICE OF 1 LEMON

½ CUP CHOPPED, FRESH SPINACH

DREDGE THE LIVER with the seasoned flour, shaking off any excess so the liver is barely dusted. Dip into the beaten egg, then dredge with bread crumbs. In a large frypan, over medium heat, melt 4 tablespoons of butter and sauté the liver until golden brown on both sides but slightly pink inside (do not overcook the liver or it will toughen; cook about 2 to 3 minutes on each side). Remove and keep warm. Pour off any fat remaining in the pan and, over medium heat, heat the remaining butter. Add the scallions and sauté for 3 minutes, or until soft. Do not brown. Stir in the beef broth, lemon juice, and spinach, simmering and stirring for 3 minutes, or until the liquid has reduced by half and the sauce has thickened. Taste for seasoning and serve the sauce over the liver slices. *Serves 4.*

Note: Frozen spinach, defrosted but not cooked, may be used, or use leftover cooked spinach, adding it at the last minute and heating through.

IRISH LAMB STEW

■■■

2 MEDIUM-SIZED POTATOES, SLICED

1 CUP FINELY SHREDDED TENDER CABBAGE

2 LARGE LEEKS (OR 1 WHITE ONION), SLICED

1 CELERY RIB, SCRAPED AND SLICED

1 SMALL CARROT, SCRAPED AND SLICED

3 POUNDS LAMB, FROM A BONED SHOULDER OR LEG, CUT INTO 1½-INCH CUBES

2 CUPS CHICKEN OR BEEF BROTH (CANNED IS GOOD)

SALT AND PEPPER TO TASTE

1 BAY LEAF

¼ TEASPOON DRIED MARJORAM

12 SMALL ONIONS, WHOLE, ROOT ENDS SCORED, SIMMERED IN 2 TABLE-SPOONS BUTTER FOR 15 MINUTES

4 CARROTS, SCRAPED, CUT INTO NUGGETS AND COOKED IN WATER UNTIL CRISP-TENDER

4 SMALL WHITE TURNIPS, COOKED IN WATER UNTIL CRISP-TENDER

1 CUP OF FRESH OR FROZEN PEAS (IF FRESH, COOK 5 MINUTES; IF FROZEN, JUST DEFROST)

CHOPPED PARSLEY

IN A STOVE-top-to-oven casserole, arrange the potatoes, cabbage, leeks, celery, sliced carrot, and lamb in layers. Pour on the broth. Add the salt, pepper, bay leaf, and marjoram. Bring to a boil on top of the stove, cover, and cook in a preheated 350° oven for 1 hour or until the lamb is almost tender. Later it will cook 20 minutes longer. Remove the lamb. Strain the liquid it cooked in, pushing the vegetables through the strainer. Return the lamb and liquid with the puréed vegetables to the casserole. Add the onions, carrots, turnips, and peas and cook on top of the stove for 20 minutes, or until the lamb and vegetables are tender. Taste for seasoning. Sprinkle with the parsley and serve from the casserole. *Serves 6.*

LEBANESE LAMB WITH PEAS

■ ■ ■

3 TABLESPOONS BUTTER
2 TABLESPOONS OLIVE OIL
3 POUNDS LEAN, BONELESS LAMB, FROM THE SHOULDER OR LEG, CUT INTO 1½-INCH CUBES
SALT AND PEPPER
2 GARLIC CLOVES, MINCED
2 TABLESPOONS FLOUR
2 CUPS BEEF BROTH
½ CUP TOMATO PURÉE
½ TEASPOON CINNAMON
18 TO 24 SMALL WHITE ONIONS, LEFT WHOLE AND ROOT ENDS SCORED
2 CUPS HULLED PEAS, SLIGHTLY UNDERCOOKED IN SALTED WATER, OR 1 PACKAGE FROZEN, DEFROSTED, BUT NOT COOKED

HEAT THE BUTTER and oil in a stove-top-to-oven casserole, over medium heat. Sprinkle the lamb with salt and pepper. Add it to the pot and evenly brown. Add the garlic and cook 1 minute. Do not brown. If any fat remains in the pot, pour it off. Sprinkle the lamb with flour and shake the pot to distribute it. Slowly add the broth, stirring. Stir in the tomato purée and cinnamon. Add the onions. Cover the pot and simmer, stirring from time to time, for 45 minutes on top of the stove, or until the lamb and onions are fork-tender. Or bring to a boil on top of the stove then transfer to a preheated 350° oven for 1 hour, or until fork-tender. Stir in the peas and cook 5 minutes. Taste for seasoning. Serve with bulgur wheat or noodles. *Serves 6.*

MIDDLE EASTERN MOUSSAKA

■■■

This is claimed by the Armenians, Greeks, Lebanese, and Syrians. We don't blame them; it's a unique dish, worth arguing about. Many of us have Americanized this by substituting the ubiquitous zucchini for the eggplant. We've even had it in the home of friends with summer squash. But that's American; use what appeals, then call the dish your own.

2 MEDIUM-SIZED EGGPLANT,
   PEELED AND CUT INTO
   ½-INCH SLICES
SALT
FLOUR
½ CUP OR MORE OLIVE OIL
SALT AND PEPPER
2 LARGE ONIONS, CHOPPED
1 GARLIC CLOVE, MINCED
1½ POUNDS LEAN GROUND
   LAMB
2 MEDIUM-SIZED RIPE TOMA-
   TOES, PEELED, SEEDED,
   AND CHOPPED

2 TABLESPOONS TOMATO PASTE
½ TEASPOON CINNAMON
¼ CUP CHOPPED PARSLEY
¾ CUP GRATED ASIAGO,
   PARMESAN, OR OTHER
   GOOD GRATING CHEESE
2½ TABLESPOONS BUTTER
2½ TABLESPOONS FLOUR
1½ CUPS MILK
PINCH NUTMEG
2 EGGS, BEATEN

SPRINKLE THE SLICES of eggplant lightly with salt. Arrange in two or three stacks on a board covered with a paper towel. Place a large plate with a weight on it over them and let stand for half an hour to allow the moisture in them to drain off. Rinse the slices with water and dry with paper towels. Dredge the slices lightly with flour. In a large frypan, heat half the oil over medium-high heat and, in a single layer, brown the eggplant slices on both sides, sprinkling lightly with salt and pepper. As they brown, transfer to paper towels to drain. Add more oil as needed. Wipe out the frypan with paper towels. Add 2 tablespoons of olive oil. When hot, cook the onions and garlic until soft. Add the ground lamb and cook, breaking up the meat with a fork, until it loses its pink color. Add the tomatoes, tomato paste, cinnamon, salt, and pepper to taste. Simmer for 15 minutes, or until the liquid has evaporated and the mixture thickened. Taste for seasoning. Stir in the parsley. In a 9-by 9-by-3-inch baking dish, arrange a layer of half of the eggplant, overlapping, if necessary. Sprinkle 3 tablespoons of the cheese over it. Spoon all the meat mixture evenly over the cheese, then sprinkle the meat with 3 tablespoons of cheese. Arrange the remaining eggplant over the meat layer, then sprinkle them with 3 tablespoons of cheese. In a saucepan, over medium heat, heat the butter. Add the flour, stirring into a smooth paste. Add the milk in small amounts and cook, stirring into a smooth, slightly thickened sauce. Add the nutmeg, salt, and pepper. Add 3 tablespoons of the sauce to the beaten eggs. Quickly stir them into the saucepan. Do not allow to boil. Spoon the sauce over the eggplant and sprinkle with the remaining cheese. Bake in a preheated 350° oven for 30 minutes, or until the top is puffed, set, and golden. Rest the dish 15 minutes before serving. *Serves 4 to 6.*

SYRIAN LAMB SHANKS

■ ■ ■

2 TABLESPOONS OLIVE OIL	½ TEASPOON GROUND MACE
4 LAMB SHANKS	4 MEDIUM-SIZED RIPE TOMA-
3 LARGE ONIONS, CUT INTO	TOES, PEELED, SEEDED,
½-INCH SLICES	AND CHOPPED, OR ONE
1 TEASPOON SALT	1-POUND CAN TOMATOES,
½ TEASPOON PEPPER	DRAINED, AND CHOPPED
1 TEASPOON GROUND ALLSPICE	1 CUP BEEF BROTH

COAT THE LAMB shanks with the olive oil. Arrange them in a stove-top-to-oven casserole just large enough to hold them snugly in one layer. Bake, uncovered, in a preheated 425° oven about 35 minutes, turning the shanks after 15 minutes to brown evenly. Arrange the onions in one layer over the lamb, seasoning with half of the salt, pepper, allspice, and mace. Spoon the tomatoes evenly over the onions, sprinkling with the remaining seasoning. Pour the beef broth around the edges; bring to a boil on top of the stove. Lower oven heat to 350°, cover pot, and bake for 45 minutes, or until the lamb shanks are fork-tender. Rice is always served with this. *Serves 4.*

ARMENIAN SHISH KEBAB
■ ■ ■

3 POUNDS BONELESS LAMB
   FROM THE LEG, CUT INTO
   1½-INCH CUBES
4 GARLIC CLOVES, MASHED
1 MEDIUM-SIZED ONION,
   CHOPPED
1 BAY LEAF
½ TEASPOON EACH GROUND
   CORIANDER, CUMIN, AND
   DRIED OREGANO

4 FRESH MINT LEAVES,
   CHOPPED
1 TEASPOON SALT
½ TEASPOON PEPPER
1 CUP DRY RED WINE
¼ CUP OLIVE OIL
JUICE OF 1 LEMON

COMBINE ALL INGREDIENTS in a large bowl and with your hands mix well to coat all of the lamb. Marinate several hours or overnight in the refrigerator, mixing 2 or 3 times. Let sit at room temperature before cooking. Skewer the meat loosely on long skewers and cook over a charcoal fire or under the broiler to your taste, basting with the marinade and turning occasionally. If desired pink, broil 10 to 15 minutes, then test; if well done, 20 minutes or more. Tomato wedges, strips of green pepper, and small onions can be alternated on the skewers with the lamb, but the pepper strips and onions should be parboiled or precooked in butter before broiling. These vegetables are an American adaptation. They are not used in this fashion in the Middle East. Serve on a bed of rice so the juices from the lamb and tomatoes can permeate the rice. *Serves 6.*

BURGUNDIAN VEAL STEW
∎ ∎ ∎

5 TABLESPOONS BUTTER
1 TABLESPOON OLIVE OIL
2 POUNDS BONELESS VEAL
FROM THE SHOULDER OR
LEG, CUT INTO 1½-INCH
CUBES
12 TO 18 SMALL WHITE
ONIONS, WHOLE, ROOT
ENDS SCORED
SALT AND PEPPER TO TASTE

2 TABLESPOONS FLOUR
1½ CUPS HOT CHICKEN OR
BEEF BROTH (CANNED IS
GOOD)
¼ CUP TOMATO PURÉE
3 SPRIGS PARSLEY
½ CUP RED BURGUNDY WINE
½ POUND MUSHROOMS,
QUARTERED

In a heavy top-of-the-stove casserole, over medium heat, heat 3 tablespoons of the butter and oil. Add the veal and onions to the pan without crowding and brown evenly. As they brown, remove them and add others. Use more butter and oil, if needed. Return all to the pot, sprinkle with salt, pepper, and the flour and stir to mix well. Add the broth, tomato purée, and parsley and stir. Cover tightly and simmer for 1 hour (stirring from time to time), or until the veal starts to become tender. Add the wine and cook half an hour, or until the veal is tender. Cook the mushrooms in 2 tablespoons of butter until brown but still crisp, add to the veal, and cook 3 minutes. Taste for seasoning. Discard the parsley. Serve with rice or noodles and a green salad. *Serves 4 to 6.*

SWISS EMINCÉ DE VEAU

(Veal Strips Cooked in Wine and Cream)

■ ■ ■

Veal is classic for this, but the breast of chicken or turkey works very well.

6 TABLESPOONS BUTTER
3 TABLESPOONS OLIVE OIL
2½ POUNDS VEAL SCALLOPS
    (OR CHICKEN OR TURKEY
    BREAST), CUT INTO STRIPS ¼
    INCH THICK, 2 INCHES
    LONG, AND ½ INCH WIDE
SALT AND PEPPER TO TASTE
2 TABLESPOONS MINCED
    SHALLOTS (OR THE WHITE
    PART OF SCALLIONS OR
    WHITE ONION)

½ CUP DRY WHITE WINE
1½ CUPS HEAVY CREAM
1 TABLESPOON CORNSTARCH
    DISSOLVED IN 2 TABLE-
    SPOONS WATER
JUICE OF ½ LEMON

HEAT 2 TABLESPOONS OF the butter and 1 tablespoon of the oil in a large frypan. Add a third of the veal strips; sprinkle lightly with salt and pepper. Over medium heat, cook the meat, turning, for 5 to 7 minutes or until golden and tender. With a slotted spoon, remove the strips, placing them in a strainer over a bowl to catch the juices. Repeat the process, cooking the strips in thirds. Cook the shallots (or whatever you use for a substitute) in the same frypan for 3 minutes, or until soft. Do not brown. Stir in the wine. Bring to a boil, lower heat, add the cream and the juices drained from the veal. Bring to a simmer and cook 10 minutes. Stir in the cornstarch mixture, blend well, simmer 1 minute. Add the veal and lemon juice. Taste for seasoning. Simmer 2 minutes, stirring. This is often served with Potatoes Roesti (see p. 203). *Serves 6.*

VEAL BRACIOLE

■■■

The Italian families that introduced these unique rolls usually used veal, but today the "braciole" has been Americanized into "birds," and beef and pork are also used.

12 4-INCH-SQUARE
    ½-INCH-THICK SLICES OF
    LEG OF VEAL, FLATTENED
    TO ¼ INCH BETWEEN TWO
    PIECES OF WAXED PAPER
    WITH A MEAT MALLET, BEING
    CAREFUL NOT TO PIERCE
    THE MEAT
TWO 1-INCH CUBES SALT PORK,
    MINCED
6 TABLESPOONS SOFT BUTTER
1 GARLIC CLOVE, MINCED
¼ CUP MINCED PARSLEY
PINCH DRY LEAF SAGE
¼ CUP RAISINS, CHOPPED

3 TABLESPOONS HALVED PINE
    NUTS
6 TABLESPOONS FRESH BREAD
    CRUMBS
6 TABLESPOONS GRATED
    ASIAGO OR PARMESAN
    CHEESE
SALT AND PEPPER
3 TABLESPOONS OLIVE OIL
2 OUNCES MARSALA WINE
½ CUP BEEF BROTH (CANNED IS
    GOOD), OR USE A SMALL
    AMOUNT OF TOMATO SAUCE
3 TABLESPOONS CHOPPED
    PARSLEY

ARRANGE THE VEAL squares on a suitable work area. Combine salt pork, butter, garlic, parsley, and sage and blend into a paste. Divide the salt pork mixture into 12 equal parts and spread 1 part on each square. Sprinkle equal amounts of raisins, pine nuts, bread crumbs, and cheese on the veal and sprinkle with salt and pepper. Roll into neat cylinders and secure with white string or toothpicks. In a large frypan, heat the oil over medium heat and evenly brown the rolls in a single layer. Transfer to a warm dish. Pour any excess fat from the pan. Return the pan to the heat and stir in the wine, scraping the bottom of the pan to release brown particles. Pour in the broth. Return the rolls to the pan, cover tightly, and simmer for 25 minutes, or until tender. If liquid cooks off, add a small amount of beef broth or water. Remove the strings or toothpicks. Arrange on a hot serving dish. Pour any liquid in the pan over the rolls, sprinkle with parsley, and serve with Potatoes Parma (see p. 202) and Baked Cherry Tomatoes (see p. 208). *Serves 4 to 6.*

AUSTRIAN PORK SCHNITZEL
■ ■ ■

Classically, veal is used in schnitzel, as it was when the dish was originally brought to Vienna from Italy, but the country folks who came here from Austria often used pork. It was cheaper, and many of us think tastier.

FOUR ¾-INCH-THICK LOIN PORK CHOPS, CAREFULLY POUNDED WITH A MEAT MALLET OR THE EDGE OF A HEAVY SAUCER, REDUCING THE THICKNESS OF THE CHOP TO ABOUT ¼ INCH (LEAVE THE BONE ON, POUNDING AROUND IT)

SALT AND PEPPER
FLOUR
2 EGGS, BEATEN
FINE, DRIED BREAD CRUMBS
3 TABLESPOONS BUTTER (OR COOKING OIL)
2 LARGE LEMONS (CUT ONE INTO HALVES AND QUARTER THE OTHER)

SPRINKLE THE MEAT with salt and pepper, then dredge with flour. Dip into the beaten eggs, then dredge with bread crumbs. Press the bread crumbs firmly into the meat, flattening it further. Refrigerate the pork until ready to cook. In a large frypan (or cook 2 at a time in a smaller one), over medium heat, heat the butter or oil and evenly brown the schnitzels. This should take about 15 minutes. They shouldn't be cooked too fast. Turn often for even cooking and browning. Add more butter or oil if needed. When the schnitzels are crisp and evenly browned, reduce the heat to low and cook another 10 minutes, again turning often, until thoroughly done. Squeeze the juice of the halved lemon over them and serve immediately while very hot with a lemon quarter. *Serves 4.*

Note: A fast way to get the most juice from the lemon: Insert the tines of a fork firmly into the lemon then squeeze around it. The fork tines will release the juice more quickly and liberally.

BULGARIAN PORK ROAST WITH APPLESAUCE GLAZE

■ ■ ■

ONE 3 ½- TO 4-POUND
  RIB-END PORK ROAST
  (CHINE BONE REMOVED FOR
  EASIER SLICING)
1 TEASPOON SALT BLENDED
  WITH ½ TEASPOON
  PEPPER

2 LARGE GARLIC CLOVES,
  HALVED
4 WHOLE CLOVES
1 CUP APPLESAUCE

Rub the pork well with the salt and pepper mixture. Fat side up, with a sharp knife, make 8 small but rather deep slits (4 on each side) evenly along both sides and, alternating, insert half a garlic clove, then a clove, using all garlic and cloves. Place the pork, fat side up, in a shallow roasting pan. Center, uncovered, in a preheated 375° oven and cook for 1½ hours. Remove from the oven, and evenly spread the applesauce on top; return to the oven and cook for 25 minutes, or until the pork is thoroughly cooked, tender, and glazed a deep, golden brown. Often a mixture of applesauce and horseradish is served with the sliced pork. *Serves 4 to 6.*

CUBAN PORK LOIN COOKED IN MILK

■■■

2 TABLESPOONS BUTTER
2 TABLESPOONS OLIVE OIL
ONE 5- OR 5½-POUND PORK
   LOIN, BONED AND TRIMMED
   OF FAT
SALT AND PEPPER
ENOUGH WARM MILK TO COVER
   THE PORK (ABOUT 1
   QUART)

1 LARGE ONION, COARSELY
   CHOPPED
1 LARGE CARROT, COARSELY
   CHOPPED
¼ TEASPOON DRIED THYME

OVER MEDIUM HEAT in a stove-top-to-oven casserole just large enough to snugly hold the pork, heat the butter and oil. Evenly brown the pork, sprinkling with salt and pepper. Pour off any fat in the casserole and cover the pork with the warm milk. Add the onion, carrot, and thyme. Bring to a boil on top of the stove, cover, and cook in a preheated 325° oven for 2 hours, or until the pork is fork-tender. Remove the pork and keep it warm. Strain the liquid. If it is too thin, simmer on top of the stove to thicken. Slice the pork and serve with the milk sauce spooned over it. Good accompaniments are Cuban Black Beans (see p. 189), fried plantains, and white rice. *Serves 6.*

CZECHOSLOVAKIAN HOT POT
■ ■ ■

3 TABLESPOONS COOKING
   OIL
3 POUNDS PORK SHOULDER,
   CUT INTO PIECES 1 INCH
   SQUARE AND ½ INCH THICK
SALT AND PEPPER TO TASTE
4 MEDIUM-SIZED ONIONS,
   THINLY SLICED
4 MEDIUM-SIZED POTATOES,
   PEELED, CUT INTO ¼-INCH
   SLICES
3 CARROTS, SCRAPED, SLICED
   SLIGHTLY THINNER THAN
   THE POTATO SLICES

2 TURNIPS, SCRAPED, SLICED
   SLIGHTLY THINNER THAN
   THE POTATO SLICES
2 CUPS FINELY SHREDDED RED
   CABBAGE (DO NOT USE
   CORE)
2 TEASPOONS CARAWAY SEEDS
1½ TO 2 CUPS CHICKEN BROTH
   OR ENOUGH TO COVER

IN A FRYPAN, over medium heat, heat the oil and brown the pork evenly, sprinkling with salt and pepper. Add more oil if needed. Remove the pork, add the onions, and cook 3 minutes, or until soft. Do not brown. In a lightly oiled casserole, arrange alternating layers of pork, onion, potato, carrot, turnips, and cabbage, sprinkling each layer lightly with salt, pepper, and caraway seeds. Make the last layer potato. Pour in enough broth to barely cover the top layer. Cook, covered, in a preheated 375° oven for 1 hour, or until the vegetables and pork are tender. The Czechs serve from the casserole and offer plenty of hearty bread and cold beer. *Serves 6.*

HAM AND PORK LOAF WITH MUSTARD SAUCE

("American" with a Scandinavian accent)

■ ■ ■

2 TABLESPOONS BUTTER
2 MEDIUM-SIZED WHITE
    ONIONS, MINCED
1 GARLIC CLOVE, MINCED
1½ POUNDS LEAN RAW OR
    COOKED HAM, GROUND
1½ POUNDS LEAN FRESH PORK,
    GROUND
SALT AND PEPPER TO TASTE
    (THE HAM COULD SUPPLY
    THE SALT)

2 EGGS, BEATEN
1 CUP FINE DRIED BREAD
    CRUMBS
1 CUP MILK
BROWN SUGAR
1 TEASPOON DRY MUSTARD
MUSTARD SAUCE (SEE
    BELOW)

IN A FRYPAN, over medium heat, melt the butter. Add the onions and garlic and cook until they are soft. Do not brown. In a bowl, combine and mix well, but lightly, with your hands, the ham, pork, salt, pepper, eggs, bread crumbs, milk, onions, and garlic. Do not overmix or it will be too solid a mixture. Lightly pack in a buttered loaf tin. Cover the loaf with a thin layer of brown sugar, sprinkle on the mustard, then another thin layer of brown sugar. Set in a pan of hot water and bake in a preheated 350° oven for 1½ hours, or until thoroughly cooked. Pour off excess fat and let stand 10 minutes before turning out onto a serving dish. Pass the Mustard Sauce at the table. *Serves 6.*

Mustard Sauce

½ PINT HEAVY CREAM, WHIPPED
¼ CUP DIJON MUSTARD

PINCH DRY MUSTARD
½ CUP MAYONNAISE

Combine and blend all ingredients into a smooth sauce.

LITHUANIAN PORK ROAST

■ ■ ■

ONE 4-POUND RIB-END PORK   1 TEASPOON SALT
   ROAST, CHINE BONE   ½ TEASPOON PEPPER
   REMOVED   ¼ TEASPOON CINNAMON
6 MEDIUM-SIZED ONIONS,
   HALVED

PLACE PORK IN a pot just large enough to hold it snugly.
Cover with water, add 3 onions, cover, and bring to a boil.
Lower heat and simmer, covered, for half an hour. Remove, pat dry, and place in a roasting pan. Season with
salt, pepper, and cinnamon. Surround with the remaining
onions. Cook, uncovered, in a preheated 325° oven for 2
to 3 hours, or until the top is crusty brown but the pork is
still juicy. This is often served with a potato cake, the
Kugeli (see p. 201). *Serves 4 to 6.*

LOIN PORK CHOPS AND SAUSAGE À LA BOULANGÈRE

■■■

In French villages, when the baker has finished his work for the day, but his wood-burning oven is still hot, village women bring casseroles of food to be baked by the baker's wife (the boulangère*) for a small fee. In the United States this has become a popular casserole party dish, the ingredients varied, using lamb, chicken, turkey, beef. But pork and sausage is classic.*

3 TABLESPOONS BUTTER
2 TABLESPOONS OLIVE OIL
6 LOIN PORK CHOPS, ½ TO ¾ INCHES THICK (SEE NOTE)
SALT AND PEPPER TO TASTE
6 SWEET ITALIAN SAUSAGES (OPTIONAL, BUT GOOD)
3 GARLIC CLOVES, MASHED
18 SMALL WHITE ONIONS, LEFT WHOLE, ROOT ENDS SCORED

3 TO 4 CUPS CHICKEN BROTH
2 CELERY RIBS, SCRAPED AND COARSELY CHOPPED
1 BAY LEAF
PINCH DRIED THYME
6 SMALL POTATOES, HALVED

IN A LARGE stove-top-to-oven casserole, heat the butter and oil. Brown the chops on both sides, sprinkling with salt and pepper. Remove the chops. Evenly brown the sausages (if used), adding more butter and oil, if needed. Remove the sausages. Add the garlic and onions and cook until golden. Pour off any fat that may remain in the casserole. Pour in 1 cup of the broth and stir, scraping the bottom of the pot to dislodge the brown particles. Return the chops and sausages to the pot. Add the celery, bay leaf, thyme, and enough of the remaining broth just to cover the contents of the pot. Bring to a boil on top of the stove. Cover tightly and cook in a preheated 350° oven for 25 minutes. Add the potatoes and cook for 20 minutes. Remove the cover, raise oven heat to 400°, and cook 15 minutes, or until everything is fork-tender. Remove and discard the bay leaf. Taste for seasoning. Serve with the broth spooned over the meat and vegetables. *Serves 6.*

Note: To guarantee tender chops, pound the chops around the bone with a meat mallet before browning. Reshape the chops with your hands.

POLISH PARTY STEW
■ ■ ■

2 TABLESPOONS BUTTER
1 TABLESPOON OLIVE OIL
3 POUNDS LEAN PORK, CUT INTO 1-INCH CUBES
3 LARGE ONIONS, SLICED
2 TABLESPOONS PAPRIKA
ONE 13 ¾-OUNCE CAN CONDENSED BEEF BROTH
ABOUT 1 CUP WATER
1 BAY LEAF
1 TEASPOON CARAWAY SEEDS, CRUSHED
SALT TO TASTE
6 MEDIUM-SIZED CARROTS, SCRAPED AND CUT INTO ½-INCH SLICES
ONE 10-OUNCE PACKAGE FROZEN, CUT GREEN BEANS

OVER MEDIUM HEAT in a stove-top-to-oven casserole, heat the butter and oil. Add pork and evenly brown, adding more butter and oil, if needed. Remove the pork, add the onions to the pot, and cook until soft but not brown. Lower heat. Add the paprika, stirring into the onions, cooking 1 minute. Return the pork to the pot, stir in the beef broth, enough water barely to cover the meat. Add the bay leaf, caraway seeds, and salt. Bring to a boil on the top of the stove. Cover and cook in a preheated 350° oven for 1½ hours, or until pork is almost tender. Add the carrots and cook 15 minutes, or until the meat is tender and the carrots are crisp-tender. Add the green beans and cook 5 minutes. Taste for seasoning. Remove and discard bay leaf. This is usually served with Polish Potato Dumplings (see p. 199) *Serves 6.*

SICILIAN PORK CHOPS WITH GLAZED ORANGE SLICES

■■■

Some American recipes are heirlooms. We've had this unique and extremely tasty dish in the home of friends whose grandparents came from Sicily. This handed-down honey was always served on Sunday. It's also dramatic. After all, how many of us have ever eaten a glazed orange slice?

½ CUP MARSALA WINE
¼ TEASPOON DRIED ROSEMARY
   LEAVES
⅛ TEASPOON CINNAMON
⅛ TEASPOON GROUND CLOVES
1 TEASPOON SALT
½ TEASPOON BLACK PEPPER
2 TABLESPOONS GRATED
   ORANGE PEEL

2 GARLIC CLOVES, CRUSHED
¼ CUP ORANGE JUICE
FOUR 1-INCH-THICK LOIN PORK
   CHOPS
2 TABLESPOONS OLIVE OIL
   GLAZED ORANGE SLICES (SEE
   BELOW)

IN A BOWL, combine and blend well all ingredients except the pork chops and the olive oil. (A trick to ensure that chops are always tender: beat both sides around the bone with a meat mallet, then reshape chops with your hands.) Place the chops in a shallow dish, pour the marinade over, and let stand at room temperature for at least 2 hours. Remove chops; reserve marinade. In a heavy stove-top-to-oven pot, over medium heat, heat the oil. Dry chops with a paper towel, add them to the pot, and evenly brown. Pour the reserved marinade over the chops, bring to a boil on top of the stove, cover tightly, and cook in a preheated 350° oven for 1 hour, or until the chops are tender. Serve on a hot serving dish, garnished with Glazed Orange Slices. *Serves 4.*

Glazed Orange Slices

3 MEDIUM-SIZED SEEDLESS
   ORANGES
¼ CUP BUTTER

2 TABLESPOONS LIGHT CORN
   SYRUP
½ CUP LIGHT BROWN SUGAR

Cut off the ends of the oranges, then, crosswise, cut into ½-inch slices. In a large saucepan, combine the butter, corn syrup, and brown sugar and cook, stirring, over medium heat, until the sugar melts and the mixture is well blended and simmering. Arrange the orange slices in the saucepan and simmer, uncovered, 3 minutes. Turn slices over, simmer 3 minutes. Slices should have a definite glaze.

POLISH BIGOS

■ ■ ■

This stew is usually made with sauerkraut, cabbage, and sausage, but it has many variations. Traditionally a hunting dish using venison, it is made everywhere with beef, pork, and other meats. It is said to be better if reheated two or three times, on two or three consecutive days. So it can be enjoyed the day it is prepared—or the day after—or the day after—or . . .

5 TABLESPOONS BUTTER
1 POUND LEAN CHUCK BEEF,
   CUT INTO SMALL, BITE-
   SIZED PIECES
1 POUND LEAN PORK, CUT INTO
   SMALL, BITE-SIZED PIECES
½ POUND VENISON, CUT AS THE
   OTHER MEATS (IF NOT
   AVAILABLE, USE AN EXTRA ½
   POUND BEEF)
SALT AND PEPPER TO TASTE
1 CELERY RIB, SCRAPED AND
   CHOPPED
1 LARGE ONION, CHOPPED
2 TART APPLES, PEELED,
   CORED, AND COARSELY
   CHOPPED
6 MEDIUM-SIZED MUSHROOMS,
   COARSELY CHOPPED
1 POUND SAUERKRAUT, FRESH,
   IF POSSIBLE (IF CANNED,
   DRAIN WELL)

2 CUPS FINELY SHREDDED
   WHITE FRESH CABBAGE
1 TEASPOON CARAWAY SEED
BOUQUET GARNI (SEVERAL
   PARSLEY SPRIGS, 1 BAY
   LEAF, AND 3 CLOVES TIED IN
   A CHEESECLOTH)
2 RIPE TOMATOES, PEELED,
   SEEDED, AND CHOPPED
1 TABLESPOON TOMATO PASTE
1 CUP DRY WHITE WINE
2 CUPS CHICKEN BROTH
1 POUND KIELBASA, SKINNED,
   AND CUT INTO 1-INCH
   ROUNDS
2 TABLESPOONS FRESH
   CHOPPED DILL (OPTIONAL)

In a large, heavy, stove-top-to-oven casserole, over medium heat, melt 4 tablespoons of butter and evenly brown the beef, pork, and venison in several batches, seasoning with salt and pepper. Transfer with a slotted spoon to a bowl. Add the remaining butter. When melted, cook the celery, onion, apples, and mushrooms until soft. Do not brown. Stir in the sauerkraut, cabbage, caraway seed, bouquet garni, tomatoes, tomato paste, wine, and 1 cup of the broth. Simmer, covered, for 10 minutes. Add the browned meats and their juices and the kielbasa. Place, covered, in a 325° preheated oven for 1½ hours, or until the meat is tender. If the liquid cooks off, add small amounts of hot broth. If too much liquid, remove the cover for the last half-hour of cooking to allow it to cook down. Discard the bouquet garni. Taste for seasoning. Sprinkle with the dill before serving. *Serves 6.*

Note: Any leftover, cooked meat can be used instead of the fresh meat, but fresh is our first choice.

EDWARD T. THOMPSON'S WATERCRESS SAUSAGE

■ ■ ■

Sausage is an American family favorite, and many are the creations dreamed up by individual cooks. In fact, sausage probably inspires more cooks to be creative than almost any other food preparation. Ed Thompson, who introduced us to this extremely tasty recipe (which also can be rolled into little balls, browned in butter, and served as a cocktail offering), shapes the sausage into patties, wraps them in foils, and freezes them. He advises that there is no need to thaw them before cooking. We guarantee that these sausage patties place a pancake supper on a new plane which may make it a weekly winter winner.

5½ POUNDS PORK SHOULDER (SKINNED AND BONED)
½ POUND PURE WHITE PORK FAT
1 TABLESPOON SALT
1 TABLESPOON BLACK PEPPER (FRESHLY GROUND IS BEST)
1 TABLESPOON WHOLE CARAWAY SEED
½ CUP CRUMBLED SAGE LEAVES
2 CUPS FINELY CHOPPED PARSLEY
2 CUPS CHOPPED SCALLIONS (GREEN ONIONS), TOPS FINELY CHOPPED, BULBS COARSELY CHOPPED
2 CUPS FINELY CHOPPED WATERCRESS LEAVES
2 TEASPOONS DRIED DILL
2 TEASPOONS DRIED SWEET MARJORAM
1 TEASPOON DRIED ROSEMARY
2 TEASPOONS DRIED OREGANO
2 TEASPOONS DRIED TARRAGON

GRIND THE PORK and fat to hamburger consistency, place in large mixing bowl, and mix the meat and fat with your hands so that they are evenly blended. Add all of the other ingredients and blend thoroughly with your hands. Put a pat of butter in a small frypan and fry a small patty of the mixture to test the seasoning, adjusting if necessary. Shape into patties, wrap in foil, and freeze.

But save a few patties for supper with mashed potatoes and maybe a little buttered broccoli. Ed Thompson would be hurt if you stowed away his unique sausage without feasting on it first.

SWEDISH MEATBALLS

■■■

This is truly a classic Swedish dish, yet many of us whip up a version and call it "American," proving again that so many of our recipes evolved from the basic ones brought by the early settlers.

4 TABLESPOONS BUTTER	¼ TEASPOON NUTMEG
1 MEDIUM-SIZED ONION	PINCH GINGER
1 POUND LEAN CHUCK BEEF	¼ TEASPOON ALLSPICE
½ POUND VEAL	SALT AND PEPPER TO TASTE
½ POUND LEAN PORK	2 TABLESPOONS FLOUR
¾ CUP ZWEIBACK CRUMBS (OR	1½ CUPS HOT BEEF BROTH
OTHER DRY CRUMBS)	(HOMEMADE, CANNED, OR
1¼ CUPS HEAVY CREAM	MADE WITH A KNORR BEEF
1 EGG, BEATEN	BOUILLON CUBE)
1 TEASPOON BROWN SUGAR	

GRIND BEEF, VEAL, and pork together twice. In a small frypan, heat 1 tablespoon of the butter over medium heat. Add the onion and cook until soft. Do not brown. In a large bowl, combine and mix well (hands are good tools) the ground meat, crumbs, half of the cream, the egg, cooked onion, brown sugar, nutmeg, ginger, allspice, salt, and pepper and shape into golf ball-sized meatballs. In a large frypan, over medium heat, melt the remaining butter and evenly brown the balls. Sprinkle with the flour, shaking the frypan to distribute it. Lower heat, pour in the stock, cover, and simmer for ¾ hour, or until thoroughly cooked. Transfer to a hot serving dish. Add the remaining cream to the sauce in the frypan. Heat to a simmer and pour over the meatballs. Should win the Nobel Prize. *Serves 6 to 8.*

VEAL KIDNEYS WITH SHERRY FRANÇAIS

■ ■ ■

6 TABLESPOONS BUTTER
½ POUND MUSHROOMS, CUT
  INTO ¼-INCH SLICES
1 TABLESPOON OLIVE OIL
4 SMALL VEAL KIDNEYS,
  TRIMMED AND CUT INTO
  ¼-INCH SLICES
¼ CUP MINCED SHALLOTS (OR
  WHITE ONION)

1½ TABLESPOONS FLOUR
SALT AND PEPPER TO TASTE
1 CUP VEAL OR CHICKEN BROTH
2 TABLESPOONS DRY SHERRY
½ CUP HEAVY CREAM
CHOPPED PARSLEY

HEAT 2 TABLESPOONS OF the butter in a medium frypan, add mushrooms, and sauté until brown but still crisp. In a large frypan, over medium heat, heat the remaining butter and oil. Add the kidneys and cook, turning until barely golden on both sides (about 5 minutes). Do not overcook or they will toughen. They should be pink inside. Remove with a slotted spoon and keep warm. Add the shallots to the pan and cook until soft. Add the mushrooms, sprinkle with the flour, and cook 1 minute. Sprinkle with salt and pepper. Pour in the broth, sherry, and cream and simmer 10 minutes, or until sauce starts to thicken. Return the kidneys to the pan and heat 1 minute. Taste for seasoning. Serve immediately with the parsley sprinkled over the top. *Serves 4.*

Chapter 7

PASTA, RICE, AND OTHER GRAINS

Today nutritionists are high on the health advantages of carbohydrates, especially pasta and rice, and also recommend a liberal intake of whole grains, corn, and wheat.

Interesting. The immigrants who taught many of us how to cook, with a kitchen heritage that grows stronger every day, have always considered these the best and most economical of foods and have passed on to us unique and flavorful ways of using them all. Some corn and rice dishes are American originals, but mainly the recipes here are passed-on gems of penny-saving ingenuity.

But back to the nutritionists. Their conclusions: pasta is one of the world's perfect foods, low in fat and high in digestibility. Four ounces of cooked pasta contain just 210 calories, about the same as two small apples. As energy-giving carbohydrate, it also contains more protein (13 percent) than potatoes, and just four ounces of pasta have all the vitamins and iron recommended by the U.S. Daily Allowances for Adults. It also rates high marks in the four groups in the U.S. Department of Agriculture's Daily Food Guide.

A complex carbohydrate, pasta has recently become the favorite of athletes. Calling it "carbo-loading," they have discovered that the body stores the energy-giving carbohydrate in pasta more readily than any other kind. Thus, the body can draw upon it for a greater length of time. Runners in the New York Marathon eat it for two or three days before the contest.

In addition, pasta provides six of the eight essential amino acids that the body requires. The standard sauces that provide the other two sound like a nutritionist's dream of what's good for us: meat, seafood, fresh vegetables, cheese, eggs, and fruit (tomatoes are a fruit).

There's a close contest between pasta and rice, perhaps with rice leading in that it impressively feeds more than half of the world. It also costs less than a nickel a serving, while providing 80 percent of daily food requirements. One pound delivers four times the food energy of a pound of potatoes.

Sometimes called the wonder food because of its versatility and benefits, rice's protein is superior to that of corn and oats, and the efficiency of protein in polished rice is 158 percent greater than that in wheat flour. Low in sodium and fat, with no cholesterol or even gluten, rice is a boon to weight watchers and those allergic to other grains. It also is easily digested, requiring only one hour, while most other foods need two to four hours. One-half cup of rice furnishes eighty-two calories of energy, enough for a person to dance for eighteen minutes, or walk for thirty-five minutes. Most of the rice we buy is also enriched, which means that it contains calcium, iron, and the B-complex vitamins. Brown rice is even better for us, as it has a bonus of fiber, oil, and vitamin E.

Probably, however, it is what we can do with pasta and rice, not what they can do for us, that makes them so popular.

FEDELINI WITH ANCHOVY-ONION SAUCE
■■■

The United States has the best onions on earth. We created the hybrid which gave us a remarkable variety of delicious onions. Again, proving that American cooking is simply a pairing of our fresh and unique products with classic recipes, we offer an Italian technique with our onions. Caution: If you aren't high on onions, skip this one.

8 TABLESPOONS BUTTER
5 MEDIUM-SIZED WHITE
   ONIONS, MINCED
TWO 2-OUNCE CANS FLAT
   ANCHOVIES, DRAINED AND
   COARSELY CHOPPED

1 POUND FEDELINI COOKED IN
   SLIGHTLY SALTED, BOILING
   WATER UNTIL *AL DENTE*
   (SLIGHTLY CHEWY) AND
   DRAINED

IN A SAUCEPAN, over medium heat, melt the butter and cook the onions until they have a slightly brown, caramel glaze. Stir in the anchovies, blending well, simmering until dissolved into the onions. Toss with the hot, drained pasta and serve immediately in warm soup bowls or plates. *Serves 4.*

Note: Fedelini is a string pasta, finer than spaghettini.

RUMANIAN NOODLES
■ ■ ■

5 TABLESPOONS BUTTER

1½ POUNDS INEXPENSIVE PORK (RIB-END CHOPS, SHOULDER, ETC.), WITH ¾ OF THE FAT TRIMMED OFF, GROUND

1 MEDIUM-SIZED ONION, MINCED

1 LARGE GARLIC CLOVE, MINCED

SALT AND PEPPER TO TASTE

3 SLICES WHITE BREAD, BROKEN INTO PIECES, SOAKED IN CHICKEN BROTH, LIQUID SQUEEZED OUT.

⅓ CUP CHOPPED PARSLEY

⅛ TEASPOON CINNAMON

½ TEASPOON CRUSHED DRY FENNEL

1 POUND NARROW EGG NOODLES, COOKED IN BOILING SALTED WATER UNTIL *AL DENTE* (SLIGHTLY CHEWY) AND DRAINED

3 EGGS

1 CUP CREAM

½ CUP GRATED ASIAGO OR PARMESAN CHEESE, OR YOUR CHOICE

IN A FRYPAN, over medium heat, melt 3 tablespoons of butter. Add the pork, onion, and garlic and cook for 15 minutes, stirring. Sprinkle with salt and pepper. Stir in the bread, parsley, cinnamon, and fennel, blending well. In a baking dish lightly rubbed with butter, arrange a layer of noodles, then a layer of the pork mixture, repeating, making the top layer noodles. Beat together eggs, cream, and cheese and pour over the top of the noodles. Dot with the remaining 2 tablespoons of butter and cook, uncovered, in a preheated 375° oven for 40 minutes, or until golden. *Serves 4 to 6.*

SPAGHETTI AND MEATBALLS

■■■

Although we never encountered this dish on our many tours of Italy in search of recipes and new food ideas, it was supposedly brought to the United States by immigrants from the south of Italy, who, it was said, ground the beef because it was tough, fashioned meatballs, and cooked them in a heavy tomato sauce. Whatever its origins, it certainly has become almost a national dish in the United States and an American family favorite.

2 POUNDS LEAN GROUND
    CHUCK BEEF
1½ CUPS GRATED ASIAGO OR
    PARMESAN CHEESE
1 GARLIC CLOVE, PUT THROUGH
    A GARLIC PRESS
1 CUP FINE FRESH BREAD
    CRUMBS
3 TABLESPOONS RAISINS,
    CHOPPED

¼ CUP CHOPPED PARSLEY
3 EGGS, LIGHTLY BEATEN
SALT AND PEPPER TO TASTE
7 TABLESPOONS BUTTER
2 TABLESPOONS OLIVE OIL
4 CUPS FILETTO SAUCE (SEE P.
    169)
1½ POUNDS SPAGHETTI

IN A LARGE bowl, combine and blend well (your hands are the best tools for this) the beef, ½ cup of cheese, garlic, bread crumbs, raisins, parsley, eggs, salt, and pepper. Shape into golf ball-sized balls. In a frypan, over medium heat, heat 3 tablespoons of the butter and oil. Add the meatballs, a few at a time (do not crowd), and evenly brown them. As they brown, transfer them to a large saucepan in which you have the Filetto Sauce heating. When all balls are cooked, simmer for half an hour in the sauce. Cook the spaghetti in boiling, salted water until *al dente* (slightly chewy), drain, and toss with 4 tablespoons of butter. Toss the pasta with half of the sauce and half of the remaining cheese. Spoon a dollop of sauce on individual servings and sprinkle with additional cheese and arrange 3 or 4 meatballs on the plate with the pasta. *Serves 6 to 8.*

FILETTO SAUCE

■■■

This can be prepared at any time and stored in the freezer.

Makes about 4 cups:

4 TABLESPOONS OLIVE OIL
4 GARLIC CLOVES, MINCED
4 LARGE ONIONS, FINELY
  CHOPPED
SALT AND PEPPER TO TASTE
2 TEASPOONS DRIED OREGANO
1 TABLESPOON DRIED BASIL

⅛ TEASPOON HOT RED PEPPER
  FLAKES, OR TO TASTE
THREE 2-POUND CANS PLUM
  TOMATOES, RUN THROUGH
  A FOOD MILL
1 TEASPOON SUGAR

IN A DEEP pot, over medium heat, heat the oil. Add the garlic and onions and cook until soft. Do not brown. Stir in the salt, pepper, oregano, basil, and red pepper flakes, blending well. Add the tomatoes and sugar. Bring to a boil, lower heat, and simmer, uncovered, for 35 minutes, or until much of the watery content has cooked off and the sauce has thickened. Do not overcook. It should be a smooth, thickish sauce, but not heavy.

TAGLIOLINI WITH GREEN GORGONZOLA SAUCE

■■■

4 TABLESPOONS BUTTER
8 OUNCES GORGONZOLA
    CHEESE, CRUMBLED
ONE 10-OUNCE PACKAGE FRESH
    SPINACH, COOKED AC-
    CORDING TO PACKAGE
    DIRECTIONS, WELL
    DRAINED, THEN PURÉED, OR
    ONE 10-OUNCE PACKAGE
    FROZEN, CHOPPED SPINACH,
    DEFROSTED AND WELL
    DRAINED

2 TABLESPOONS BEEF BROTH
⅓ CUP DRY MARSALA WINE
⅓ CUP HEAVY CREAM
2 GARLIC CLOVES, MINCED
1 POUND TAGLIOLINI, COOKED
    UNTIL *AL DENTE* (SLIGHTLY
    CHEWY), AND DRAINED
½ CUP GRATED ASIAGO OR
    PARMESAN CHEESE

IN A SAUCEPAN, over medium-low heat, melt the butter and the Gorgonzola cheese, stirring until smooth and well blended. Raise heat slightly, stir in the spinach, beef broth, and Marsala, and simmer 5 minutes. Gradually add the cream, stirring, then blend in the garlic. Simmer 5 minutes. Taste for seasoning, adding salt if needed. Toss with the hot pasta, sprinkling the grated cheese on top of each serving. *Serves 4 for a main course or 6 for a first course.*

TURKEY TETRAZZINI

■■■

For us, this recipe is representative of how ethnic food becomes "American." My Italian mother-in-law, Maria Limoncelli, was not one to waste food, and had a magic way with leftovers. After a Thanksgiving or Christmas turkey, instead of dreading the leftover bird, we always looked forward to dinners with her where we applauded her versatility. Today, this recipe has been adopted by her in-laws, all American, but with mixed ethnic backgrounds—Scotch, German, English, Jewish.

12 TABLESPOONS BUTTER
5 TABLESPOONS FLOUR
2 CUPS MILK
1 CUP HEAVY CREAM
SALT AND PEPPER TO TASTE
¼ TEASPOON NUTMEG
½ POUND FRESH SMALL
  MUSHROOMS, QUARTERED
3 CUPS LARGE, BITE-SIZED
  PIECES COOKED TURKEY
  (WITHOUT SKIN)

10 OUNCES ¼-INCH-WIDE
  NOODLES, FETTUCCINE OR
  TAGLIATELLE
1 CUP GRATED ASIAGO OR
  PARMESAN CHEESE
⅓ CUP FINE, DRIED BREAD
  CRUMBS

IN A SAUCEPAN, over medium heat, melt 5 tablespoons of butter. Stir in the flour and cook, stirring into a smooth paste. Add the milk and cream, a small amount at a time, stirring into a smooth, light sauce. Stir in salt, pepper, and nutmeg. Set aside. In a frypan, sauté the mushrooms in 3 tablespoons of the butter over medium heat until tender but still firm. Stir in the turkey and cook for about 30 seconds, mixing well but gently. Season with salt and pepper. Cook the noodles until *al dente* (slightly chewy) in boiling salted water. Drain. Place in a warm bowl with 3 tablespoons of the butter, melted, half of the cheese, and half of the sauce. Toss well, then gently toss in the turkey and mushrooms (with the butter they cooked in). Place in a shallow (2 inches deep), buttered dish. Spoon remaining sauce over the top, then sprinkle the remaining cheese and the bread crumbs. Dot with the remaining butter and place in a preheated 350° oven for 30 minutes, or until the sauce bubbles and the top is golden. *Serves 6.*

ZITI WITH AN EASY BOLOGNESE SAUCE
■■■

5 TABLESPOONS BUTTER
6 MEDIUM-SIZED FRESH MUSH-
  ROOMS, THINLY SLICED
½ POUND (ABOUT 8) CHICKEN
  LIVERS, TRIMMED AND CUT
  INTO SMALL BITE-SIZED
  PIECES
2 TABLESPOONS OLIVE OIL
2 GARLIC CLOVES, MINCED
1½ POUNDS LEAN GROUND
  BEEF
SALT AND PEPPER TO TASTE
4 CUPS FILETTO SAUCE (SEE P.
  169)

½ CUP HEAVY CREAM
1 POUND ZITI (A SHORT,
  HOLLOW PASTA, OR ANY
  SHORT, HOLLOW PASTA),
  COOKED IN BOILING
  SALTED WATER UNTIL *AL
  DENTE* (SLIGHTLY CHEWY),
  DRAINED, AND TOSSED WITH
  4 TABLESPOONS BUTTER
1 CUP GRATED ASIAGO OR
  PARMESAN CHEESE

SAUTÉ MUSHROOMS IN 2 tablespoons of butter for 1 minute, and set aside. Sauté chicken livers in 3 tablespoons of butter until slightly pink inside and set aside. In a deep pot, over medium heat, heat the olive oil. Add the garlic and cook until soft. Do not brown. Add the beef and cook, breaking the meat up with a fork until it starts to brown but still has some pink color. Season with salt and pepper. Stir in the Filetto Sauce and heat to a simmer. Add the mushrooms and livers and cook 5 minutes. Stir in the cream. Simmer 2 minutes. Toss the hot pasta with half of the hot sauce and half a cup of the cheese. Serve with a dollop of sauce spooned on top of individual servings. Sprinkle with the remaining cheese. *Serves 6 for a first course or 4 for a main course.*

DIRTY RICE

■ ■ ■

The name given this rice dish is not very appetizing, just as any restaurant called "The Rusty Nail" is not very appetizing. But we like chicken giblets, so it appealed to us, and we found it delicious when we had it at the rural bayou home of a duck-hunting guide in the Lake Charles area of Louisiana.

4 TABLESPOONS BUTTER
1 TABLESPOON OLIVE OIL
1 LARGE ONION, FINELY CHOPPED
1 GARLIC CLOVE, MINCED
1 LARGE GREEN PEPPER, SEEDS AND CORE REMOVED, AND FINELY CHOPPED
1 CELERY RIB, SCRAPED AND FINELY CHOPPED
½ POUND CHICKEN GIZZARDS AND HEARTS, TRIMMED AND FINELY CHOPPED

½ POUND CHICKEN LIVERS, TRIMMED AND COARSELY CHOPPED
SALT AND PEPPER TO TASTE
1 CUP LONG GRAIN RICE
2 CUPS BOILING CHICKEN BROTH (OR USE A KNORR CHICKEN BOUILLON CUBE DISSOLVED IN BOILING WATER)
½ CUP CHOPPED PARSLEY

IN A DEEP, heavy-bottomed pot, over medium heat, heat 2 tablespoons of the butter and the olive oil. Add the chopped vegetables and simmer for 10 minutes, or until soft. Do not brown. Add the chicken gizzards, hearts, and livers and cook until the pink color has left them but they are still tender (overcooking will toughen them) and most of the liquid has cooked off (about 10 minutes). Season with salt and pepper. In another pot, heat the remaining butter. Stir in the rice and coat well with the butter. Add the hot broth, cover pot, lower heat, and simmer 20 minutes, or until the rice is tender and the liquid has been absorbed. Add the rice to the vegetable–giblet mixture with 3 tablespoons of the parsley and mix with a fork. Mound on a hot serving dish and sprinkle with the remaining parsley. *Serves 6.*

RICE PILAF

■ ■ ■

6 TABLESPOONS BUTTER
½ CUP RAISINS
½ CUP PINE NUTS OR CHOPPED
   WALNUTS
1 SMALL ONION, CHOPPED
1 MEDIUM-SIZED ONION,
   FINELY CHOPPED

1 CUP UNCLE BEN'S CON-
   VERTED LONG-GRAIN RICE
2 CUPS CHICKEN BROTH
SALT AND PEPPER TO TASTE
2 TABLESPOONS CHOPPED
   PARSLEY

COOK RAISINS IN 1 tablespoon of butter long enough to plump them; set aside and keep warm. Brown pine nuts in 1 tablespoon of butter; set aside and keep warm. Sauté small onion in 1 tablespoon of butter until slightly golden; set aside and keep warm. In a saucepan, over medium heat, melt the remaining butter. Add the medium-sized onion and the rice and cook until the onion is soft and slightly golden, stirring frequently. Do not brown. Pour in the broth, bring to a boil, cover, and cook over low heat until the broth has been absorbed, about 25 minutes. Just before serving, fluff the rice with a fork and mix in the warm raisins, nuts, onion, and parsley. Taste and add salt and pepper, if needed. *Serves 4.*

Variation

1 RECIPE RICE PILAF (SEE
    ABOVE), BUT DO NOT ADD
    THE RAISINS, NUTS, OR EXTRA
    ONION
1 CUP BROWN GRAVY (HOME-
    MADE IS BEST)
2 TABLESPOONS DRY SHERRY
5 TABLESPOONS BUTTER
4 CHICKEN LIVERS, CUT INTO
    SMALL, BITE-SIZED PIECES

SALT AND PEPPER TO TASTE
8 SMALL MUSHROOM CAPS
ONE 7-OUNCE CAN WHITE
    GRAPES, DRAINED
1 TABLESPOON COGNAC
½ CUP GRATED ASIAGO OR
    PARMESAN CHEESE
2 TABLESPOONS CHOPPED
    PARSLEY

In a saucepan, over medium-low heat, combine the gravy
and sherry. In a frypan, over medium-high heat, melt 2
tablespoons of butter. Add the livers, sprinkle with salt and
pepper, and cook briskly, turning, until browned on the
outside and slightly pink inside (about 3 minutes). Transfer with a slotted spoon to the gravy pan. Add 1 tablespoon of butter to the frypan; when melted add the
mushrooms and cook 2 minutes, or until crisp-tender.
Transfer the mushrooms to the gravy pan. Add the grapes
and cognac. Stir and taste for seasoning. Keep warm. Stir
the remaining butter and the cheese into the hot rice. Fill
a hot buttered ring mold with the rice, press down with a
wooden spoon, and unmold onto a hot, round serving
dish. Fill the center of the rice ring with the chicken
liver–mushroom–grapes mixture. Sprinkle with the parsley. *Serves 4.*

RICE WITH EGG, LEMON, AND CHEESE ALLA MARIA CIFELLI LIMONCELLI

■ ■ ■

3 TABLESPOONS BUTTER
3 CUPS COOKED LONG-GRAIN
 RICE (COOKED IN CHICKEN
 BROTH)

JUICE OF 1 LEMON
3 EGGS
½ CUP GRATED ASIAGO OR
 PARMESAN CHEESE

IN A SAUCEPAN, over medium heat, melt the butter; stir in the rice, fluffing it up with a fork and heating it through. Lower heat. In a bowl combine and beat together the lemon juice, eggs, and cheese. Blend the mixture thoroughly with the hot rice. Cook, stirring until the eggs have set. *Serves 6.*

PORK FRIED RICE

■ ■ ■

2 EGGS
4 TABLESPOONS SOY SAUCE
¼ TEASPOON GINGER
½ TEASPOON MONOSODIUM
GLUTAMATE
2 TABLESPOONS PEANUT OIL
1½ CUPS LEAN RAW PORK, CUT
INTO ½-INCH CUBES
2 GARLIC CLOVES, MINCED

5 WHOLE, SMALL SCALLIONS
(GREEN ONIONS), THINLY
SLICED DIAGONALLY (SEPA-
RATE WHITE AND GREEN
PARTS)
3 CUPS COOKED LONG-GRAIN
RICE (COOKED IN CHICKEN
BROTH)

COMBINE EGGS, SOY sauce, ginger, and monosodium glutamate in a bowl and beat. In a saucepan, over medium
heat, heat the oil and brown the pork evenly. Lower heat
and cook, stirring (stir-frying) until the pork is fork-tender.
Add the garlic and cook until soft. Add the white part of
the scallions and stir-fry 3 minutes; then the green part
and cook 2 minutes. They should be crisp-tender. Stir in
the cooked rice. When hot and well blended with the pork,
add the beaten egg mixture. Stir-fry until the eggs set.
Serves 6.

RICE CROQUETTES

■ ■ ■

2 CUPS COOKED MEDIUM-GRAIN
RICE (COOKED IN CHICKEN
BROTH)
2 TABLESPOONS HEAVY CREAM
2 SMALL (OR 1 JUMBO) EGGS,
BEATEN
1 TABLESPOON MINCED PARSLEY
3 TABLESPOONS MELTED
BUTTER

SALT AND PEPPER TO TASTE
½ CUP GRATED ASIAGO OR
PARMESAN CHEESE (OR
ANY SHARP CHEESE)
FLOUR
1 LARGE EGG, BEATEN
BREAD CRUMBS
FAT FOR DEEP FRYING

COMBINE AND BLEND well the rice, cream, eggs, parsley, butter, salt, pepper, and cheese. Form into cylinders 1 inch by 2 inches or form into patties. Lightly dredge with flour, dip into the egg, and dredge with bread crumbs. Refrigerate for 2 hours. Heat the fat to 390° (a small bread cube will brown in about half a minute). Lower a few of the croquettes into the hot fat. Do not crowd them. Cook 2 to 4 minutes, or until golden. Drain on paper towels and keep warm in a 250° oven while you are cooking the others. *Serves 6.*

RICE RING
■ ■ ■

3 TABLESPOONS BUTTER
1 SMALL WHITE ONION, FINELY
   CHOPPED
1½ CUPS MEDIUM-GRAIN RICE,
   WHITE OR BROWN

3 CUPS CHICKEN BROTH
SALT AND PEPPER TO TASTE
¼ CUP FINELY CHOPPED
   PARSLEY

IN A SAUCEPAN, over medium heat, melt the butter. Add the onion and cook until soft. Do not brown. Stir in the rice, cook 1 minute, coating the rice well with the butter. Add the broth and bring to a boil. Lower heat, cover tightly, and cook until the rice is tender and the broth has been absorbed (about 30 to 40 minutes). Stir in the parsley. Season with salt and pepper. Press firmly into a well-buttered ring mold. Place in a pan of hot water and bake in a preheated 350° oven for 20 minutes. Run a knife around the edge of the ring and carefully turn out onto a hot serving dish. If desired, chopped raisins, slivered, toasted almonds, grated cheese, or curry can be added to the rice before it is baked. Fill the ring with creamed mushrooms, curried shrimp or lobster, creamed chicken, or chicken livers to which a little sherry wine has been added. *Serves 4 to 6.*

GREEN RISOTTO
■ ■ ■

1 MEDIUM-SIZED ONION,
MINCED
2 TABLESPOONS BUTTER
3 CUPS SLIGHTLY UNDER-
COOKED, LONG-GRAIN RICE
(COOKED IN CHICKEN
BROTH AND QUITE FIRM),
WELL DRAINED
1 CUP FINELY CHOPPED
PARSLEY
1 CUP FINELY CHOPPED FRESH
SPINACH

4 BASIL LEAVES, FINELY
CHOPPED
1 CUP COARSELY GRATED
FONTINA OR GRUYÈRE
CHEESE
½ CUP GRATED ASIAGO OR
PARMESAN CHEESE
SALT AND PEPPER TO TASTE
3 EGGS
1 CUP MILK

COOK THE ONION in a large frypan, over medium heat, in the butter until soft. Do not brown. Stir in the rice, parsley, spinach, basil, cheeses, salt, and pepper. Remove from the heat and blend well. Beat together eggs and milk. Combine the rice mixture with the egg–milk mixture, blending well. Spoon into a well-buttered baking dish, set in a pan of hot water, and bake in a 350° oven for 30 minutes, or until set. *Serves 6.*

RISOTTO MILANESE
■ ■ ■

5 TABLESPOONS BUTTER
1 LARGE ONION, FINELY
  CHOPPED
1 GARLIC CLOVE, MINCED
2 CUPS LONG-GRAIN RICE
4 CUPS CHICKEN BROTH
  (CANNED OR HOMEMADE)

SALT AND PEPPER TO TASTE
¼ TEASPOON POWDERED
  SAFFRON
1 CUP GRATED ASIAGO OR
  PARMESAN CHEESE

IN A HEAVY-bottomed saucepan, over medium heat, melt the butter. Add the onion and garlic and cook until soft. Do not brown. Add the rice, stir until well coated with butter. Pour in the broth, add the salt, pepper, and saffron. Bring to a boil, cover, turn the heat to low, and cook about 20 minutes, or until the rice is tender (not too soft) and broth has been absorbed. If necessary, add more hot broth in small amounts. Stir in the cheese, taste for seasoning. *Serves 6 to 8.*

CORNMEAL CAKES

■ ■ ■

1 RECIPE OF POLENTA (SEE P. 185)
½ CUP GRATED ASIAGO OR PARMESAN CHEESE
TWELVE 1-INCH CUBES FONTINA CHEESE
FLOUR

2 EGGS, BEATEN
FINE FRESH BREAD CRUMBS
VEGETABLE OIL FOR DEEP FRYING

ADD THE GRATED cheese to the polenta while it is still very warm and stir until the cheese has melted. Spoon the mixture onto a wet board or plate in 12 equal portions. As they cool, push a cube of the Fontina cheese into the center of each. Mold the polenta into an oval shape, being sure that the cheese is well encapsulated. Lightly dredge each portion with flour. Dip in the beaten eggs, then dredge with the bread crumbs. Refrigerate for two hours. Fry in deep oil until golden. Drain on paper towels and serve as soon as possible just as they are, or with a spoonful of tomato sauce (homemade or commercial) over each. *Serves 4 to 6.*

BURGUNDIAN GAUDES

■■■

The French also have a unique way with cornmeal.

2 CUPS MILK
1 CUP WATER
1 TEASPOON SALT
1½ CUPS FINE CORNMEAL
1 EGG, BEATEN
½ CUP GRATED GRUYÈRE OR
  PARMESAN CHEESE

1 CUP HEAVY CREAM
2 OUNCES DRY WHITE WINE
¼ CUP FINE FRESH BREAD
  CRUMBS
2 TABLESPOONS MELTED
  BUTTER

HEAT THE MILK, water, and salt to a boil. Slowly stir in the cornmeal, stirring constantly. Transfer to a double boiler. Cook, covered, for 1 hour, stirring frequently to prevent lumping. If mixture becomes too thick before end of cooking time, add small amounts of hot water, but at end of cooking time the cornmeal should be so thick that your wooden spoon will stand in it. Quickly stir in the egg. Spread the mixture in a shallow, buttered baking dish. It should be 1½ inches thick. Let cool until set. Combine and blend cheese, cream, and wine and pour over cornmeal. Sprinkle with the bread crumbs and dribble with the melted butter. Place in a preheated 400° oven for 20 minutes, or until the top is golden. This is a good accompaniment for any meat dish with a dark sauce. *Serves 6.*

GRITS SOUFFLÉ

■ ■ ■

2 CUPS MILK
2 CUPS WATER
1 CUP GRITS
1 TEASPOON SALT
2 TABLESPOONS MINCED ONION
1 STICK (¼ POUND) BUTTER

1½ CUPS GRATED CHEDDAR
   CHEESE
3 EGG YOLKS
¾ CUP MILK
3 EGG WHITES, STIFFLY BEATEN

IN A SAUCEPAN, bring the milk and water to a boil. Stir in the grits, salt, and onions. Lower heat and simmer, stirring constantly, until mixture is very thick. Add the butter and cheese and stir until melted. Quickly beat egg yolks and milk together and stir in. Fold in the beaten egg whites and pour into a shallow, buttered baking dish. Bake in a preheated 350° oven for 1 hour, or until set. Good with any stew-type dish. *Serves 6.*

POLENTA
■ ■ ■

The Italians' versatile way with cornmeal.

1 QUART WATER
1½ TEASPOONS SALT
1 CUP YELLOW CORNMEAL

1 EGG, BEATEN
2 TABLESPOONS BUTTER

IN A HEAVY saucepan, heat the water and salt to a boil. With
the water still boiling, gradually add the cornmeal, stirring
constantly. Lower heat and, stirring constantly, cook until
the mixture is very thick (the consistency will be that of
mashed potatoes). Quickly stir in the butter and egg,
stirring until the butter has melted. Serve immediately
with a mushroom sauce, tomato sauce or gravy. Italians
like to serve this with stews, sausage, and game dishes. It
is also excellent served with a nugget of Gorgonzola or
blue cheese poked into the center of each serving, or with
Chicken Cacciatore with Red Wine and Tomato (see p.
98), spooning the tomato sauce over the polenta. It can
also be spread out onto a buttered, shallow baking dish or
a board and refrigerated until firm, then cut into any
shape and fried in butter and oil and served with cheese
and/or a sauce on top. *Serves 4.*

VIRGINIA SPOONBREAD

■■■

2 EGGS, BEATEN IN A LARGE
   BOWL UNTIL LIGHT
1 CUP BUTTERMILK
1 CUP MILK
½ CUP WHITE CORNMEAL
2 TEASPOONS BAKING POWDER

½ TEASPOON BAKING SODA
½ TEASPOON SALT
2 TABLESPOONS MELTED
   BUTTER, OR BACON
   DRIPPINGS

ADD ALL INGREDIENTS to the beaten eggs and stir until well blended. Pour into a shallow, buttered baking dish and bake in a preheated 375° oven about 30 minutes, or until set and custardy. Serve immediately. *Serves 4 to 6.*

Chapter 8

VEGETABLES

Vegetables not only have a way of balancing our meals and our diets, they have a way of surprising as well.

For example, how many of us know that we in the United States eat four times as many potatoes as any other vegetable, that it appears on our menus more often than any other food?

It's also a fact that although we spend only 2 percent of our food dollar on potatoes, we receive from that small amount more than 25 percent of all our energy and nutrient requirements.

If our diet consisted of nothing but potatoes, we'd get all of the riboflavin (B_2), one and one-half times the iron, three to four times the thiamine (B_1) and niacin (B_3), and more than ten times the amount of vitamin C that the body requires. Yet, with all of these advantages, the potato contains only 1 percent fat. Ounce for ounce it has no more calories than an apple and has less calories than equal weights of avocados, pears, rice, or bran flakes.

What about the tomato, superstar of the vegetable world? How many know that it isn't a vegetable at all, but a fruit, actually a berry? That because of its large U.S. consumption (2.5 billion pounds of fresh tomatoes yearly) the tomato is rated number one in supplying "total" vitamins and minerals in our diets?

And what about the ugly duckling of the vegetable world, the turnip? How many realize that it is always a bargain in markets, available for pennies, and that when properly prepared (as in the Turnip Custard that follows) it can be among the most elegant of foods?

Vegetables were always treated with respect, almost reverence, by our forebears, many vegetables supplying the entire meal, and they cooked them in many unusual ways. They also had rules: Buy them as fresh as possible (or better still, raise them) and never overcook them.

Today it has become a fad among some dieters to eat nothing but vegetables. Fine. But we believe that vegetables complement and complete a meal that otherwise would lack luster and also nutrients.

Also, what a spark it is to discover a new way to serve vegetables that will surprise and please not only guests but ourselves.

We hope we have brought the American family a few surprises in this chapter, remembering, of course, that it was the very early American family that made most of these recipes possible.

CUBAN BLACK BEANS

■■■

1 POUND DRIED BLACK BEANS,
PICKED OVER, RINSED
THOROUGHLY, AND SOAKED
IN COLD WATER TO COVER
FOR 5 HOURS
1 GREEN PEPPER, WHITE RIBS
REMOVED, HALVED, AND
SEEDED
1 MEDIUM-SIZED ONION, STUCK
WITH 2 CLOVES
1 BAY LEAF

¼ TEASPOON DRIED OREGANO
5 TABLESPOONS OLIVE OIL
1 GREEN PEPPER, WHITE RIBS
REMOVED, SEEDED, AND
CHOPPED
1 MEDIUM-SIZED ONION,
CHOPPED
1 GARLIC CLOVE, MINCED
SALT TO TASTE
½ TEASPOON SUGAR
¼ CUP WINE VINEGAR

DRAIN THE BEANS and place them in a pot with the halved
green pepper, the onion with the cloves, bay leaf, oregano,
and 2 tablespoons of olive oil. Barely cover the beans with
cold water. Bring to a boil, lower heat, and simmer, uncovered, for 1 hour, or until the beans are soft and there is
very little liquid left in the pot. (Do not salt the beans
while they are cooking. If the liquid cooks off before the
beans are soft, add small amounts of *hot* water.) Remove
the pepper halves, the onion with the cloves, and the bay
leaf and discard. Mash a few spoonfuls of beans against
the side of the pot and then stir them with the other beans
to make a thick sauce. Sauté the chopped green pepper,
onion, and garlic in 3 tablespoons of olive oil until soft and
slightly golden (do not brown) and stir into the beans.
Dissolve the sugar in the vinegar, add to beans, and taste
for seasoning, adding more salt, if needed. Simmer, uncovered, for 10 minutes. The beans should not be soupy
but have a thick consistency. Serve with Cuban Pork Loin
Cooked in Milk (see p. 152). *Serves 6.*

STRING BEAN SAVORY
■■■

Often string beans are considered a rather "blah" offering. Not this one!

2 POUNDS SMALL, TENDER STRING BEANS, TRIMMED, COOKED IN A SMALL AMOUNT OF BOILING, SALTED WATER UNTIL TENDER-CRISP, THOROUGHLY DRAINED, AND CUT INTO 1-INCH PIECES
6 TABLESPOONS BUTTER
¼ POUND SMALL FRESH MUSHROOMS, CUT INTO ¼-INCH SLICES

3 TABLESPOONS FLOUR
2 CUPS LIGHT CREAM
2 OUNCES SHERRY
¾ CUP GRATED GRUYÈRE CHEESE
SALT AND PEPPER TO TASTE
3 TABLESPOONS BREAD CRUMBS

IN A FRYPAN, over medium heat, melt 2 tablespoons of butter and cook the mushrooms for 2 minutes. Remove with a slotted spoon and reserve. Add 2 tablespoons of butter to the frypan. When melted, stir in the flour and cook, stirring, into a smooth paste. Gradually add the cream and cook, blending into a smooth, medium-thick sauce. Stir in the sherry and add half the cheese, simmering until the cheese has melted. Season with salt and pepper. Butter a shallow baking dish and arrange the string beans and mushrooms in an even layer and mask with the sauce. Sprinkle with the remaining cheese and then with the bread crumbs. Dot with remaining butter. Cook in a preheated 350° oven for 20 minutes, or until the sauce is bubbling and the top is golden. *Serves 6 to 8.*

SOUFFLÉED BROCCOLI

■ ■ ■

2 BUNCHES (ABOUT 1½ POUNDS EACH) BROCCOLI
2 TABLESPOONS BUTTER
1 CUP SLICED WHITE ONIONS
2 TEASPOONS LEMON JUICE
½ TEASPOON SALT
1 CUP SHREDDED SHARP CHEDDAR CHEESE
1 LARGE EGG, LIGHTLY BEATEN

TRIM AND SEPARATE broccoli. Peel the stems. Cook in a small amount of boiling, salted water for 10 minutes, or until crisp-tender. In a frypan, melt the butter over medium heat and cook the onions until soft. Cut the broccoli into chunks and purée with onions in a food processor or blender. Transfer to a bowl and blend in the lemon juice, salt, and ¾ of the cheese. Fold in the egg. Spoon into a buttered, shallow baking dish. Sprinkle the remaining cheese on top. Bake in the center rack position of a preheated 350° oven for 20 minutes, or until puffed and golden. *Serves 6 to 8.*

DANISH RED CABBAGE
(Roedkaal)

■ ■ ■

ONE FIRM HEAD (ABOUT 3
    POUNDS) RED CABBAGE
2 TABLESPOONS BUTTER
1 MEDIUM-SIZED ONION,
    MINCED
1 MEDIUM-SIZED APPLE,
    PEELED, CORED, AND
    MINCED

2 TABLESPOONS SUGAR
¼ CUP CIDER VINEGAR
½ TEASPOON CARAWAY SEED
SALT AND PEPPER TO TASTE
2 TABLESPOONS CURRANT
    JELLY

WASH THE CABBAGE and remove the tougher outside leaves; quarter (cut out and discard the core) and shred. In a large pot, over medium heat, melt the butter and cook the onion until soft. Add the cabbage, apple, sugar, vinegar, caraway seed, salt, and pepper. Blend well. Cover, bring to a boil, then lower heat and simmer, cooking for 30 minutes, or until the cabbage is tender. Stir occasionally, adding small amounts of hot water, if necessary. It should be moist, but not soupy. If too much moisture, remove cover, raise heat, and cook off the excess, watching carefully so the cabbage does not scorch. Stir in the currant jelly and simmer for 10 minutes. We like this with roast pork. *Serves 6.*

CORN CREOLE

■ ■ ■

3 TABLESPOONS BUTTER
¼ CUP FINELY CHOPPED GREEN
  PEPPER
1 SMALL WHITE ONION (OR 3
  SCALLIONS, WHITE PART
  ONLY), CHOPPED
1 LARGE, RIPE TOMATO,
  PEELED, SEEDED, CHOPPED,
  AND DRAINED

6 EARS CORN, COOKED IN
  BOILING WATER, KERNELS
  CUT OFF THE COB
SALT AND PEPPER TO TASTE
½ CUP GRATED CHEDDAR
  CHEESE

IN A SAUCEPAN, over medium heat, heat half of the butter.
Add the green pepper and onion and cook until soft. Do
not brown. Add the tomato and cook 5 minutes. Add the
corn and cook 3 minutes, or until thoroughly heated.
Season with salt and pepper. Stir in the remaining butter
and cheese until melted and serve. *Serves 4 to 6.*

CORN FRITTERS
■■■

2 EGGS
¼ CUP MILK
1 CUP SIFTED, ALL-PURPOSE
   FLOUR
1 TEASPOON SALT
2 TEASPOONS SUGAR

1 TEASPOON BAKING POWDER
1 TABLESPOON MELTED BUTTER
2 CUPS FRESH OR FROZEN
   CORN KERNELS, COOKED,
   CHOPPED, AND DRAINED
FAT FOR DEEP FRYING

BEAT EGGS WELL with milk. In a large bowl, sift together flour, salt, sugar, and baking powder. Stir the egg–milk mixture into the bowl with the dry ingredients. Add and blend in the butter and corn. Drop the batter by tablespoonfuls into the hot fat, kept hot on medium heat. (The fat is hot enough when a small bread cube dropped in browns almost instantly.) Do not cook too many at one time; they expand somewhat and might stick together. Cook until lightly browned. Drain well on paper towels. Serve just as they are or with a mushroom sauce or with maple syrup. *Serves 6.*

CREAMY CORN PUDDING

■ ■ ■

1 EGG
1 TABLESPOON SUGAR
SALT AND PEPPER TO TASTE
1 HEAPING TABLESPOON
    CORNSTARCH

ONE 16-OUNCE CAN CREAM-
    STYLE CORN
1 CUP MILK

IN A BOWL large enough to hold all ingredients, beat together the egg, sugar, salt, pepper, and cornstarch. Add
and blend well the corn and milk. Pour into a deep,
buttered baking dish. Bake in a preheated 350° oven for
1 hour, or until set (a knife blade inserted just off center
will come out clean). *Serves 4 to 6.*

ITALIAN EGGPLANT
■ ■ ■

*This is an extremely popular "American" dish, cooked in all
sections of the country.*

3 EGGPLANTS (ABOUT 3-BY-
    5-INCHES), CUT LENGTHWISE
    INTO ½-INCH-THICK SLICES
SALT
FLOUR
PEPPER TO TASTE
ABOUT 1 CUP OLIVE OIL

2½ CUPS TOMATO SAUCE
    (HOMEMADE OR
    COMMERCIAL)
1 CUP GRATED ROMANO OR
    OTHER GRATING CHEESE
½ POUND MOZZARELLA
    CHEESE, THINLY SLICED

LIGHTLY SALT THE slices of eggplant and arrange them in
two even stacks on several layers of paper towels. (to
absorb moisture). Set a plate on top and place a weight on
the plate (a brick, flat iron, or heavy pot will do the job).
Allow to set at least half an hour. Wipe off the slices with
paper towels. Dredge lightly with flour and season with
pepper. In a large frypan, heat ⅓ cup of the oil and cook the
eggplant slices, a few at a time, until golden on both sides,
adding more oil as needed. Drain on paper towels. Coat
the bottom of a glass, rectangular casserole lightly with
tomato sauce. Arrange layers of eggplant, covering with
sauce, grated cheese, and Mozzarella, repeating layers until
all ingredients have been used. The top should be covered
with sauce and sprinkled with grated cheese. Bake, uncovered, in a preheated 350° oven for 30 minutes, or until
bubbling and golden. *Serves 6.*

ONION SOUFFLÉ

■■■

4 LARGE WHITE ONIONS, SLICED
2 TABLESPOONS BUTTER
2 TABLESPOONS FLOUR
½ CUP MILK
½ CUP CREAM

SALT TO TASTE
½ TEASPOON SUGAR
½ TEASPOON PAPRIKA
3 EGG YOLKS, BEATEN
3 EGG WHITES, STIFFLY BEATEN

COOK THE ONIONS in boiling water to cover. When the onions begin to get tender, strain and cover with fresh hot water and continue to cook until very soft. Place in a strainer and drain well. Mince the onions. In a saucepan, over medium heat, melt the butter. Add the flour and stir into a smooth paste. Gradually add the milk and cream and cook, stirring into a thick sauce. Stir in the salt, sugar, paprika, and onions. Remove from the heat and quickly stir in the egg yolks. Fold in the egg whites. Pour into a buttered soufflé dish and bake in a preheated 350° oven for 30 minutes, or until set, puffed, and golden. *Serves 4.*

STUFFED PEPPERS

■ ■ ■

6 LARGE FRESH GREEN   BREAD CRUMBS
    PEPPERS   OLIVE OIL
STUFFING FOR ITALIAN STUFFED
    ZUCCHINI (OMITTING THE
    PULP OF THE ZUCCHINI) (SEE
    P. 211)

CUT A SLICE from the top of the peppers. Remove the seeds, core, and white ribs. Parboil in boiling water for 5 minutes. Drain and cool. Lightly salt the insides. Fill with the stuffing. Set in a baking dish just large enough to hold the peppers snugly. Pour in half an inch of water. Sprinkle the top of the peppers with bread crumbs, then olive oil, and bake in a preheated 400° oven for 30 minutes, or until the peppers are tender and the top golden brown. As with the Italian Stuffed Zucchini, you can cook and serve the stuffed peppers with the tomato sauce or not, according to your taste. If cooking with the tomato sauce, do not use the bread crumbs or olive oil. *Serves 6.*

POLISH POTATO DUMPLINGS
■■■

3 MEDIUM-SIZED IDAHO
   POTATOES, PEELED,
   COOKED IN BOILING, SALTED
   WATER UNTIL TENDER,
   DRAINED, DRIED OVER HEAT,
   AND PUT THROUGH A
   POTATO RICER

1 EGG, BEATEN
⅓ CUP FLOUR
2 TABLESPOONS FINE, DRY
   BREAD CRUMBS
½ TEASPOON SALT
¼ TEASPOON PEPPER
1 TABLESPOON MINCED PARSLEY

IN A LARGE bowl, beat the potatoes and egg together. Then beat in the flour, bread crumbs, salt, pepper, and parsley. With lightly floured hands, shape into 1-inch balls. Drop dumplings atop a stew, such as Polish Party Stew (see p. 157), cover, and simmer for 10 to 15 minutes. *Serves 4.*

GERMAN POTATO PANCAKES

■ ■ ■

1½ CUPS GRATED RAW POTATOES	1 TABLESPOON GRATED ONION
2 EGGS, BEATEN	1 TEASPOON SALT
1 TABLESPOON FLOUR	3 TABLESPOONS BUTTER
	1 TABLESPOON OLIVE OIL

PLACE THE GRATED potatoes in a dish towel and squeeze moisture out. Place in a bowl and stir in the eggs, flour, onion, and salt, blending well. Shape into ¼-inch-thick, 3-inch cakes. In a frypan, over medium heat, heat the butter and oil and brown the potato cakes on both sides, until crisp. Add more butter and oil, if needed. We love these with George Herz's German Pot Roast (see p. 132). *Serves 4.*

JOHN PETROKAITIS'S KUGELI

■ ■ ■

This is a unique potato cake created by Lithuanians and served in many of their homes in the United States.

6 MEDIUM-SIZED IDAHO
    POTATOES
3 EGGS, BEATEN
½ POUND BACON, MINCED,
    SAUTÉED UNTIL CRISP,
    AND DRAINED ON PAPER
    TOWEL

1 MEDIUM-SIZED ONION,
    MINCED
ONE 5.33-OUNCE CAN EVAPO-
    RATED MILK
SALT AND PEPPER TO TASTE

PEEL AND GRATE the potatoes. Blend the eggs with the potatoes. Stir in the bacon, onion, and milk. Season with salt and pepper. Spoon into a casserole and bake, uncovered, in a preheated 350° oven for 40 minutes, or until golden brown. Test like a cake. If a toothpick or the thin blade of a knife emerges clean, the *kugeli* is done. *Serves 6.*

POTATOES PARMA

■■■

5 MEDIUM-SIZED POTATOES, COOKED IN SALTED WATER UNTIL TENDER
2 EGG YOLKS, BEATEN
7 TABLESPOONS BUTTER
SALT AND PEPPER TO TASTE
⅛ TEASPOON NUTMEG
2 TABLESPOONS MINCED CHIVES
5 TABLESPOONS GRATED ASIAGO OR PARMESAN CHEESE
FLOUR
2 EGGS, BEATEN IN A SHALLOW DISH
FINE FRESH BREAD CRUMBS
1 TABLESPOON OLIVE OIL

DRAIN THE POTATOES and dry them out over low heat. When thoroughly dried (be careful not to scorch them), put them through a potato ricer into a bowl. Add the egg yolks, 4 tablespoons of butter, salt, pepper, nutmeg, chives, and grated cheese and blend well. Cool. When cool enough to handle, form cylinders 3 inches long and 1 inch in diameter. Dredge the potato cylinders lightly with flour, dip into the beaten eggs, roll in the crumbs. Over medium heat, heat the remaining butter and the oil in a large frypan and evenly brown the potato cylinders, adding more butter, if necessary. *Serves 4 to 6.*

SWISS POTATOES ROESTI

■■■

6 MEDIUM-SIZED (ABOUT 2
  POUNDS) POTATOES

12 TABLESPOONS BUTTER
SALT AND PEPPER TO TASTE

COOK THE POTATOES in their skins in boiling water for 15 minutes. Cool, peel, and grate them on the medium blade of a hand grater or the appropriate blade of a food processor. They should be in very thin strips about ½ inch by 1 inch. Cook in 6 individual portions or in 1 large cake.

For individual portions, melt 2 tablespoons of butter in a small frypan. Add ⅙ of the potatoes to the pan, mix with the butter, and shape into a small cake, patting it down gently with a spatula. Sprinkle with salt and pepper. Brown on one side, shaking pan to prevent sticking, then turn to brown the other side. The potatoes should be crusty brown. Keep the cakes warm in a heated oven while you prepare the others.

To make 1 large cake, heat only 10 tablespoons of butter in a large frypan, over medium heat. Add all of the grated potatoes, mix with the butter and, with a spatula, gently press into a large flat cake. Sprinkle with salt and pepper. Brown the bottom, shaking pan back and forth to prevent sticking. Lay a plate (larger than the frypan) over the frypan. Hold tightly and invert the frypan so the potato cake falls out onto the plate, then slide it back into the frypan (brown side up) to brown the other side. If the cake breaks up a little, just pat it back into shape with the spatula. *Serves 4 to 6.*

SCALLOPED POTATOES
WITH THREE CHEESES

■ ■ ■

4 LARGE BAKING POTATOES,
   PEELED AND CUT INTO
   1/8-INCH SLICES
PINCH DRIED THYME
SALT AND PEPPER
2 TABLESPOONS BUTTER, AT
   ROOM TEMPERATURE
1/3 CUP CRUMBLED BLUE CHEESE,
   AT ROOM TEMPERATURE

1/3 CUP SMALL CUBES OF
   MONTEREY JACK CHEESE,
   AT ROOM TEMPERATURE
3/4 CUP MILK
3/4 CUP CREAM
1/4 CUP GRATED ASIAGO OR
   PARMESAN CHEESE
1/2 CUP ADDITIONAL HOT CREAM
   (OPTIONAL)

PLACE THE POTATO slices in a saucepan. Add the thyme and
cover with boiling water. Bring to a boil, cover, lower heat
and simmer 3 minutes. Do not overcook, or the potatoes
will break up. Drain thoroughly and carefully. Blend butter, blue cheese, and Monterey Jack into a paste, using a
fork, blender, or food processor. Butter a shallow dish
large enough to hold 2 layers of overlapping potato slices.
Arrange half of the potato slices, overlapping on the bottom. Sprinkle with salt and pepper and dot with butter–
cheese paste. Arrange the remaining potato slices on top,
overlapping. Heat together the milk and cream and pour
over the potatoes. Sprinkle with the grated cheese. Bake in
a preheated 350° oven for 1 hour, or until the top is
golden, the potatoes are tender, and the liquid has been
absorbed. If liquid cooks off before potatoes are tender,
pour over the additional cream and continue to bake until
the top is golden and liquid absorbed. If the top starts
getting too brown before potatoes are tender, cover loosely
with a sheet of aluminum. *Serves 6.*

SPANISH GARLIC POTATOES

■ ■ ■

2 TABLESPOONS OLIVE OIL
2 TABLESPOONS BUTTER
3 GARLIC CLOVES, MINCED
4 LARGE POTATOES, PEELED
  AND CUT INTO ¼-INCH
  SLICES
1 TABLESPOON CHOPPED
  CHIVES
½ TEASPOON SAVORY

1 CUP BABY LIMA BEANS, FRESH
  OR FROZEN, SLIGHTLY
  UNDERCOOKED
1 TEASPOON SALT
½ TEASPOON PEPPER
¾ CUP HOT CHICKEN BROTH
3 TABLESPOONS CHOPPED
  BROADLEAF PARSLEY

IN A LARGE, shallow, stove-top-to-oven casserole (Corning stove-toppers are good) that will hold all of the potatoes in a single overlapping layer, heat the oil and butter over medium heat. Add the garlic and cook one minute. Do not brown. Arrange the potatoes in one overlapping layer over the garlic, sprinkling with the chives and savory. Evenly distribute the lima beans over the potatoes, sprinkling with salt and pepper. Pour the broth around the edge of the vegetables. Cover tightly and cook in a preheated 350° oven for 40 minutes, or until the potatoes and limas are tender and the broth has been absorbed. Sprinkle with the parsley before serving. *Serves 4 to 6.*

RATATOUILLE

■■■

⅓ CUP OLIVE OIL

2 MEDIUM-SIZED WHITE ONIONS, THINLY SLICED

2 GARLIC CLOVES, MINCED

2 SMALL SWEET RED PEPPERS, CORED, SEEDED, WHITE RIBS REMOVED, AND CUT INTO THIN STRIPS

1 SMALL GREEN PEPPER, CORED, SEEDED, WHITE RIBS REMOVED, AND CUT INTO THIN STRIPS

2 MEDIUM-SIZED EGGPLANTS, CUT INTO STRIPS ¼ INCH THICK AND ½ INCH WIDE

2 MEDIUM-SIZED ZUCCHINI, CUT INTO STRIPS ¼ INCH THICK AND ½ INCH WIDE

1 TABLESPOON FLOUR

4 LARGE, RIPE, FIRM TOMATOES, PEELED, SEEDED, AND CHOPPED

SALT AND PEPPER TO TASTE

½ TEASPOON CORIANDER SEEDS, CRUSHED

4 FRESH BASIL LEAVES, CHOPPED

2 TABLESPOONS CHOPPED PARSLEY

IN A LARGE saucepan, over medium heat, heat the oil and cook the onions and garlic until soft. Do not brown. Add the peppers and cook 5 minutes. Sprinkle the eggplant and zucchini with the flour. Add them to the pan along with the tomatoes, salt, pepper, and coriander seeds. Cover tightly and simmer 45 minutes, or until the vegetables are soft and mixture thickens. Taste for seasoning. If vegetables are very soft but there still seems to be too much liquid, remove the cover, raise the heat, and cook to thicken, being careful not to burn. Serve hot as a vegetable course or cold with lemon juice and olive oil as an hors d'oeuvre. Sprinkle basil and parsley on top. *Serves 6.*

NEW ENGLAND HUBBARD SQUASH

■ ■ ■

Here's a way to make the prosaic squash a prestigious prize winner.

2 TABLESPOONS BUTTER
2 TABLESPOONS FLOUR
1 CUP LIGHT CREAM
½ TEASPOON MACE
4 EGG YOLKS
1 TABLESPOON LIGHT BROWN
  SUGAR

2 TABLESPOONS DARK RUM
2 CUPS COOKED, MASHED
  HUBBARD SQUASH
4 EGG WHITES, STIFFLY BEATEN

IN A DEEP saucepan, over medium heat, melt the butter, stir in the flour, blending into a smooth paste. Gradually add the cream, stir in the mace, blending into a thickish, smooth sauce. Remove from the heat and cool. Beat in the egg yolks one at a time. Stir in the sugar and rum, then blend in the squash. Fold in the egg whites. Pour into a buttered 1-quart soufflé dish to which a wax collar has been attached. Cook in a preheated 350° oven for 35 minutes, or until lightly browned, puffed, and set. *Serves 6.*

BAKED CHERRY TOMATOES

■■■

1 QUART CHERRY TOMATOES
(AT LEAST 8 TOMATOES
FOR EACH PERSON)
½ CUP FINE, FRESH BREAD
CRUMBS

1 GARLIC CLOVE, MINCED
1 TABLESPOON OLIVE OIL
½ TEASPOON DRIED OREGANO
SALT AND PEPPER

CUT A VERY thin slice from the stem end of each tomato and invert them on a board or plate covered with paper towel to drain. Combine bread crumbs, garlic, oil, and oregano in a bowl and stir with a fork to blend well. Lightly coat the bottom of a shallow baking dish (in which the tomatoes will snugly fit in a single layer) with olive oil. Arrange the tomatoes, cut side up, in the dish. Sprinkle with salt and pepper, then with the bread crumb mixture. Cook in a preheated 400° oven for 10 minutes, or until top is golden. They should not be too well done, but still quite firm. *Serves 4 to 6.*

BULGUR WHEAT-STUFFED TOMATOES
■ ■ ■

6 LARGE, RIPE, FIRM TOMATOES
2 TABLESPOONS BUTTER
1 TABLESPOON OLIVE OIL
1 MEDIUM-SIZED ONION, FINELY CHOPPED
1 SMALL GARLIC CLOVE, MINCED
1 CUP BULGUR WHEAT
¼ TEASPOON DRIED OREGANO
½ TEASPOON POWDERED CUMIN
2 CUPS CHICKEN BROTH (HOMEMADE OR CANNED)

SALT AND PEPPER TO TASTE
3 TABLESPOONS CHOPPED PARSLEY
2 TABLESPOONS RAISINS, CHOPPED
6 STUFFED GREEN OLIVES, CHOPPED
6 TABLESPOONS GRATED ASIAGO, PARMESAN, OR OTHER GRATING CHEESE

Cut a slice from the stem end of the tomatoes and, leaving a rather thick shell, remove the center pulp, discarding the seeds and chopping the pulp. Set aside pulp. Lightly salt the inside of the tomatoes, inverting to drain. In a saucepan, over medium heat, heat the butter and oil. Add the onion and garlic and cook until soft. Do not brown. Add the bulgur wheat and cook 1 minute, stirring. Stir in the oregano, cumin, and broth and season with salt and pepper. Bring to a simmer, cover, lower heat, and simmer 15 minutes, or until the liquid has been absorbed. Stir in the tomato pulp, parsley, raisins, and olives. Taste for seasoning. Heap the wheat mixture into the tomato shells. Place on a small baking sheet or shallow baking dish, sprinkle with the cheese, and bake in a preheated 350° oven for 15 minutes, or until the cheese is golden. *Serves 6.*

DIANE HUNTER'S
AMERICAN TURNIP CUSTARD

■ ■ ■

2 CUPS COOKED, MASHED
  TURNIPS (ABOUT 1 POUND
  RAW)
2 EGGS, BEATEN
1 CUP HOT MILK

2 TABLESPOONS MELTED
  BUTTER
1 TEASPOON GRATED ONION
¼ TEASPOON MACE
SALT AND PEPPER TO TASTE

SLIGHTLY COOL THE turnips. Stir in all other ingredients, blending well. Pour into a shallow 1-quart baking dish. Set this in another dish of boiling water, with the water coming halfway up the dish. Bake on the center rack in a preheated 325° oven for 45 minutes, or until set. A knife blade inserted just off center will come out clean. *Serves 4.*

ITALIAN STUFFED ZUCCHINI

■ ■ ■

6 ZUCCHINI, ABOUT 3 BY 5
   INCHES
4 TABLESPOONS OLIVE OIL
1 LARGE ONION, CHOPPED
1 GARLIC CLOVE, MINCED
SALT AND PEPPER TO TASTE
1 POUND GROUND LEAN LAMB
   OR BEEF
1½ CUPS COOKED RICE (*AL
   DENTE*, SLIGHTLY CHEWY)
½ CUP PINE NUTS OR CHOPPED
   WALNUTS

1 EGG, BEATEN
5 FRESH MINT LEAVES,
   CHOPPED
½ TEASPOON GROUND CUMIN
½ TEASPOON DRIED THYME
½ CUP GRATED ASIAGO,
   PARMESAN, OR OTHER
   GRATING CHEESE
ONE 1-POUND, 12-OUNCE CAN
   TOMATOES
½ CAN BEEF BROTH (CANNED IS
   GOOD)

CUT THE SQUASH lengthwise and scoop out the pulp (reserve it), leaving a ¼- to ½-inch-thick shell. Lightly salt the shells and invert to drain. Chop half of the pulp (discard the remainder). In a frypan, over medium heat, heat half the oil. Add half the onion and garlic and cook until soft. Do not brown. Sprinkle with salt and pepper. Add the pulp and cook 1 minute. Add the lamb (or beef). Cook, breaking up the meat with a fork until it loses its pink color. Add the rice, nuts, egg, mint, cumin, thyme, cheese, and one tomato from the can, chopped. Blend, taste for seasoning, and dividing equally, mound the stuffing in the zucchini shells. Arrange the filled squash in a shallow baking dish just large enough to hold them snugly. In the frypan, cook the remaining onion and garlic in the remaining oil. Add the tomatoes that you have broken up (your hands are good for this) and the beef broth and cook 15 minutes, or until the sauce slightly thickens. Spoon the tomato sauce over the stuffed zucchini and around them. Cover with the baking dish top or aluminum foil and bake in a preheated 375° oven for 30 minutes, or until the squash shell can be pierced easily with a fork. Serve with the tomato sauce spooned on top. *Serves 6.*

Chapter 9

DESSERTS

The American family's favorite dessert is also one of the world's oldest: ice cream. About 98.8 percent of us consume 4.1 billion pounds a year, just under one hundred scoops for every man, woman, and child in the United States, which comes out to 42.83 pints per person annually. Favorites: vanilla, chocolate, Neapolitan (a combination of vanilla, chocolate, and strawberry), chocolate chip, strawberry, fudge swirl, butter pecan, cherry, butter almond, and French vanilla.

Who are the biggest ice cream freaks? Consumption is highest among children two to seventeen and adults forty-five and older. And ice cream fans, relax: Research has proven that the higher the education level, the more ice cream is eaten. In other words, we who eat ice cream are smart, probably much smarter than those who don't. Why? It's good for us, much better than gooey, rich cakes and pies, loaded with sugar and calories.

Of course, moderation is the key. Don't eat a quart, or even a pint, even though it's one of the best of all sources for calcium and also supplies much needed protein. What other dessert can make that claim? Calories? Half a cup contains fewer than half the calories of a slice of apple pie or frosted yellow cake and about 60 percent fewer calories than a cup of low-fat, fruit-flavored yogurt. A serving of our favorite, vanilla, averages 140 calories, compared with 150 for a cup of whole milk, and 160 calories for a half-cup of frozen yogurt.

This is not meant to turn the reader off other desserts. They bring a dramatic and glorious ending to any dinner and deserve top billing in every host's or hostess's accomplishments. And, since strawberries are another American favorite, we offer several versions.

Dedicated dessert lovers, in this country we do many original and unique things with ordinary ingredients like pumpkins, apples, peaches, blueberries, even cream cheese. For many of us, no dinner is complete without a dessert, and even though we are today thinking more about weight and calories, on those special occasions when we entertain we all like to serve a tempting offering to climax the evening and exhibit our culinary ability.

But ice cream is America's first choice. We didn't invent it, but we "discovered" and perfected it, along the way eating more of it than any people on earth.

As with many of our favorite foods, ice cream came from Italy. It began in a primitive form in A.D. 62, when Roman Emperor Nero sent slave runners to the Apennines Mountains to rush back with snow and ice, which were flavored with honey and crushed fruit.

In the thirteenth century Marco Polo brought back to Italy from Asia recipes for water ices, believed to have been enjoyed in Asia for centuries. "Italian" ices became the rage in Venice and soon throughout Italy. Even today, Italy is famous for its ices.

When Catherine de Medici left Florence to marry Henry II of France, she brought with her secret recipes for Italian sherbet, thus introducing the French to what they later claimed were their own *sorbets.*

Italy kept its fine hand in the introduction of ice cream. In 1660, when the Cafe Procopia was founded in Paris by Italian Francisco Procopia, its most popular desserts were ices and ice cream.

In the mid-eighteenth century, our most famous president, George Washington, purchased a "cream machine for ice" and spent $200 a year indulging himself, but it was Thomas Jefferson who wrote the first recipe for ice cream in America (having enjoyed it in Italy), and Dolly Madison who created a trend in 1812, when she served ice cream in the White House.

But ice cream didn't even begin to take off until 1846, when Nancy Johnson invented the first hand-cranked freezer. Ice cream became available to the public in 1851, when Jacob Fussell established the first commercial ice cream plant in Baltimore. Its most popular form, the ice cream cone, appeared in 1904 at the St. Louis World's Fair.

The Italian hand is still strong in the world of ice cream. Bruno Valbona, an ingenious executive with Waring, perfected the electric Waring Ice Cream Parlor for the home, which produces two quarts of ice cream in thirty minutes. Ordinary ice cubes are packed around the cream can, which is filled with the chilled mix. Ice cubes are then sprinkled lightly with table salt, a cup of cold water is poured over them, and then the Ice Cream Parlor goes to work. Result: superb homemade ice cream.

And it is the Italians, with their IL Gelataio, the most remarkable ice cream machine ever made, who have given Americans new impetus to make ice cream at home, absolutely without effort. Seeing the ingenious machine at work, we couldn't resist obtaining one. A product of the Simac Appliances Corporation (14 East Sixtieth Street, New York, N.Y. 10022), the Italian-made, compact IL Gelataio fits on any counter top and, in reality, is a small, super-effective freezer with just two switches and a minute timer. Press "Chill," turn the timer to five minutes, then pour the chilled ice cream mix into the stainless steel bowl, cover it with its plastic cover, press the "Churn" switch, set the timer for 20 minutes, and without further effort from you, the paddle churns the mixture into the smoothest, most delicious ice cream we have ever tasted. For ice cream lovers, it's the most impressive invention to come out of any country. After we finish dinner we routinely invite guests to the kitchen to watch us make ice cream and receive their portion. It's a dramatic experience.

With a half-dozen other good machines on the market, and with the American family increasingly making ice cream at home, it is appropriate to lead this chapter with several recipes that are favorites of ours and that do well in the ice cream machines designed for home use.

Homemade ice cream will be a revelation to those who have never tasted it. When you make it yourself you know what's going into it. Commercial ice cream (most of which doesn't have cream or anything resembling it, except inexpensive dried skim milk and chemical flavorings and stabilizers) is cheaply made, with much air whipped into it to increase its bulk and make it economical to sell at reasonable prices. Its butterfat content is also very low.

When you make your own you can use pure heavy cream, fresh fruits, and natural flavorings. There really is no comparison; once you've made your own you'll never buy commercial ice cream again. Ice cream machines for the home are sensible and rewarding investments.

Our first ice cream choice is vanilla, as so much can be done with it, combining it with various fruits and flavorings to produce a quick and unusual dessert. Our favorite is a very simple one: a homemade chocolate sauce dolloped on freshly made vanilla, topped with redskin peanuts. So fast and delicious and with various taste textures: the rich cream, the smooth chocolate, and the salty peanuts.

But it's fun to create different kinds of ice cream, so we offer a few here that may encourage and inspire you to get creative with the most cooperative of all desserts.

In working with the following recipes, refer to the instructions that came with your ice cream machine for amounts, methods, and so on. Some make a quart, some two quarts, so the machine's capacity will dictate amounts used.

We find it effective to blend the ice cream mixture in a pitcher (large enough to hold all ingredients), then immediately refrigerate it before placing it in the "cream can." The pitcher makes it easier to pour the mixture into the cream can without spilling, and the prior chilling speeds up finishing the ice cream.

PLAIN VANILLA ICE CREAM
■■■

2 CUPS HEAVY CREAM
2 CUPS LIGHT CREAM
1 CUP SUPERFINE SUGAR

2 TEASPOONS PURE VANILLA
    EXTRACT
2 EGG WHITES, BEATEN TO A
    FROTH (NOT STIFF)

PLACE ALL INGREDIENTS into a large pitcher, stirring well, until sugar is dissolved. Refrigerate. Then pour mixture into the container of the ice cream freezer and proceed according to the manufacturer's directions. *Serves 6 to 8.*

FRENCH VANILLA ICE CREAM
■ ■ ■

This is a famous, creamy, rich vanilla, made so by the addition of egg yolks.

4 EGG YOLKS
1 CUP SUPERFINE SUGAR
2 CUPS HEAVY CREAM

2 CUPS LIGHT CREAM
2 TEASPOONS PURE VANILLA
   EXTRACT

IN A HEAVY pot, combine egg yolks and sugar, beating with a whisk until lemony in color and well blended. In another pot pour the cream and, over medium heat, bring just to the boil. Remove from heat. Add half a cup of the cream to the beaten egg yolk pot, beating rapidly. Add the rest of the cream, still beating rapidly and blending well. Heat the egg yolk–cream mixture almost to the boil. *Do not boil* or it will curdle. Pour into a cold pitcher, blend in the vanilla extract, and refrigerate to chill thoroughly. Before churning, stir well again, then pour into the container of the ice cream freezer and proceed according to the manufacturer's directions. *Serves 6 to 8.*

CHOCOLATE ICE CREAM
■■■

4 OUNCES UNSWEETENED
   CHOCOLATE
4 OUNCES SEMISWEET
   CHOCOLATE

FRENCH VANILLA ICE CREAM
(SEE P. 217)

IN A SAUCEPAN, over low heat, place the chocolates. Set the saucepan in another pan of boiling water, stirring the chocolate until soft and smooth. (Or, if you have a microwave oven, simply melt the chocolate in a glass measuring cup.) Prepare the mixture for French Vanilla Ice Cream, adding the smooth, melted chocolate. Blend well, chill, then proceed according to manufacturer's directions. *Serves 6 to 8.*

STRAWBERRY ICE CREAM
■ ■ ■

FRENCH VANILLA ICE CREAM
  (SEE P. 217)
2 TEASPOONS WILD STRAW-
  BERRY LIQUEUR

1 PINT FRESH STRAWBERRIES,
  HULLED, WASHED, DRAINED,
  AND PURÉED IN A FOOD
  PROCESSOR

MAKE THE FRENCH Vanilla Ice Cream mixture, substituting 2 teaspoons of wild strawberry liqueur for the vanilla extract. Blend the strawberries into the mixture, chill, and proceed according to manufacturer's directions. *Serves 6 to 8.*

MAPLE WALNUT ICE CREAM

■ ■ ■

PLAIN VANILLA ICE CREAM
  (SEE P. 216)
2 TEASPOONS MAPLE SYRUP
  EXTRACT

1 CUP COARSELY CHOPPED
  WALNUTS

PREPARE THE PLAIN Vanilla Ice Cream mixture, substituting
2 teaspoons of maple syrup extract for the vanilla extract.
Blend in walnuts, chill, and proceed according to manufacturer's directions. *Serves 6 to 8.*

ICE CREAM POUROVERS
■■■

ICE CREAM IS one of those delicious and unusual desserts that take other flavors and enhance them. The combinations are almost without limit. It's simple. To a generous serving of vanilla ice cream, pour over a liqueur, creme de cacao, Tia Maria, Vandermint, cherry herring, creme de menthe, Tuaca. Or try a little rum on orange ice or cassis on raspberry sherbet. It's surprising what a unique liqueur and ice cream or sherbet do for one another!

QUICK APRICOT PARFAIT

■■■

1 LARGE DIP VANILLA ICE CREAM
2 TABLESPOONS APRICOT JAM, MELTED

3 TABLESPOONS WHIPPED CREAM

PLACE ICE CREAM in a parfait or wine glass. Drench with the melted jam. Top with whipped cream. *Serves 1.*

FAST PEACH MELBA

■ ■ ■

1 THICK SLICE SPONGE CAKE
1 LARGE DIP PEACH ICE CREAM
2 TABLESPOONS RASPBERRY
   PRESERVES, MELTED

3 TABLESPOONS WHIPPED
   CREAM
1 TABLESPOON TOASTED
   SLIVERED ALMONDS

PLACE THE SLICE of cake on a dessert dish. Top with the ice cream. Drench with the raspberry sauce. Top with whipped cream and almonds. *Serves 1.*

MELON SORBET

■■■

Here's a palate-pleasing surprise that will surprise guests and give you a new three-star rating as a host or hostess.

1 CUP SUPERFINE SUGAR
1 CUP WATER
1 VERY RIPE MEDIUM-SIZED
  CANTELOUPE, SEEDED,
  FLESH TAKEN FROM RIND,
  CUT INTO PIECES, AND
  PURÉED IN A FOOD
  PROCESSOR

½ CUP FRESHLY SQUEEZED
  LEMON JUICE

IN A SAUCEPAN, combine the sugar and water, and bring to the boil over medium heat, stirring. Immediately reduce heat to low and simmer, stirring, until the sugar has dissolved. Remove from heat, cool, and place in a cold bowl. Add lemon juice to melon, blend into the syrup, and refrigerate for 3 hours. Pour into the container of the ice cream machine and proceed according to manufacturer's directions. *Serves 6.*

FRESH PEACH ICE CREAM
■ ■ ■

PLAIN VANILLA ICE CREAM (SEE   4 VERY RIPE PEACHES, PEELED,
  P. 216)   PITTED, AND PURÉED IN A
3 TEASPOONS PEACH CORDIAL   FOOD PROCESSOR

MAKE THE PLAIN Vanilla Ice Cream mixture, substituting 3
teaspoons of peach cordial for the vanilla extract. Blend
the peaches into the Plain Vanilla mixture, chill, and
proceed according to manufacturer's directions. *Serves 8.*

AMARETTO ICE CREAM CAKE

■ ■ ■

THREE 8-INCH SPONGE CAKE
   LAYERS
½ CUP AMARETTO LIQUEUR
1 PINT VANILLA ICE CREAM,
   SLIGHTLY SOFTENED
1 PINT CHOCOLATE ICE CREAM,
   SLIGHTLY SOFTENED

2 CUPS HEAVY CREAM, STIFFLY
   WHIPPED
½ CUP SHAVEN SEMISWEET
   CHOCOLATE, OR COMMER-
   CIAL CHOCOLATE SPRINKLES

SPRINKLE SPONGE CAKE layers with all but 2 tablespoons of the amaretto. Spread the vanilla ice cream on one layer, press another cake layer on top, and spread with the chocolate ice cream. Press the third cake layer on so the layers adhere to one another. Add the remaining 2 tablespoons of amaretto to the whipped cream and spread over the top and sides of the cake, completely covering it. Freeze until ready to serve. Just before serving, decorate with the chocolate shavings or sprinkles. *Serves 6 to 8.*

PECAN ICE CREAM PIE

■ ■ ■

Makes two 9-inch pies:

¼ POUND BUTTER, MELTED
1 CUP ALL-PURPOSE FLOUR
¼ CUP LIGHT BROWN SUGAR
1 CUP FINELY GROUND PECANS
2 QUARTS OF YOUR FAVORITE

ICE CREAM (WE FAVOR
VANILLA OR BUTTER PECAN),
SOFTENED JUST ENOUGH
TO SPREAD

IN A BOWL, combine and blend well the butter, flour, brown sugar, and half of the pecans. Divide mixture and pat onto the bottom and sides of two 9-inch glass pie plates, forming shells. Place shells in a preheated 350° oven for 10 minutes. Remove and cool. Divide the ice cream and smoothly spread onto the pie shells. Sprinkle with the remaining ground pecans and freeze until ready to serve.

DUTCH APPLE CAKE
■ ■ ■

2 CUPS SIFTED ALL-PURPOSE
  FLOUR
1 TABLESPOON BAKING POWDER
1 TEASPOON SALT
¼ CUP SUGAR
⅓ CUP BUTTER
2 EGGS
½ CUP MILK
½ TEASPOON VANILLA

4 TART APPLES, PEELED,
  CORED, QUARTERED, AND
  EACH QUARTER CUT INTO 3
  SLICES
½ TEASPOON CINNAMON
¼ CUP SUGAR
2 TABLESPOONS MELTED
  BUTTER

SIFT TOGETHER FLOUR, baking powder, salt, and sugar into a large bowl. Cut the butter into the flour mixture with a pastry blender, or use your fingers. Beat together eggs milk and vanilla lightly and stir in with a fork. Spread the batter evenly in a buttered 9-by-9-by-2-inch baking dish. Arrange the apple slices on top of the batter, distributing evenly and overlapping if necessary. Blend cinnamon and sugar and sprinkle over the apples. Dribble on the melted butter. Bake in a preheated 400° oven for 30 minutes, or until the apples are soft and a toothpick inserted in the pastry comes out clean. *Serves 6 to 8.*

AMERICAN CHEESE CAKE

■■■

One of the most economically satisfying and customer-appreciated breakthroughs in the cheese industry was the U.S. invention of cream cheese, a creation that has so many uses that it is impossible to list them all. But paramount is the cheese cake. Just about everyone dotes on this coupling of American culinary ingenuity. Here's an American classic.

24 GRAHAM CRACKERS, CRUSHED
¾ CUP PLUS 3 TABLESPOONS SUGAR
¼ CUP BUTTER, MELTED
4 EGG YOLKS
FOUR 3-OUNCE PACKAGES PHILADELPHIA CREAM CHEESE, AT ROOM TEMPERATURE
2 TEASPOONS PURE VANILLA EXTRACT
1⅛ TEASPOONS ALMOND EXTRACT
4 EGG WHITES, STIFFLY BEATEN
1 PINT SOUR CREAM
SUGAR—CINAMON

BLEND CRUSHED GRAHAM crackers, ¼ cup of sugar and butter. Pack the mixture evenly against the bottom and sides of a 9-inch, straight-sided pie plate, forming a shell. Refrigerate while preparing the filling. In a large bowl, beat the egg yolks until light and lemony in color. Beat in ½ cup of the sugar. Add the cream cheese, one package at a time, beating well after each package is added. Blend in 1 teaspoon of vanilla extract and the ⅛ teaspoon almond extract. Beat the egg whites until stiff, flavoring with 1 teaspoon of vanilla extract, and fold in. Pour onto the graham cracker shell. Bake on center rack position in a preheated 325° oven for 20 minutes, or until set. Remove from oven and cool. Blend sour cream, 3 tablespoons of sugar, and 1 teaspoon of almond extract well. Spoon the mixture evenly over the cooled cheese cake. Dust lightly with sugar-cinnamon. Place on center rack position in a preheated 350° oven and cook for 10 minutes. Cool. Then refrigerate. Serve cool. *Serves 6 to 8.*

BANANAS AU RHUM FLAMBÉ
■ ■ ■

½ CUP BUTTER
½ CUP LIGHT BROWN SUGAR
4 MEDIUM-SIZED RIPE, FIRM
   BANANAS, CUT INTO HALVES
   LENGTHWISE

½ CUP DARK RUM, HOT
4 DIPS HARD VANILLA ICE
   CREAM

IN A FRYPAN, over low heat, heat the butter and sugar, stirring until the sugar has dissolved. Handling carefully, arrange the banana halves in one layer in the butter–sugar mixture and simmer 2 minutes on each side. Pour on the rum and ignite. When the flame dies, on individual serving dishes, lay a banana half on either side of a dip of the ice cream and spoon the butter–sugar sauce over ice cream and banana. *Serves 4.*

CRÈME BRÛLÉE

■ ■ ■

2 CUPS HEAVY CREAM
2 CUPS LIGHT CREAM
3 TABLESPOONS SUGAR
8 EGG YOLKS

2 TEASPOONS VANILLA EXTRACT
LIGHT BROWN SUGAR WITH NO
  LUMPS IN IT

HEAT THE CREAM in a double boiler until barely hot (if too hot, the eggs will curdle). Add the sugar and stir until dissolved. Beat the egg yolks until light and lemony in color. Add to the cream. Blend well. Strain into a shallow glass baking dish (the custard should be about 1½ inches thick). Place the dish in a pan of hot water with the water coming about halfway up the side of the baking dish and bake in a preheated 325° oven 45 minutes, or until set. A knife blade inserted just off center will come out clean. Do not overcook. Cool, then place in the refrigerator until thoroughly chilled. Preheat oven broiler. Cover the surface of the custard with a ¼-inch-thick, smooth layer of soft, lump-free brown sugar. Place dish under the broiler and watch constantly (the sugar must not burn) until the sugar has melted and forms a brown, smooth, almost shellac-like glaze. When entire surface is glazed, remove and cool. Then refrigerate to chill through. *Serves 6 to 8.*

DEEP-DISH BLUEBERRY PIE

■■■

As American as apple pie (especially if made with huckle-berries).

2 CUPS PLUS 3 TABLESPOONS ALL-PURPOSE FLOUR
½ TEASPOON SALT
⅔ CUP SHORTENING, HALF BUTTER, HALF VEGETABLE SHORTENING
ABOUT ⅓ CUP ICE WATER

2½ QUARTS BLUEBERRIES (OR HUCKLEBERRIES), WASHED AND DRAINED
⅔ CUP SUGAR
1 TABLESPOON LEMON JUICE
3 TABLESPOONS BUTTER
1 EGG

SIFT 2 CUPS OF flour and the salt into a bowl. Add the shortening and cut in with a pastry blender. Then, mixing with a fork, add just enough water to hold the pastry together. Do not overmix. Roll into a ball and refrigerate until ready to use. Lightly butter a deep-dish pie plate. In a bowl, carefully, but well, mix the berries, sugar, 3 table-spoons of flour, and the lemon juice. Spoon into the pie dish, building up the center so the berries can support the pastry. Dot with the butter. Roll out the pastry, slightly larger than the rim of the dish, moisten the edges, and cover the berries. Press the edge of the pastry against the rim of the pie dish and flute. Cut several slits in the top. Brush lightly with a mixture made of 1 egg beaten with 1 teaspoon of water. Bake in a preheated 450° oven for 10 minutes, then at 350° for 20 minutes, or until the pastry is golden brown. If the edge gets brown before the rest of the pastry, rim it with a 3-inch strip of aluminum foil. Serve with soft vanilla ice cream. *Serves 6.*

Note: This also can be made with a flaky biscuit dough topping.

FRESH FRUIT CUP

■ ■ ■

2 SWEET SEEDLESS NAVEL
   ORANGES
½ TEASPOON GRATED ORANGE
   RIND
1 PINT FRESH STRAWBERRIES,
   HULLED, WASHED, DRAINED,
   AND HALVED
1 PINT FRESH RASPBERRIES,
   WASHED AND DRAINED,
   OR ONE 10-OUNCE PACKAGE
   OF FROZEN, DRAINED

1 PINT BLUEBERRIES, WASHED
   AND DRAINED
½ CUP SUGAR
3 TABLESPOONS LIGHT RUM
½ CUP CURRANT JELLY
1 TABLESPOON BOILING WATER

WITH A SHARP knife, cut away the rind and white part of
the oranges and section them. In a large bowl, combine
the orange rind, orange sections, strawberries, raspberries,
blueberries, sugar, and rum, blending well. Combine the
currant jelly and boiling water in a Pyrex measuring cup;
set in a pan of simmering water, stirring until the jelly
dissolves. Pour the jelly over the fruits and chill until
ready to serve. *Serves 6.*

HUGUENOT TORTE

■■■

1½ CUPS SUGAR
3 TABLESPOONS FLOUR
2½ TEASPOONS BAKING POWDER
¼ TEASPOON SALT
2 EGGS
1 CUP CHOPPED TART APPLES
(PEEL AND CORE BEFORE
CHOPPING)

1 CUP CHOPPED WALNUTS
1 TEASPOON VANILLA EXTRACT
½ PINT HEAVY CREAM,
WHIPPED

SIFT TOGETHER SUGAR, flour, baking powder, and salt. In a large bowl, beat the eggs until light and lemony in color. Gradually add the dry ingredients, beating well after each addition. Mix in the apples, nuts, and vanilla. Pour into a generously buttered 9-inch spring mold. Bake in a preheated 300° oven for about 1 hour, or until the top is golden and crusty. Cool. Remove rim of spring mold and serve cake with a topping of whipped cream. *Serves 6.*

COLD LEMON SOUFFLÉ

■ ■ ■

1 TABLESPOON (1 ENVELOPE)
   UNFLAVORED GELATIN
¼ CUP COLD WATER
3 EGG YOLKS
1 CUP SUGAR
½ CUP LEMON JUICE
GRATED RIND OF 1 LEMON
   (NONE OF THE WHITE
   PART)

1 TEASPOON VANILLA EXTRACT
3 EGG WHITES, STIFFLY BEATEN
2 CUPS HEAVY CREAM, STIFFLY
   BEATEN

STIR THE GELATIN into the water. Beat the yolks until light and lemony in color. Add the sugar, small amounts at a time, and beat well after each addition. Beat in the lemon juice, rind, and vanilla. Dissolve the gelatin over hot water until it is transparent and liquid. Stir well into the egg yolk mixture. Place in the refrigerator until it just begins to set. Carefully and thoroughly fold the egg whites, then the cream into the egg yolk mixture. Spoon into individual soufflé dishes. Refrigerate. Before serving, grate bitter chocolate curls over the top of each or garnish with several perfect fresh raspberries. Or spoon into a large soufflé dish with a collar (depending on the size of the dish) and garnish with the chocolate or raspberries. This dessert also freezes well for a short period. *Serves 8.*

GEORGIA PEACH COBBLER
■■■

½ CUP PLUS 1 TABLESPOON
  SUGAR
1 TABLESPOON CORNSTARCH
  OR MINUTE TAPIOCA
4 CUPS SLICED FRESH PEACHES
1 TEASPOON LEMON JUICE
¾ CUP WATER

⅛ TEASPOON NUTMEG
1 CUP ALL-PURPOSE FLOUR
1½ TEASPOONS BAKING POWDER
½ TEASPOON SALT
3 TABLESPOONS BUTTER
½ CUP MILK

BLEND ½ CUP OF the sugar and the cornstarch in a saucepan. Stir in the peaches, lemon juice, water, and nutmeg. Cook, stirring constantly, until the mixture comes to a simmer. Simmer and stir 1 minute. Pour the hot fruit into an ungreased 2-quart baking dish. Place in a preheated 400° oven to keep hot while preparing the biscuit topping. Sift together flour, 1 tablespoon of sugar, the baking powder, and the salt into a bowl. Add the butter and cut it in with a pastry blender. With a fork, stir in the milk and mix until the dough forms a ball. Drop 6 large spoonfuls onto the hot fruit. Bake 25 minutes, or until the biscuits are golden brown. *Serves 6.*

SOUTHERN PECAN PUMPKIN PIE

■■■

2 LARGE EGGS
⅓ CUP WHITE SUGAR
⅓ CUP LIGHT BROWN SUGAR
1 TABLESPOON MOLASSES
1 TABLESPOON FLOUR
¾ TEASPOON SALT
¼ TEASPOON CINNAMON
⅛ TEASPOON GINGER
⅛ TEASPOON CLOVES
ONE 1-POUND CAN PUMPKIN
2 TABLESPOONS MELTED
  BUTTER

2 CUPS "HALF AND HALF" (HALF
  MILK, HALF HEAVY CREAM)
DEEP 9-INCH PIE SHELL,
  PARTIALLY BAKED
2 TABLESPOONS BUTTER
1 CUP UNSALTED PECAN
  HALVES
¼ CUP (PACKED) LIGHT BROWN
  SUGAR, NO LUMPS

BEAT TOGETHER EGGS, sugars, molasses, flour, salt, cinnamon, ginger, and cloves in a large bowl. Add the pumpkin, melted butter, and half and half to the bowl with the egg mixture. Blend thoroughly. Pour into the pie shell and bake in a preheated 450° oven for 15 minutes. Lower heat to 375° and bake 35 minutes, or until a knife blade inserted just off center comes out clean. In a frypan melt the butter. Add the pecans and stir to coat well with the butter. Add the pecans to the brown sugar and stir with a fork to coat with sugar. Arrange in an orderly fashion on the pie and place under a broiler for 1 to 2 minutes, watching carefully (so as not to burn the sugar) until the sugar has melted and the pecans have developed a glaze. *Serves 6 to 8.*

STRAWBERRY GLACÉ PIE

∎∎∎

This is Sandra Hall's Fourth-of-July Special.

1 CUP SUGAR
2 HEAPING TABLESPOONS
 CORNSTARCH
1 CUP COLD WATER
¼ CUP STRAWBERRY JELLO
 POWDER (ABOUT ½ A
 3-OUNCE PACKAGE)

1½ QUARTS FRESH STRAWBER-
 RIES, HULLED, WASHED,
 AND DRAINED
ONE 9-INCH PIE SHELL,
 THOROUGHLY BAKED AND
 COOLED
WHIPPED CREAM

IN A SAUCEPAN combine and blend the sugar, cornstarch, and cold water. Cook over low heat, stirring constantly, until thick and clear. Add the gelatin powder, stirring until dissolved. Select ⅓ of the strawberries fairly uniform in size and set aside. Slice the remaining berries onto the pastry shell. Arrange the whole berries in an orderly fashion on top. Pour the sauce over and chill several hours. Pipe the whipped cream on top or just offer with a dollop of cream on each serving. *Serves 6.*

STRAWBERRY ROLL

■■■

4 EGG YOLKS
½ CUP SUGAR
¾ CUP SIFTED FLOUR
¾ TEASPOON BAKING POWDER
1 TEASPOON VANILLA
4 EGG WHITES, STIFFLY BEATEN
1 CUP HEAVY CREAM,
   WHIPPED AND SWEETENED
   TO TASTE

CONFECTIONER'S SUGAR
1 QUART STRAWBERRIES,
   HULLED, WASHED, WELL
   DRAINED, SLICED, AND
   SWEETENED TO TASTE

IN A BOWL, beat the egg yolks until light and lemony in color. Gradually beat in the sugar, then the flour, baking powder, and vanilla. Fold in the egg whites. Butter a jelly roll pan, line with waxed paper, and butter the waxed paper. Evenly pour in the batter. Bake in a preheated 400° oven for 10 minutes. Reduce heat to 350° and bake 10 minutes, or until golden. Remove from the oven, place a damp kitchen towel over the cake, and refrigerate until ready to fill. Loosen the sides of the sponge sheet with a spatula. Sprinkle with confectioner's sugar. Place a sheet of waxed paper longer than the pan over the pan, holding the ends of the paper firmly against both ends of the pan, and invert the sponge onto the paper. Carefully peel off the paper. Spread the sponge sheet with the whipped cream. Strain the strawberries, saving the liquid that has collected in the bowl. Arrange ⅔ of the berry slices on the whipped cream. Combine the remaining slices with the liquid and coarsely mash them. Roll the sponge sheet, using the paper underneath to help raise and move it along. Sprinkle the top with confectioner's sugar. Cut into serving pieces and spoon some of the mashed berries and liquid on each serving. *Serves 6.*

NEW ENGLAND STRAWBERRY SHORTCAKE

■ ■ ■

A Fourth-of-July special since both wild and cultivated strawberries are ripe at this time.

2 CUPS ALL-PURPOSE FLOUR
1 TABLESPOON BAKING POWDER
3 TABLESPOONS SUGAR
½ TEASPOON SALT
6 TABLESPOONS BUTTER
1 EGG BEATEN
ABOUT ⅓ CUP MILK
MELTED BUTTER

1 QUART STRAWBERRIES,
    HULLED, WASHED, DRAINED,
    SLICED, AND SWEETENED
    WITH SUGAR TO TASTE
1 CUP HEAVY CREAM, WHIPPED
    AND SWEETENED, OR 1 CUP
    SOUR CREAM, SWEETENED

SIFT TOGETHER FLOUR, baking powder, sugar, and salt in a large bowl. Add the butter in pieces and with a pastry blender or your fingers work it in until the mixture has the texture of coarse meal. Stir in the egg and enough of the milk to make a soft, manageable dough. Turn out onto a lightly floured board and knead about half a minute. Divide the dough into halves and pat each half into an 8-inch circle. Set one in a lightly buttered 8-inch cake pan. Brush the top with melted butter. Lay the second layer on top. Bake in a preheated 450° oven 15 minutes, or until firm to the touch and golden. Cool. Run a spatula around the sides of the pan and invert cake onto a wire rack. When cool, carefully remove bottom layer and set onto a serving dish. Spoon on half the berries. Set second layer on top and spoon on the remaining berries. Top with the whipped cream or sour cream. *Serves 6.*

J.D.S.'S STRAWBERRIES ROMANOFF

■ ■ ■

This is a superb offering that lifts ice cream onto a new dessert plane, a lofty one that will tempt you to try again and again.

1 QUART FRESH, RIPE STRAW-
    BERRIES, WASHED, HULLED,
    AND WELL DRAINED
2 TABLESPOONS SUPERFINE
    SUGAR
2 OUNCES GRAND MARNIER

2 OUNCES COGNAC
1 PINT STRAWBERRY ICE CREAM
1 PINT VANILLA ICE CREAM
1 PINT ORANGE SHERBET
1 CUP WHIPPED CREAM

PLACE THE STRAWBERRIES in a large glass serving bowl. Sprinkle with the sugar, then pour the Grand Marnier and cognac over them. Carefully, with two spoons, toss the strawberries with the liqueurs and sugar so that everything is well blended. Refrigerate. Five minutes before you are ready to serve, add the ice creams and the sherbet. Blend well with the strawberries and liqueurs. Blend in the whipped cream and serve in chilled champagne glasses. *Serves 6 to 8.*

INDEX

243

Cookbooks

Cooking for every lifestyle

☐ **BETTER HOMES AND GARDENS NEW COOK BOOK**
(22528-6 • $4.50)

The Cookbook used in more American kitchens than any other is now better than ever! Over 1200 delicious recipes plus meal planning guides and menus, and hundreds of recipes for appliances, easy meals and great new entertainment ideas.

☐ **THE FANNIE FARMER COOKBOOK** (23488-9 • $5.95)

A heritage of good cooking for a new generation of cooks. Since 1896 when Fannie Merritt Farmer published the first BOSTON COOKING-SCHOOL COOKBOOK, it has been the culinary bible for generations of American women. The original has been continually updated by her heirs, and, now, 86 years and 12 editions later, THE FANNIE FARMER COOKBOOK is better than ever.

Special Cooking Needs

☐ **THE ARTHRITIC'S COOKBOOK** by Dong & Bank
(25349-2 • $3.95)
☐ **COOKING WITHOUT A GRAIN OF SALT** By J. Bagg
(23418-8 • $3.95)
☐ **RECIPES FOR DIABETICS** (23257-6 • $3.95)

And don't miss these other Bantam Cookbooks

☐ **MICROWAVE COOKERY** By Deacon (24021-8 • $3.95)
☐ **CROCKERY COOKERY** By Hoffman (24021-8 • $3.95)
☐ **ATHLETE'S KITCHEN** By Nancy Clark (23211-8 • $3.95)
☐ **LAUREL'S KITCHEN** By Robertson, Flinders & Godfrey
(22565-0 • $4.95)
☐ **COMPLETE BOOK OF PIES** By J.D. Scott & M. Scott
(24681-X • $4.50)
☐ **THE FRENCH CHEF'S COOKBOOK** By Julia Child
(24789-1 • $4.50)

Available wherever Bantam Books are sold or use this handy coupon for ordering

---

Bantam Books, Inc., Dept. KP3, 414 East Golf Road, Des Plaines, Ill. 60016

Please send me the books I have checked above. I am enclosing $_____ (Please add $1.50 to cover postage and handling.) Send check or money order— no cash or C.O.D.'s please.

Mr Ms _____

Address _____

City State _____ Zip _____

KP3—3/86

Please allow four to six weeks for delivery. This offer expires 9/86.
Prices and availability subject to change without notice.